Irving Babbitt in
Our Time

Irving Babbitt in Our Time

Edited by

George A. Panichas and Claes G. Ryn

The Catholic University of America Press
Washington, D.C.

1986

Library of Congress Cataloging-in-Publication Data
Main entry under title:
Irving Babbitt in our time.

Includes index.
1. Babbitt, Irving, 1865–1933—Addresses, essays,
lectures. I. Panichas, George Andrew. II. Ryn,
Claes G., 1943–
B945.B124I78   1986   191   85-21260
ISBN 0-8132-0625-1

It is the critic's business to grapple with the age in which he lives and give it what he sees it needs.
                                        —Irving Babbitt

He related for you a multitude of separate and apparently disconnected tendencies to the great central currents of thought. . . . He had given you theses about literature, about life, which you would spend a lifetime in verifying.
                                        —Stuart P. Sherman

Contents

Editors' Note

Irving Babbitt in Our Time grows in part out of an interdisciplinary conference, "Irving Babbitt: Fifty Years Later," which was held on November 18–19, 1983, at The Catholic University of America in Washington, D.C., to commemorate the fiftieth anniversary of Babbitt's death. The conference was sponsored by CUA's Department of Politics, The Marguerite Eyer Wilbur Foundation, and The Intercollegiate Studies Institute.

The essay by the late Dr. Folke Leander was previously published in Sweden in 1954 by the University of Gothenburg. It is reprinted in this volume to make it available to a wider audience. The essays by Mr. Joseph Baldacchino; Dr. Richard B. Hovey; and Mr. T. John Jamieson were written exclusively for this volume. The remaining essays, originally presented during the conference, have been substantially revised.

The editors wish to express special thanks to Miss Mary E. Slayton for her generous assistance in preparing the manuscript, the Chronology, and the Index. The Chronology should help to rectify the long absence of a systematic year-by-year biographical portrait of Irving Babbitt.

The editors are grateful to Dr. Charles Driscoll Murphy and Professor Paul Gottfried for helpful comments on the manuscript.

Introduction

MORE THAN A HALF century separates us from Irving Babbitt's
death on July 15, 1933. Since then, much has happened in
American letters and culture to confirm Babbitt's critiques and
warnings regarding what he viewed as an alarming decline in
standards of life, literature, and thought. "We live, fifty years
after Babbitt," Austin Warren writes, "in a time when his
predictions have come true." Babbitt gave his witness as a
teacher and a thinker during forty years of unbroken service,
"under fire," on the educational battlefront. To the very end of
his life he spoke out on the indissolubly connected issues—
literary, educational, economic, political, philosophical, and religious—that help define a way of life and ultimately shape
moral character and ethos. He spoke out on these issues with a
courage and a conviction rarely encountered in the intellectual
community. "To have standards," he tirelessly insisted, "means
practically to select and reject; and this again means that one
must discipline one's feelings or affections, to use the older
word, to some ethical center." These words sum up the standards of discrimination that he saw as necessary at all levels of
life and thought. And they are words that remind us of the
fitness, the measure, and the centrality, which, as Matthew
Arnold asserts, are the soul of good criticism.

When we inspect Babbitt's witness and weigh his testimony in
the context of our time we become increasingly aware of an
inspired teacher and thinker who speaks out not only as a

modern but also as our contemporary. Babbitt still speaks to us today, to our condition, as it were. Babbitt's achievement has enduring and visionary qualities and a meaningfulness that, in its cosmopolitan dimensions, goes beyond the frontiers of the academy and even beyond the nets of nation, language, and custom. His achievement emerges from a vision at once dynamic and consistent. No other critic and teacher in the twentieth century has more tenaciously dared, or been able, to look beneath the surfaces or venture beyond the perimeters of our modern world in the astonishing ways that Babbitt did. He is to be counted among the first and keenest of the "keen-sighted few," to use his own term, who must belong to that small remnant of wisdom and renewal that Isaiah has in mind when he proclaims: "For though thy people . . . be as the sand of the sea, yet a remnant of them shall return" (X, 22).

Babbitt's achievement prompts endless frequentation, such is its intellectual richness and critical discernment and its ability to direct our attention to the things that matter, "the permanent things." To say that Babbitt speaks to us as our contemporary is to say that we can and ought to return to his writings for "wisdom and renewal." His ideas have, to be sure, long been opposed and subjected to misunderstanding and misrepresenta-tion by those forces in our society that scorn first principles and depict, in Joseph Joubert's apt phrase, "the moral sense in ruins." Babbitt himself labeled these forces as "a false liber-alism" and a "sham spirituality," terms as applicable in our time as they were in Babbitt's. His writings provide a diagnosis of precisely those doctrines that would shake the foundations and imperil the order of a civilized society. In our time his teachings and writings should also provide a corrective to the teachings and writings of those influential spokesmen in the American intelligentsia who, demonstrating, in Babbitt's words, "the confusion between moral and material progress," take it upon themselves to make policy, mold public opinion, and legislate conduct both within and without the academy. The insidious results of reductionist and brutally empirical practices, glorify-ing expansionist habits that lack the rectitude, continuity, and force found in moral principle, are painful and even shattering as they stubbornly confront us. They are results that help to validate the thrust of Babbitt's diagnosis, as well as the urgent need for us to study what he has written for its corrective strengths and relevance to conditions in our time, as is evident in this passage from *Democracy and Leadership* (1924):

... the latter stages of the naturalistic dissolution of civilization with which we are menaced are, thanks to scientific "progress," likely to be marked by incidents of almost inconceivable horror. The danger of power without wisdom, of a constantly increasing material organization combined with an ever-growing spiritual anarchy, is already so manifest that unless there is a serious search for a remedy we may conclude that the instinct for self-preservation that is supposed to inhere in mankind is a myth.

Babbitt's contribution as a teacher and a thinker can be seen as transcending any institutional or organizational designation. In its spiritual quality and moral character his contribution has a uniquely multidimensional and universal significance. Too often and too conveniently his worth and meaning have been consigned almost exclusively to the particulars of the movement known as the New Humanism. Yet any careful estimation of his work and thought discloses a mind that transcends special and specializing categories of intellect. The sapiential aspects of his thought, to put it another way, reveal a mind and a strength of character that defy both compartmentalization and departmentalization. In short, Babbitt addresses himself to all essential categories and conditions of human existence in their interconnections.

"Universally," Henry James once declared, "relations stop nowhere." Babbitt reveals, in this respect, the visionary element that distinguishes him from the purely academic or the secularly parochial and elevates his thought to that higher plane that the Greek word *paideia* connotes. For no less than the ancients whom he much admired and emulated, Babbitt was convinced that education and culture are not a discrete technique, an autarchic art, or an abstract theory, splintered from the historical situation. Rather they are a continuous and integral part of a nation's life. This consummate process, Babbitt insisted, includes reverence for a sense of measure and proportion that both emerges from and brings about a true union of will, imagination, and reason.

Literature and life, Babbitt insisted, are indivisible: Literary studies need to be justified on cultural and disciplinary grounds. The study of literature must, in effect, become a discipline of ideas and imagination: a discipline that must distinguish between the significant and the insignificant, between literature that has an ethical or moral center and literature that is subservient to the flux of relativism. Babbitt saw literary studies as fundamental to the larger educational process, specifically of the "old education" aiming for a humanistic training for wisdom and not for a humanitarian "training for service and power." He sought quality and standards and not quantity and "ideals": "True democracy consists not in lowering the standard but in giving everybody, so far as possible, a chance of measuring up to the standard." Insofar as he regarded the modern age as revolutionary and expansionist, with the traditional supports disappearing in society, he believed that the idea of quality and selection in cultural life must be sustained. In the study of literature, as in the whole of education, he saw a common problem that relates to the even greater crisis of modern civilization. "What seems to me to be driving our whole civilization toward the abyss at present is a one-sided conception of liberty, a conception that is purely centrifugal, that would get rid of all outer control and then evade or deny openly the need of achieving inner control." Without a sufficiently stringent discipline of ideas, imagination, and character, Babbitt believed, the temper of the sham "liberals" would triumph, spurning the past and barely tolerating the present—"the true home of their spirit is that vast, windy abode, the future." The main task of education, and of the teacher of literature, was that of defining general terms; the phenomena for which the terms stand should be studied positively, critically, and concretely, especially as reflected in major literary currents and works.

For Babbitt the critic's central task, no less than the teacher's, was one of selection and judgment, and not of comprehension and sympathy only. That the final test of art is not its originality but its truth to the universal constituted for Babbitt the guiding principle of criticism. The truth of art, to be sure, is for Babbitt not intellectual in nature. Its insight is intuitive: Art gives us concrete experience, not concepts. But Babbitt also insists that intuitive insight can vary greatly in depth and fullness. Some imaginative creations, having lost a sense of the ethical essence of life, either distort or trivialize existence.

Particularly in nineteenth-century art and literature, he detected eccentric and centrifugal, even pathological, tendencies. He felt that these tendencies, continuing into the twentieth century, signaled a rejection of those representative qualities of vision, and of permanence, that he found in ancient Greece. Although Babbitt stressed the insufficiency of the notion of art as imitation, he found in the Greeks an admirable sense of the universal: "The original man for the Greek was one who could create in the very act of imitating the past. Greek literature at its best is to a remarkable degree a creative imitation of Homer." For Babbitt the universal in art is expressed through *creative* imitation. Creativity without the ordering sense of the universal becomes idiosyncratic or offensive. Original genius must not allow humility and decorum to be outstripped by the temperamental excesses of self-expression and restless self-concern. Babbitt thought it important that a work be assessed not just in terms of the fulfillment of a particular aesthetic aim but in terms of whether its aim is intrinsically valuable as both an intelligible and an aesthetically compelling expression of the essence of life.

The main business of the critic must be one of rating "creation with reference to some standard set above his own temperament and that of the creator." Original genius must be disciplined to ethical reality: "Once eliminate the high impersonal standard, the ethical norm that sets bounds to the eagerness of the creator to express himself, and the eagerness of the creator to thrill to this expression, and it is hard to see what measure of a man's merit is left save his intoxication with himself; and this measure would scarcely seem to be trustworthy."

The role of the "ethical imagination," which blends creativity and high seriousness in the Aristotelian sense, was for Babbitt a defense against the lures of "decadent aestheticism." Relentless in his censure of "romantic eleutheromaniacs," "the corrupters of the conscience in general," he held that "we must begin by creating standards." A reverence for boundaries and limits was, for Babbitt, essential; he endorsed fully Goethe's words that in limitation one first shows himself the master. But in much of modern art and literature, he argued, expression triumphs over form, a process that he associated with the Rousseauistic view of art. "There is no place in the process for the sharply drawn line of demarcation, for the firm and fast distinction. Definite standards are swallowed up in a universal relativity." The creator's need to mediate between "the outward push of expression" and "the circumscribing law" remained for Babbitt a crucial one, particularly if beauty is to be acquired that is pertinent to man. The need for mediation between the One and the Many informed Babbitt's view that extremes are barbarous. Although critical of neoclassical formalism and rigidity he cited form and symmetry as properties essential to beauty. The outstanding work of beauty has the form of the ethical imagination. While there are lesser forms of beauty, the epithet "beautiful" must not be applied indiscriminately. A skyscraper, he noted, is hardly beautiful: "Now sky-scrapers may be picturesque, or vital, or what you will, though they are usually not much more than a mixture of megalomania and commercialism."

Babbitt was fearful of the dehumanization of life and literature in the absence of firm principles of judgment. In Oscar Wilde and Paul Verlaine, for example, he saw the Rousseauistic side of romanticism: "The latest romanticists have discredited themselves, which is not perhaps a serious matter; but they have also thrown a certain discredit on art and literature, and this is far more serious." For Babbitt there was no special mystery or paradox regarding the genres and the boundaries of art: ". . . a clear-cut type of person, a person who does not live in either an emotional or intellectual muddle, will normally prefer a clear-cut type of art or literature." It was first of all to the ancient Greeks, to the *exemplaria graeca,* that Babbitt refered for our emulation: to their redeeming way of mediating between the One and the Many; to their sense of "vital unity, vital measure, vital purpose"; to their high standards of art, which at its best is a triumph of restraint. Aristotle's law of measure, in aesthetics as combined with the modern idea of the creative imagination, should be, first and always, the impelling principle of life and literature. In life it helps us to distinguish between appearance and reality; in literature it acts as a defense against the excesses of the romantic imagination and particularly of the romantic religion of love: "There is in fact no object in the romantic universe—only subject. This subjective love amounts in practice to a use of the imagination to enhance emotional intoxication, or if one prefers, to the pursuit of illusion for its own sake." All this leads, Babbitt felt, to the confusion of values, found, for example, in William Hazlitt, who "converts criticism itself into an art of impassioned recollection," with "its cult of Arcadian illusion and the wistful backward glance to the vanished par-adise of childhood and youth when illusion was most spon-taneous."

In the literature of the modern world, as in life, Babbitt perceived the consequences of a human situation when "things are in the saddle and ride mankind." For the individual and for society the consequences are intuitive, ethical and intellectual anarchy. The critic, and especially the moral critic, Babbitt believed, has the responsibility of resisting such tendencies and habits of mind. Precise analysis, clear definitions of general terms, firm application of principles and standards, keen aware-ness of the value of traditional beliefs: These are some of the qualities, besides aesthetic openness and sensibility, that a critic must bring to bear in pursuit of his task.

Matthew Arnold exemplified for Babbitt the critical function

that he himself sought to fulfill in America: "Arnold always
assumes a core of normal experience, a permanent self in man,
and rates a writer according to the degree of his insight into this
something that abides through all the flux of circumstance, or,
as he himself would say, according to the depth and soundness
of this writer's criticism of life." (At the same time Babbitt did
not fail, as his most famous student, T. S. Eliot, did not fail, to
point to Arnold's inability to rise far enough above the naturalistic level in his dealings with religion.) Arnold had worked out
a positive and critical humanism, pertinent, Babbitt averred, to
culture and society in modern democracy. Thus he saw in
Arnold a critic who was ahead not only of his own time but also
of ours: "Not to get beyond the idea of material organization as
a remedy for moral anarchy is still to linger in the zones of
illusion peculiar to the nineteenth century."

Arnold's belief in a high quality of leadership, in terms of
secured (and secure) standards and discipline, through the
interaction of education and government, is also the belief that
Babbitt argues for in his *Democracy and Leadership*. The real enemy of democracy is an anarchy of values that prepares the way
for ruthless power seeking. The corrective of anarchy is not a
material and naturalistic efficiency but a humanistic or religious
discipline. To have such a discipline, Babbitt noted, there must
be standards, but to attain standards there must be critics who
are concerned with defining and applying them. To be sure, he
confessed, "We have no end of clever people, but clever people
without standards."

Babbitt considered Arnold's essay on Joseph Joubert "one of
the best critical essays ever written in English." Babbitt was
sparing in outbursts of admiration; he was not, as has been
observed, "an easy prey to imaginative enchantment of any
kind." His standards were usually so strict that he excluded
more than he included when passing judgment and assigning
value. With Arnold, he recognized in Joubert a great critic, at
once simple, brave, studious, and severe; one who, as Arnold
wrote in the last sentence of his essay, "nourished on some
secret tradition, or illumined, perhaps, by a divine inspiration,

kept aloof from the reigning superstitions, never bowed to the gods of Canaan." Joubert, Babbitt said, possessed a true spirituality.

Babbitt's estimation of Joubert appears in *Masters of Modern French Criticism* (1912), which, as Babbitt wrote in his preface, is a criticism of critics. The discussion of Joubert (and of other leading French critics of the nineteenth century, e.g., Chateaubriand, Sainte-Beuve, Taine, Brunetière) shows Babbitt at his best. His qualities of mind and of critical discrimination, of style, methodology, and scholarship, are immediately evident and provide an index to the integrity of his achievement, as well as a rebuttal of repeated charges by his detractors that he was an unsound critical thinker and a petulant writer. ("Professor Babbitt frowns a good deal and thrusts viciously," claimed one commentator.) His combination of courage of judgment and pithiness of statement radiates throughout this essay and throughout the book. He never indulges in the kind of uncritical praise that, in Babbitt's own words, becomes "too full of admiration for unregulated sympathy." Even his admiration for Joubert is qualified and balanced: "Joubert tends to see only the benefits of order just as Emerson tends to see only the benefits of emancipation. In the name of what he conceives to be order, he would be too ready to deliver society over to the Jesuits and fix it in a sort of hieratic immobility." These two sentences illustrate Babbitt's mastery of words and his powers of condensation and concentration. What Joubert wrote of himself can also be applied to Babbitt: "If there is a man tormented by the accursed ambition to put a whole book in a page, a whole page in a phrase, and that phrase in a word, it is I."

If Joubert leaned too much on the side of reaction in his politics and religion, he nevertheless preserved, as Babbitt emphasized, remarkable poise and balance in his literary opinions: "He did not, like so many moderns, go mad over the powers of suggestiveness." Joubert exemplified the merits that raise the art of criticism above impressionism and relativity. He knew how to combine sympathy with selection; how to temper expansion by concentration—"Joubert has not a trace of our modern megalomania." Babbitt called him "the critics' critic much as Spenser has been called the poets' poet" and recognized his remarkable literary perceptiveness: "Like Emerson he possessed the gift of vision, 'the eye of the spirit, the instinct of penetration, prompt discernment; in fine, natural sagacity in discovering all that is spiritual.' " Babbitt valued in Joubert the critic as sage. Joubert joins to his sense of unity a fine perception of the local and impermanent. His overall quality as a critic is revealed by the fact that he had standards but held them fluidly. He was willing to concede much to the element of relativity without seeing literature merely as the reflection of mobile conditions. Joubert perceived an "enduring something in man and aimed at it"; he focused on abiding relations. *"Il y a quelque chose d'immuable dans l'homme!"* In short, Joubert exemplified both humanistic criticism and the dignity of criticism. In his appraisal of Joubert, Babbitt offered a "collective criticism," not only a theory of criticism but also a theory of conduct, a theory of education, a philosophy of life.

In art as in criticism, Babbitt contended, one must always be on guard against the impressionism that culminates in "the fatality and finality of temperament." The mere impressionist cancels the principle of judgment; he slides into a quagmire of illusion and relativity. To counter the existing conditions that conduce such a vulgarization of sensibility, Babbitt appealed on an international scale to "the judgment of the keen-sighted few." The true critic, as well as the great artist, mediates between the One and the Many, the unchanging and the changing. "What we are seeking is a critic who rests his discipline and selection upon the past without being a mere traditionalist; whose holding of tradition involves a constant process of hard and clear thinking, a constant adjustment, in other words, of the experience of the past to the changing needs of the present." He pointed to Emerson as a model of this critical spirit, as one who can help us delineate critical standards, despite the fact that Emerson also contains a baffling blend of Rousseauism ("in denying intrinsic evil in human nature") and of insight. "The oversoul that Emerson perceives in his best moments is the true oversoul and not the undersoul that the Rousseauist sets up as a substitute."

The "humanistic Goethe," the Goethe who renounced Rousseauistic reverie and turned from dreaming to doing and classical balance, is still another model of one who can initiate us into the critical habit. In Goethe, Babbitt saw a modern who taught man the need to live and to think on the human path, without escapist illusions and with a sense of man's concrete moral responsibilities. Goethe attained and personified that existential wisdom for which Babbitt himself always sought: "No inconsiderable part of wisdom consists in just this: not to allow the mind to dwell on questions that are unprofitable in themselves or else entirely beyond its grasp." Such merely abstract speculation can be a flight from the kind of ethical action that provides the only sure answer to man's questions regarding the meaning of life. The problem of finding firm and yet flexible standards constituted for Babbitt the modern predicament, which is analogous in many of its ramifying difficulties and results to the problem that faced Socrates: how to "recover that firm foundation for human life which a misuse of the intellectual spirit was rendering impossible."

Babbitt must be viewed as a generalist critic and cultural thinker comparable with Carlyle, Arnold, and Emerson—possibly inferior to them, as is sometimes claimed, in the literary quality of his style, but superior in intellectual depth and scope. "He is a defender of tradition, an historian of ideas and tendencies, a moralist, a popularizer of general ideas: anything and everything, in fact, except a critic or a student of criticism." So wrote a distinguished American literary critic, J. E. Spingarn, in 1913, his words epitomizing the charge so often leveled at Babbitt: that he had no aesthetic theory and failed to answer the central questions: What is art? What is literature? What is criticism? Spingarn, who undoubtedly spoke for many others, objected not so much to Babbitt's social and cultural views as to his aesthetic theory, which he claimed "is vitiated by moralistic and intellectualistic errors." Above all, Spingarn continued, Babbitt shows his "confusion of ethical bias with aesthetic thought": "He does not care what art or criticism is, but he does care that young men and women should have discipline, training, tradition, ideals." Babbitt does not see, according to Spingarn, that "disciplined art and undisciplined art are both art; or perhaps we should say that disciplined minds as well as undisciplined ones may express themselves in art."

What Spingarn and other opponents of Babbitt's method emphasized is that Babbitt's literary approach can be rejected at the same time that his ethical outlook can be praised. Babbitt was dismissed as doctrinaire, or intellectualistic, as insensitive to the literary experience. Later another critic, perpetuating Spingarn's objections, was to write of Babbitt: ". . . his literary criticism was inquisitorial, shrill—*criticism manquée*—because he sacrificed aesthetic to ethical vision." Even admirers of Babbitt's critical ethos, of literary criticism that sees the continuation of literary questions into general questions, voiced the fear that a critical practitioner, by placing moral edification above appreciation of genius, might lose his detachment and become too much a servant of his mind.

"Experience . . . has other uses," Babbitt maintained, "than to supply furnishings for the tower of ivory; it should control the judgment and guide the will; it is in short the necessary basis of conduct." That he equated the sense of beauty with the moral sense; that his literary standards were ethical absolutes, involving a violation of immediacy; that he "fatally" separated two orders of intuitions, the sensuous or aesthetic from the spiritual or intellectual; that he placed inordinate stress on control of the artistic imagination; that he expounded his views with "a feverish quickstep that arises from almost an excess of earnestness": these are summary and often simplistic charges continually brought against Babbitt that should finally be checked against what he actually wrote. His ideas need to be carefully studied without the confining prejudices characteristic of rigid doctrines of *l'art pour l'art*.

The criticisms directed against Babbitt's ideas about art and literary criticism vastly simplified or distorted his position and even betrayed lack of familiarity with his writings. Babbitt never confused the intuition that is intrinsic to art with reason or ethics. He never believed that literature achieves greatness by letting reason control the imagination. For all his concern with the ethical content of art, his alternative to romantic and "realist" amoralism was not didacticism or some form of aesthetic intellectualism. On the contrary, he criticized such notions at length and emphatically rejected them. Yet Babbitt also insisted that poetry, as intuition, can have more or less fullness and depth in expressing the essence of life. His appreciation of classical art and his stress on what is ethically universal did not stop him from affirming the modern idea of the creative imagination. Indeed, precisely in the fusion of the elements of aesthetic creativity and apprehension of the universal is found Babbitt's originality in aesthetics. The failure of so many commentators to grasp the nature of this achievement raises some serious questions about the state of modern aesthetics and literary criticism. Contrary to the charge of Spingarn and others, Babbitt possesses an elaborate aesthetic theory, but it has yet to be adequately understood.

The fact remains that he viewed, and appraised, literary situations as cultural situations. He damned much, whether in art or in criticism, a fact that must be taken into account in weighing the charges against him. "There are critics who have founded," he wrote, "a considerable reputation on the relationship that exists between their own mediocrity and the mediocrity of their readers." In his view of the critical function there was no room for endearing diplomacy and niceties. The critical act of judgment—and a judgment is intensely personal as well as impersonal—requires a mental toughness that is both a rejection of "unprofitable subtleties," to use Bacon's term, and a refusal of elegance: "The significant struggle is between the sound and the unsound individualist." For the modern critic, Babbitt contended, the main problem was how to "escape from the quicksands of relativity to some firm ground of judgment." He had little tolerance for dilettantes and *jouisseurs littéraires,* leading one critic to observe, ". . . Babbitt never takes a holiday.

There is 'work' to be done, ethical work, seven days a week."

By dint of his conviction and sense of mission, and by the power of his achievement and character, Babbitt gained a remarkable presence in the house of intellect. Even well before his death in 1933 he was internationally recognized as an American literary scholar and cultural thinker of unusual intellectual power, learning, and insight. He had many admirers in Europe, perhaps especially in France, and outside of the West as far away as China. Professor René Wellek, although not generally sympathetic to Babbitt, speaks of his "real critical power and acumen." Wellek says of Babbitt and his leading disciples that "they have a power of abstraction and generalization and a fervid 'engagement' in ideas unknown to earlier American scholarship."

In one way or another the discussion about this legendary teacher and critic involved practically every leading figure in American literature, scholarship, and journalism in the first half of this century. Babbitt has been at the center of one of the most intense and long-lasting intellectual controversies in modern American history. Among his admirers are such thinkers, educators, and men of letters as Paul Elmer More, T. S. Eliot, Louis Mercier, Gordon Keith Chalmers, Walter Lippmann, Richard Weaver, Leo Ward, Austin Warren, and, in a later generation, Nathan Pusey, Walter Jackson Bate, Russell Kirk, and Peter Viereck. His critics have included Edmund Wilson, Sinclair Lewis, H. L. Mencken, Ernest Hemingway, J. E. Spingarn, R. P. Blackmur, Arthur Lovejoy, Jacques Barzun, and Allen Tate. But the writings of some of these critics show that they too have been indelibly affected by his ideas. Although not always mentioned by name, Babbitt has remained a presence in the American intellectual consciousness.

The intensity of the opposition to Babbitt in the dominant literary and intellectual circles of the 1920's and 1930's and later has made it risky for young scholars to take up his work or associate writing with his name. A lingering climate of more or less open hostility has discouraged careful attention to Babbitt's ideas and has also served to conceal or deemphasize such influence as he has nevertheless exerted, and continues to exert. Scholars drawing upon and developing his ideas form a partly submerged tradition.

Only a thinker of rare stature could have stimulated so much and such persistent controversy. Still, Irving Babbitt's thought and influence have yet to be fully comprehended and assessed. On the whole, his critics have neglected to deal in a systematic, scholarly fashion with his actual arguments. Too often they have directed their charges against more easily refuted caricatures of his ideas. This pattern of avoidance may be taken as a sign that, in an intuitive way, these critics do recognize the importance of his work and its potential for unsettling accustomed habits of thought.

Half a century after Babbitt's death the evidence is accumulating of a resurgence of interest in his work. New editions of some of his books and an expanding secondary literature testify conclusively to the continuing pertinence of his thought. The time has come for a thorough and judicious reconsideration of his lasting contribution and also for a greater measure of recognition and restitution. There is a need to set aside the careless and even willful distortions of his ideas that originated long ago in the heat of controversy. The many misinterpretations of Babbitt, relating, for example, to his ideas of the inner check and the moral imagination, can be attributed only in small part to ambiguities and weaknesses in Babbitt's own writing. Patient scholarly examination of his work as a whole that is sensitive to the subtleties of his position and that places it in its historical and philosophical context discloses a challenging and fully intelligible, if sometimes difficult, doctrine of life and letters.

The editors of this volume cannot claim that it deals comprehensively with Babbitt's far-reaching work. But the book seeks to present, or at least to suggest, some of the necessary work of reconsideration and critical reassessment, and is the first collective volume of its kind. The authors represent several academic disciplines and a diversity of scholarly emphases. Babbitt's ideas are thus explored in the interdisciplinary and transdisciplinary setting that he himself identifies in these words of lasting consequence in our time—and, indeed, for all time: "When studied with any degree of thoroughness, the economic problem will be found to run into the political problem, the political problem in turn into the philosophical problem, and the philosophical problem itself to be almost indissolubly bound up at last with the religious problem."

Washington, D.C.   G.A.P.
April 1985   C.G.R.

Russell Kirk

The Enduring Influence of
Irving Babbitt

OF THE MAKING of books there is no end. Most men of letters of our century, much reviewed though they may be in their day, are quite forgotten a year or two after they have departed from our midst—if not forgotten well before that fatal event. It cannot be otherwise: too many books are published, more with every year that passes, for even the most devoted bibliophile to glance at more than a tiny percentage of them, let alone bear many of them in mind some decades later. The production of books grows inordinately; in the age of television, the number of oldfangled "common readers" diminishes sadly.

More than seventy-five years have elapsed since Irving Babbitt published his first book; more than a half a century has passed since Babbitt's death. We hear lamentations that Babbitt has been ignored, denounced, and nearly forgotten; I heard such mournful voices at the time I first encountered Babbitt's writings, in 1936 or 1937. And yet several of Babbitt's books have recently appeared in new editions; essays and even books about him and his work and ideas continue to appear occasionally.

Babbitt was born only a few months after the end of the Civil War. His influence has endured far longer than that of most eminent men of letters. And through his disciples, especially T. S.

Eliot, Babbitt's ideas have been widely disseminated among reflective people, even though many readers may be unaware of
the source. Interest in Babbitt is not one of literary antiquarian-
ism, for his thought survives as an energizing power within many
men and women who contend against the sensual and the dark.
"The dead alone give us energy," says Le Bon.

While he lived, Irving Babbitt was intemperately assailed by
a diversity of critics, more eager to discover failings in the "movement" called the New Humanism than to recognize any promise
in such a renewal of old truths. Yet in the fullness of time, not
a few of those critics came to entertain opinions interestingly similar to Babbitt's convictions—though usually without acknowledg-
ing the resolute scholar at Harvard. Rebecca West, for instance,
called Babbitt "this drill-sergeant." But if one turns to Rebecca
West's later writings, one might fancy that Dame Rebecca, like
T. S. Eliot, had studied with Babbitt at Harvard. Consider the
whole tone and temper of her moving book *The Court and the
Castle: A Study of the Interactions of Political and Religious Ideas in
Imaginative Literature* (1958). Consider especially the book's final
sentence: "It is a tendency of creative literature, when it rises
above a certain level, to involve itself with statecraft and with
religion: to exist and to belong to Him."

Nevertheless, today's inveterate social radical detests Babbitt
as ferociously as did his counterpart of some decades ago. This
attitude is sufficiently suggested in Oscar Cargill's book *Intellectual America: Ideas on the March* (1941). Cargill calls Babbitt a
pedant, "the nearest approach to Scaliger the New World has
seen." He is particularly enraged by *Literature and the American
College: Essays in Defense of the Humanities* (1908), Babbitt's first
book.

We know not in what superstitious eighteenth century sectarianism
Babbitt was reared, but his lack of salivary control at the mere mention of *science* or *democracy* suggests the rural hymn singer and sermon
note-taker, rather than the cosmopolitan. Had he read his Aristotle, he
would have been prepared for Bacon, for he would have seen that
philosophy and literature are built upon the science which he con-
demns. How could any but rustics rally behind such a leader?

Or take Granville Hicks, then a Marxist, who declared that the New Humanists had nothing to say to mill hands, Colorado beet-toppers, and screw-tighteners on the Ford assembly line. It is true that mill hands, beet-toppers, and screw-tighteners, with few exceptions, are not given to studying the works of professors of French literature or of Sanskrit. Nor do they assiduously read the productions of Oscar Cargill and Granville Hicks. Yet it remains true, in Coleridge's words, that "In every state, not wholly barbarous, a philosophy, good or bad, there must be. . . . Nor is this the less true, because the great majority of men live like bats, but in twilight, and know and feel the philosophy of their age only by its reflections and refractions." The philosophy of Irving Babbitt, after all, has turned out to accord more with American common sense than has the Marxist dialectic.

When Irving Babbitt died, I was a fourteen-year-old boy living in a house by the railroad yards at Plymouth, Michigan—a few miles from the Rouge plant where men tightened screws for Mr. Ford. Although my grandfather subscribed to *The Bookman,* I had not then heard of Professor Babbitt. I topped beets only now and again, but I picked cherries whenever the season came round. I confess that I was quite unaware of being an oppressed proletarian, ripe for redemption by such literary gentlemen as Mr. Hicks and Mr. Cargill. Indeed, my family shared all the prejudices of Professor Babbitt, even though we possessed none of his books.

One day in 1933 my mother disclosed to my father and me that our remaining capital consisted of one $20 bill, concealed in her copy of Kipling's novel *The Light That Failed.* The possession of that sum reassured, rather than dismayed, a cherry-picking boy. The Great Depression is said to have undone the New Humanism. But the New Humanism never was a political movement, intended to take power nationally: it was an endeavor to renew mind and conscience. The political and social events of the past half-century have increased, rather than diminished, the pertinence of the ideas of Babbitt and his colleagues to the American mind and the American character.

The Great Depression, or more precisely the Roosevelt recession, sent me to college, for lack of anything better to do. And at Michigan State College I became a student and a friend of John Abbot Clark, a good-natured, thoroughgoing disciple of Babbitt's. As a freshman or a sophomore, I read all Babbitt's books; Professor Babbitt then had been dead only three or four years, but he seemed to the boy at Michigan State one of the sages of antiquity, along with Longinus and Quintilian, for we studied him in John Clark's course in the history of criticism.

When I read Babbitt, a conscience spoke to a conscience. I felt a strong sympathy of mind and character. The feeling might have been stronger still, had I then known that Babbitt's first American ancestor, like mine, had settled at Plymouth, on Massachusetts Bay, early in the seventeenth century, and that Babbitt, like me, had been reared in a household given to talking about ghosts and perceiving them. ("He had been immersed in childhood in an atmosphere of spiritualism," William Giese writes of the young Babbitt, who could hold "none of the common inhibitions as to belief in what transcends ordinary experience.") Unlike me, Babbitt did not go so far as to publish tales of supernatural phenomena. But I was aware, in 1936 and 1937, of a different sort of spiritual link between Babbitt and my callow self.

The convictions Babbitt expressed so logically and powerfully were the convictions held by my family for generations. Whether Babbitt had aught to say to Colorado beet-toppers, he spoke movingly to a boy from the railroad yards outside Detroit. He has influenced me more strongly than has any other writer of the twentieth century. It was through Babbitt that I came to know Edmund Burke, and Babbitt, as much as Burke, animates my book *The Conservative Mind.*

I was impressed especially, in my first year of college, by *Literature and the American College,* so ridiculed by Oscar Cargill a few years later. What I did not expect in 1937 was that I would bring out in 1956 a paperback edition of that little book, the forlorn hope of the New Humanism.

"What Is Humanism?" is the first chapter of *Literature and the*

American College. The rest of Babbitt's books enlarged upon this topic. Humanism is the belief that man is a distinct being, governed by laws peculiar to his nature; there is law for man, and law for thing. Man stands higher than the beasts that perish because he recognizes and obeys this law of his nature. The disciplinary arts of *humanitas* teach man to put checks upon his will and his appetite. Those checks are provided by ethical will and reason—not by the private rationality of the Enlighten-ment, but by the higher reason that grows out of a respect for the wisdom of our ancestors and out of the endeavor to appre-hend that transcendent order which gives us our nature. The sentimentalist, who would subject man to the rule of impulse and passion; the pragmatic materialist, who would treat man as a mere edified ape; the leveling enthusiast, who would reduce human personality to a collective mediocrity—these are the enemies of true human nature. Against them Babbitt directed all his books.

For Babbitt, the goal of education is ethical. In college, as at all other levels of education, the student learns to distinguish between good and evil. It is this humane tradition and discipline that keeps us civilized and maintains a tolerable civil social order. Babbitt knew, as Lynn Harold Hough wrote, "that he lived in a world where undisciplined and expansive emotion was running riot." This world was proceeding to dedicate itself to the study of subhuman relationships, which it mistook for the whole of life; it was sinking into a meaningless aestheticism, an arid specialization, and a mean vocationalism. "If by science you meant the discovery and the use of every truth you could find in every realm," Dr. Hough continues, "nothing would have pleased Babbitt more than to be regarded as the exponent of the scientific mind. But he believed that the naturalistic scientist ignored truths even more important than those which he discovered, and so he set men going wrong." Babbitt's revival of an understanding of true humanism was intended to remind his generation of the real aim of education, the study of the greatness and the limitations of human nature.

Against the humanist, Babbitt set the humanitarian. The

humanist struggles to develop, by an act of will, the higher
nature in man; the humanitarian believes in "outer working
and inner *laissez faire,*" material gain and emancipation from
ethical checks. What the humanist desires is a working in the
soul of man; what the humanitarian wants is the gratification of
appetites. Bacon symbolized for Babbitt the utilitarian aspect of
humanitarianism: the lust for power over society and physical
nature. Rousseau symbolized for him the sentimental aspect of
humanitarianism, the treacherous impulse to break what Burke
called "the contract of eternal society" and to substitute for
moral obligation the worship of a reckless egoism.

The central sentence in all Babbitt's writings, Paul Elmer
More tells us, is this:

The greatest of vices, according to Buddha, is the lazy yielding to the
impulses of temperament *(pamāda);* the greatest virtue *(appamāda)* is
the opposite awakening from the sloth and lethargy of the senses, the
constant exercise of the active will. The last words of the dying Buddha
to his disciples were an exhortation to practice this virtue unre-
mittingly.

Just so were they the first and last words of Irving Babbitt. To
egoism and appetite, which so oppress our time, Babbitt opposed humanism, the study of man's essential nature, with its
strict ethical disciplines. Humane studies are those that teach a
man his dignity, rights, and duties. They inform him that he is
a little lower than the angels, but infinitely higher than the
beasts.

This theme is illustrated by Babbitt in a variety of ways. His
observations on leisure, originality, the classics, the doctor's degree, and the study of literature in our colleges, written nearly eighty years ago, remain thoroughly relevant to our present
discontents; our problems in education are precisely the problems upon which Babbitt touched. My book *Decadence and
Renewal in the Higher Learning* owes much to Babbitt.

We are eight decades closer to that total collapse of humane
disciplines which Babbitt, in an era of optimism, saw as a grisly
possibility. The very imminence of our peril has awakened some
minds to the veracity of Babbitt's vaticinations. Will and appe-

tite have gone unchecked in a great part of the world, and humanism fights only a rear-guard action here in America. Whether we can restore order in personality and society depends, in no small part, upon whether there still exists among us a remnant sufficiently educated to understand Babbitt's words and boldly resolute to clothe them with flesh.

The present condition of Harvard University, rich in financial endowments but a far cry from Newman's idea of a university, suggests how far we have descended since Babbitt's years there. Babbitt perceived the beginning of the end of the old Harvard in the radical curricular alterations of Charles W. Eliot; that was done in the green tree; it is as well that Babbitt cannot behold what is done in the dry. A woman anthropologist of my acquaintance was invited to discuss the possibility of accepting a permanent post at Harvard. She, incidentally, has read something of Babbitt. She wrote to me, "Honestly, I would be in moral agony, working at Harvard!"

"Our colleges and universities could render no greater service than to oppose to the worship of energy and the frantic eagerness for action an atmosphere of leisure and reflection," Babbitt wrote in the final paragraph of *Literature and the American College*. One does not find that desired atmosphere at today's swollen Harvard, where all the emphasis is upon power.

When I spoke at Harvard near the end of the war in Vietnam, it was shortly after a serious public discussion of making a just peace was broken up by student radicals with bullhorns, who threatened to bring down the house, literally, by concerted stamping upon the old floor. My student host, on returning to his residence hall, found his doorstep encumbered by a dying German graduate student whose skull had been smashed by a mugger. The Harvard police apologized for the incident. They said that once upon a time they had been able to detect criminal intruders upon Harvard Yard, but that nowadays "We can't tell them from the students." And the town of Cambridge today, ugly and impossibly noisy, would horrify Babbitt.

Harvard is America writ small. Are we condemned, then, in Babbitt's words, "to live in a perpetual devil's sabbath of

whirling machinery, and call it progress"? Will the humane
understanding of existence be extinguished altogether?

Perhaps not. We need to recall the observation of T. S. Eliot
that there are no gained causes, because there are no lost causes:
we fight the same battles over again from age to age—if, as Eliot
suggests, "with shabby equipment always deteriorating."

> There is only the fight to recover what has been lost
> And found and lost again and again: and now, under conditions
> That seem unpropitious. But perhaps neither gain nor loss.
> For us, there is only the trying. The rest is not our business.

Perhaps the conditions for recovery today are not quite so
unpropitious as they may seem. America has been chastened by
adversity to some degree, many of Babbitt's predictions of our
prospects having been fulfilled. Politically, the American people
seem inclined once more toward politics as the art of the possible. As for schooling, a large part of the public has become
aware that our system of public instruction is a sorry failure for
most purposes—at least there is much talk of sweeping reforms.

The churches stand in disrepute; yet there are signs of a
widespread yearning for the life of spirit; while ideology, the
pseudo religion of fanatic politics, has made little real headway
among us. For a renewal of faith in the transcendent, a sign
seems required. May that sign be a great miracle paradoxically
verified by modern science and technology—the Shroud of
Turin? Despite Babbitt's tactical decision not to adventure in
the realm of dogmatic religion, such an overwhelming vindication of the central mystery of Christianity would justify also the
enduring belief in a supernatural reality that Babbitt held, what
Giese calls "a mist-enshrouded Ultima Thule on the far edge of
his humanism."

The future being unknowable, historical determinists frequently are undone. John Dewey's brummagem paradise of
egalitarian uniformity, devoid of imagination or faith, certainly
has not come to pass. Perhaps once more men and women will
strive to renew the moral imagination. "A common soldier, a

child, a girl at the door of an inn, have changed the face of fortune, and almost of Nature," Burke wrote in 1790. (Burke's "common soldier" is Arnold of Winkelried, the Swiss who broke in upon the spears at Sempach; his child is Hannibal, taking at the age of twelve his oath to make undying war upon Rome; his girl at the inn is Joan of Arc.)

I do not maintain that the ideas of Irving Babbitt, fifty years after his death, will abruptly change the face of fortune, and almost of Nature. Yet certain events, unpredictable but conceivable, may restore a climate of opinion favorable to humane learning. It has become sufficiently clear to a great many people that American education has not been developing good character among the rising generation and that such notions as "values clarification" in schools give us confusion worse confounded. The unpleasant practical consequences of a nonethical or antiethical schooling are all about us. In such circumstances, Babbitt and his friends might obtain a wider popular hearing than ever they did fifty or sixty years ago; or, to speak more precisely, the disciples of Babbitt, who seem to increase in number in this decade, may find the struggle against a mechanistic or sentimental humanitarianism not wholly lost.

Yes, the influence of Irving Babbitt endures. Babbitt once suggested that although people of his school of thought were welcome to use his ideas, they might find it imprudent to use his name. Half a century later, let us audaciously use his name, too. "Prevailing opinions," Disraeli remarked, "generally are the opinions of the generation that is passing." The hegemony of utilitarianism, pragmatism, and naturalism has been shaken, though it still dominates uneasily the universities and most of the serious press. Even the leading lights of the natural sciences begin to recant. My point is made by the late Arthur Koestler, in *The Roots of Coincidence* (1972):

We have heard a whole chorus of Nobel Laureates in physics informing us that matter is dead, causality is dead, determinism is dead. If that is so, let us give them a decent burial, with a requiem of electronic music. It is time for us to draw the lessons from twentieth-century post-mechanistic science, and to get out of the strait-jacket which

nineteenth-century materialism imposed on our philosophical outlook. Paradoxically, had that outlook kept abreast with modern
science itself, instead of lagging a century behind it, we would have
been liberated from that strait-jacket long ago.

Along with determinism, mechanism, and materialism, in the
dawning age, there may be buried Dewey's pragmatism and
Marx's dialectic. The humane tradition, so long harried and
hounded, may survive the death of its enemies. In literature, in
politics, in religion, in economics, in the natural sciences we
may hear the words *humane* and even *humanist* as terms of
approbation, used with increasing frequency.

If such a renewal comes to pass, it will be the legacy in large
part of Irving Babbitt, who with fortitude labored to redeem the
time. I remind you of the parable of the sower and the seed. The
tares came up thickly, in 1933 and thereafter, among the worst
of those weeds Dewey's "Religious Humanist Manifesto." But
Babbitt's seeds of genuine humanism, planted deeply, are
germinating still.

George A. Panichas

Babbitt and Religion

AS A TEACHER and a critic, Irving Babbitt has come to represent a man of character, an Anglo-Saxon moralist, a New England mind, "the last of the great American Puritans." In his person, as in his teaching, Babbitt was to communicate solidity, robustness, austerity, tenacity, integrity. Even his physical appearance identified him as quintessentially Yankee: a man above average height, powerfully built, with a radiant complexion and dark blue eyes. *"Qui est ce monsieur, si beau, si distingué? Il a l'air d'un dieu!"* someone in his Parisian audience was heard to observe.[1]

His was essentially a masculine disposition. Ascetical and ethereal traits are not part of this disposition; nor was there anything valetudinarian or epicurean in what he projected. Combativeness was at the center of his character and task. He was a man of immense, tactile energy: a polemical dialectician with a probative mind and prophetic message, working from axiomatic principles to inevitable conclusions. Not the idealism of Plato, but the positivism of Aristotle is what inheres in Babbitt's thought. And what is fundamental and experiential, secular and empirical in the best sense, characterizes the articles of Babbitt's humanist creed.

This creed must be assessed in the contexts of what Babbitt

1 Quoted in *Irving Babbitt: Man and Teacher,* ed. Frederick Manchester and Odell Shepard (New York, 1941), 229.

calls "the immediate data of consciousness," that is, those viable and verifiable elements that are distinct and different from the metaphysical and supernatural and from what he termed "a mystical-transcendental mist." In defense of his creed he was indefatigable: "Nor shall my sword sleep in my hand" are words that Babbitt might have easily written. The ancient Greeks used the adjective *gennaios* to designate a man who is high-minded, brave, manly. This word, which describes Babbitt's mission as teacher and critic, is central to "the courage to be" and "the courage of judgment." Irving Babbitt had both.

This profile can hardly do justice to the strength of conviction and "the terrible earnestness" that Babbitt disclosed in his long ministry as a teacher and a critic. Even his foes paid him respect for his effort in behalf of what they happily considered to be lost causes. "He was so powerful a teacher that the very presence of him," writes Alfred Kazin in *On Native Grounds,* "the slow stubborn consecration of his ideal, was moving. In the face of so much inertia, cynicism, and triviality in others, the total absence of anything like his force in American criticism, his moral effectiveness was profound."[2]

For the most part, Babbitt has been denied full recognition as a religious man, as a man of spiritual insight. Kazin dismisses Babbitt as "a commonplace skeptic," "a Yankee Republican and a Tory materialist," who lacked religious history and religious sensibility. And Paul Elmer More, Babbitt's coadjutor and friend, opined in his obituary essay that Babbitt's life, though obedient to "the unrelenting exactions of conscience," was not a life of steady growth in Grace. "I can remember him," More reminisces, "in the early days stopping before a church in North Avenue, and, with a gesture of bitter contempt, exclaiming: 'There is the enemy! there is the thing I hate.'"[3] This incident has long influenced a common perception of Babbitt as anti-religious. Nothing could be, or has been, more misrepresentative of Babbitt's religious importance, which a Hindu crystallizes

2 New York, 1942, p. 300.
3 "Irving Babbitt," *On Being Human* (Princeton, N.J., 1936), p. 37.

in these words: "Oh, Babbitt, he is a holy man, a great saint!"[4] Austin Warren further defines the special nature of his mentor's saintliness by including Babbitt among the "New England Saints"—Jonathan Edwards, Ralph Waldo Emerson, Edward Taylor, Charles Eliot Norton. "My saints are," Warren emphasizes, "none of them, canonized; but they are, whether priests, and of whatever 'communion,' men I recognize, and celebrate, as those to whom reality was the spiritual life, whose spiritual integrity was their calling and vocation."[5]

But the hagiographic titles assigned to Babbitt by his Oriental admirer and his Harvard pupil have enjoyed little approval. Babbitt has always been a victim of those who, like Kazin, see him as a fanatic reactionary and those who, like F. O. Matthiessen, see his "conception of human nature . . . [as] high principled, but arid and inadequate."[6] These impressions of Babbitt, like More's recollection of Babbitt gesticulating at a Cambridge church, have led to a distorted image. Perhaps his friends and his enemies wanted him to be something more than he could be. To the question, "Does not criticism consist above all in comprehending?" Babbitt was to reply, "No, but in judging." That reply takes the measure of the man. It adumbrates, with economy of emotion and expression, his severe magistrative orientation and his absolute honesty. Babbitt did not fudge; there is an astonishing transparency in his total contribution that makes it difficult to accept the charge that he was plagued by "abstract spiritual manliness." What identifies Babbitt is the absoluteness and the concreteness of his views: the commitment and the pertinacity, the belief and faith, of one who avows principles of life and order. A central quality of his achievement is the absence of corruptions, of anomalies, of fantasies, of roles, of turnings. Babbitt wears no masks. The centrality of his thought is its virtue of honesty, its integrative *gennaiotēs,* to use that informing Greek word.

4 *On Being Human,* p. 42.
5 *New England Saints* (Ann Arbor, Mich., 1956), p. v.
6 *American Renaissance* (London, Toronto, New York, 1941), p. 231.

"The saints come to us," Henri Daniel-Rops tells us, "as the *judges* of their own period and society."[7] One must read Babbitt's particular form of saintliness in the contexts of these words. Daniel-Rops also reminds us that "a saint is a scandal," that he creates " 'a troublesome commotion.' " No words better characterize both the treatment and the effects of Babbitt's endeavors. But for Babbitt not to have held any one of these saintly dimensions would have made him merely another humdrum critic.

It was as a teacher-saint that Babbitt was to conduct his dedicated ministry, "without confusion of the planes of being": that is, as a worldly counterpart of a saint, one who, in a quintessentially human rather than a superhuman sense, aspires for moral excellences in this world. His arena was his classroom; his pupils were both his catechumens and his concelebrants. No other teacher in this century has more powerfully or memorably exemplified selfless commitment to the art of teaching, to *humanitas.* His writings were the products of his teaching, that is, lectures transposed from the lectern to the printed page, there to become permanent principles of character and conscience. Babbitt was to sanctify the whole process of teaching as a moral act and to elevate it to its maximum point of meaning. "Here was a new kind of teacher: not reducible to a learned expositor, he taught with authority," Warren recalls. "If, to doctrinal 'liberals,' he was patently reactionary, he defended an academic freedom precious and perishable—the freedom to judge. . . . He was concerned with principles, with tracing lines of intellectual development."[8] Babbitt's pupils readily testify to the greatness of his teaching, which he summarized repeatedly with his admonition, "Live at the center." Even those pupils who disagreed with him and those adherents who diverted from his ideas testify to the influence Babbitt exerted on them. To read his pupils' reminiscences and tributes is to become aware of one who is, as the Chinese are wont to say, "a

7 "Introduction: Holiness in History and Holiness Today," Roland Cluny, *Holiness in Action* (New York, 1963), p. 10.

8 *New England Saints,* p. 149, p. 152.

teacher of men." For them his classes were an intellectual and spiritual experience and, ultimately, "spiritual exercises." Master of "self-reverence, self-knowledge, self-control," he disclosed those gifts and disciplines of the teacher-saint possessing a great soul, one whom Babbitt's own master of "unsurpassed humanism," Aristotle, speaks of as *megalopsychos*.

Few would deny Babbitt recognition as a teacher-saint. But that recognition is diminished frequently by the concomitant indictment of Babbitt's humanism as being, at the very least, religiously vacuous and of Babbitt himself as being a teacher-saint who is also a heretic standing some distance from or outside the church and holding a position short of a commitment to Christianity. Babbitt's brand of humanism, as Marion Montgomery charged, is overtly Hellenic and not New Testament. That is to say, Babbitt represents a gnostic mentality whereby the Greek spirit threatens to engulf faith in speculative philosophy. "Aristotle without St. Thomas," Montgomery reminds us in the course of indicting Babbitt, "like Plato without St. Paul, is an incomplete champion against secular relativism."[9] The substance of this indictment of Babbitt is not new, but goes back to what remains a definitive statement, T. S. Eliot's *After Strange Gods: A Primer of Modern Heresy* (1934), in which Babbitt is included with D. H. Lawrence, Ezra Pound, and the early Yeats as modern heretics, that is, men who are not necessarily unbelievers, but who emphasize a doctrine too strongly and obsessively, to the point of falsehood. In two earlier essays, "The Humanism of Irving Babbitt" (1927) and "Second Thoughts about Humanism" (1928), Eliot had also delineated his critique of Babbitt's religious position, or what he calls "the weaknesses of humanism."[10]

Eliot's case against Babbitt's doctrine of humanism can be summarized as follows: Insofar as humanism refuses the orthodox religious view, it seeks to be an alternative to religion; it stresses the role of human reason, not the revelation of the

9 See review of George A. Panichas, *The Courage of Judgment: Essays in Criticism, Culture, and Society* (Knoxville, Tenn., 1982), in *Christianity and Literature* (Winter 1983), p. 83.

10 These two essays are included in *Selected Essays* (New York, 1960), pp. 419-438.

supernatural. As such Babbitt's humanism is essentially a by-product of liberal Protestant theology. In the end, Babbitt is trying to make his form of humanism work without religion, even as he himself remains detached from any fundamental religious belief. Babbitt has come to know many philosophies and religions and has assimilated them so thoroughly that he cannot commit himself to any. Eliot could not accept Babbitt's emphasis on the appliance of the "inner check" in controlling the human personality's centrifugal pull. Orthodox religion alone, he insisted, was capable of providing not only the "external restraints," but also "a single spiritual core and a dogmatic creed." ("Only Christianity helps to reconcile me to life, which is otherwise disgusting," Eliot once wrote to More.) However admirable Babbitt's concern "with the discipline and training of emotion," Eliot says, the end, the *telos,* of humanism is futile: "What is the higher will to *will,* if there is nothing either 'anterior, exterior, or superior' to the individual?" What Eliot has to say is underlined by Allen Tate in his essay on "The Fallacy of Humanism" when he observes: "His [Babbitt's] doctrine of re-straint does not look to *unity,* but to abstract and external *control*—not to a solution of the moral problem, but to an attempt to get the moral results of unity by main force, by a kind of moral fascism."[11]

The depiction of Babbitt as a heretic who somehow trans-figured into a moral fascist has long been with us. It has con-spired to strip him of those genuine religious qualities that per-vade his humanist faith and that reveal him as a great spiri-tual figure. If there are seeds of heresy in Babbitt, they are neither perverse nor diabolic. His heresy can be interpreted as a neces-sary aspect of the life of the church, as a supplement to it in the contexts of what Edmund Burke terms "the dissidence of dis-sent." The church and the heretics, it has been observed, form a far more vital union than either one will admit. Above all, then, the religious significance of heresy is what needs to be grasped

---

11 *Memoirs and Opinions 1926–1974* (Chicago, 1975), p. 171. Here the original title of this essay has been changed to "Humanism and Naturalism."

and understood. But before examining this significance in Babbitt, it is best to earmark the major traits of a great heretic in the
words of Swiss theologian Walter Georg Nigg: "He is the extreme
antithesis of the indifferentist. . . . He courageously accepts the
consequences of his actions. His fervor can teach us the meaning
of loyalty to truth. We may even say that the heretic embodies the
religious spirit in concentrated form."[12]

Dr. Nigg goes on to say that the heretic typifies a repressed
interpretation of religion; that unresolved problems come to life
in a heretic; that a heretic seeks to advance an overlooked or
misunderstood religious concept, so that religious values previously unknown are discovered. "Only great men have brought
forth heresies," Saint Augustine tells us. The heretic often
resembles the saint; the piety of the latter contrasts with the
rebellion of the former to underscore a mission on the part of
one who is simultaneously a witness, an outlaw, and even a
martyr. It should be remembered that the term heresy is a
transliteration of the Greek *hairesis,* meaning an act of choosing,
a course of action or thought, and finally the philosophical
principles of one who professes them. At its most destructive
stage, heresy destroys unity and induces spiritual alienation; at
its most constructive, in the words of Leopold Ziegler, heresy is
"necessary for the tradition, so that it will remain in flux and not
congeal into rigidity."

No less than the Blaise Pascal of the *Lettres Provinciales,* whom
Unamuno termed "an orthodox heretic," Babbitt could also
say, "I stand alone," as he sought to uphold the sovereignty of
conscience to the point of heresy. Pascal, a religious visionary
who both attracted and repelled Babbitt, was long the subject of
one of his Harvard courses and much discussed in his writings.
The spiritual core of Pascal's personality appealed to Babbitt,
whose own religio-humanistic position is epitomized in Fragment 378 of the *Pensées:* "To leave the mean is to abandon
humanity. The greatness of the human soul consists in knowing
how to preserve the mean. So far from greatness consisting in

12 *The Heretics* (New York, 1962), p. 10.

leaving it, it consists in not leaving it." Babbitt, who distrusted "the Jansenist emphasis on thunderclaps and visible upsets of grace," admired the Pascal who differentiated the man of faith from the naturalist, the traditional disciplines from pure naturalism, true faith from "the horrible flux of all things," faith from worldliness. It is the Pascal who finally exclaims, "Joy, certainty, peace," whom Babbitt embraces and whom he equates with the "peace, poise, [and] centrality" he especially admires in Buddhism. Babbitt's admiration of Pascal shows sympathy not with the ascetical and the mystical, with what he speaks of as the Pascalian "expressions of the theological terror," but rather with the conviction and strength that resist the morbid and discouraging.

Spiritual strenuousness remained Babbitt's major tenet of faith: "Work out your own salvation with diligence." Buddha's words dramatize Babbitt's religious orientation, one that clearly disavowed "dogmatic or revealed religion" and the doctrine of Grace. G. K. Chesterton, in opposing Superhumanism to Humanism, regarded the latter as one of those "spiritual experiments outside the central spiritual tradition." "Humanism may try to pick up the pieces; but can it stick them together?" Chesterton asks. "Where is the *cement* which made religion corporate and popular, which can prevent it falling to pieces in a débris of individualistic tastes and degrees?"[13]

Babbitt's qualified acceptance of Pascal is indicative of his discernment of institutional religion and its fundamental ideas. His endorsements were selective and limiting. In the religious realm, as in the educational, Babbitt was motivated by a positive critical spirit informed by his absolute rejection of any romantic tendency culminating in man's "expansive conceit" that produces ignorance and blindness. His religious views have a decidedly generalist cast and belong to what should be called the universal moral order. In contemporary religious parlance, Babbitt could be termed an "ecumenist," though this word would be apt to imply nonselective and nondefined religious

13 "Is Humanism a Religion?" *The Bookman* (May 1929), p. 241.

elements that Babbitt would find antipathetic. Babbitt's religious search goes beyond the frontiers of historical Christianity
and is more inclusive in its figures, goals, and essences, as he
makes clear when he writes: ". . . if there is such a thing as the
wisdom of the ages, a central core of normal human experience,
this wisdom is, on the religious level, found in Buddha and
Christ and, on the humanistic level, in Confucius and Aristotle.
These teachers may be regarded both in themselves and in their
influence as the four outstanding figures in the spiritual history
of mankind."

This statement identifies the comprehensive features of Babbitt's religious quest, even as it points to its heterodox features.
Yet to insist on Babbitt's religious deviationism does him a disser-
vice. Any fair consideration of his thought will corroborate
Professor Louis J.-A. Mercier's contention that, for Babbitt, man
is a rational animal in whom there is felt "the presence of a
higher will ultimately divine." Indeed, in one of his later essays,
"Humanism: An Essay at Definition," Babbitt affirms Pascal's
belief that the humanist must finally take part in the debate
between naturalists and supernaturalists. Babbitt proceeds to
state a principle of belief that elucidates the religious character
of his humanism: "For my own part, I range myself unhesitat-
ingly on the side of the supernaturalists. Though I see no evidence that humanism is necessarily ineffective apart from dogmatic and revealed religion, there is, as it seems to me, evidence that
it gains immensely in effectiveness when it has a background of
religious insight."

In their thrust and ramification Babbitt's religious ideas and
acceptances are cautious. Any excess of rarefied religious sentiment or spirituality is checked. One cannot, he iterates, pass
from the human to the religious level too quickly; the world
would be better if men "made sure that they were human before setting out to be superhuman." There are priorities to be
observed, levels of growth to be attained, particular paths to be
followed, and adjustments to be made if humanism and religion
are to have a gainful encounter. At the same time, as Babbitt
avers, "Humanistic mediation that has the support of medita-

tion may correctly be said to have a religious background. Mediation and meditation are after all only different stages in the same ascending 'path' and should not be arbitrarily separated."

Humanism can work in harmony with religion in opposition to what Babbitt sees as a common foe when he writes: "The chief enemies of the humanist are the pragmatists and other philosophers of the flux who simplify this problem for themselves by dismissing the One, which is a living intuition, as a metaphysical abstraction." "Humanism: An Essay at Definition" occupies a high place in an understanding of Babbitt's religious views. Its chief value is corrective. Babbitt was keenly aware of the misunderstanding and misrepresentation of his attitude toward religion. His statements in this essay have a concentrated purpose, not only in definition but also in clarification. He is painstaking in formulating his religious views. "It is an error to hold that humanism can take the place of religion," he emphasizes. "Religion indeed may more readily dispense with humanism than humanism with religion." Here Babbitt is speaking to critical friends, to the Paul Elmer More who asks in trepidation: "Will not the humanist, unless he adds to his creed the faith and the hope of religion, find himself at the last, despite his protests, dragged back into the camp of the naturalist? If we perish like beasts, shall we not live like beasts?"[14]

These are defiant, even embarrassing, questions that Babbitt answered with the patience and dignity of the great teacher that he was. So much more was demanded of Babbitt than of others, perhaps because he, more than others, meditated on first causes and ultimate ends. If anything, Babbitt's orientation was one of opportunities and strivings. Between humanism and the Christian communions Babbitt sought for a basis of cooperation in a united struggle against "the humanitarian programme." "The weakness of humanitarianism from both the humanistic and the religious point[s] of view," he declared, "is that it holds out the hope of securing certain spiritual benefits . . . without any ascent

---

14 "A Revival of Humanism," *The Bookman* (March 1930), p. 9.

from the naturalistic level." What is constant in Babbitt's religious thought is his stress on man's need for a morality of
ascent, the ultimate standard of spiritual effort and life. That
man needs to submit his ordinary self to some higher will is, for
Babbitt, a central religious tenet. In this submission there reside
the elements of awe and humility and the ultimate attainment
of peace. He advances the ethical dimension of religion. As he
remarks: "The final reply to all the doubts that torment the
human heart is not some theory of conduct, however perfect,
but the man of character." Though Babbitt repeatedly warns of
the perils of intellectual unrestraint, he is critical of the Christian
tendency to get rid of the intellect in order to get rid of the pride
of the intellect. Unfailingly Babbitt keeps his eye on the universal center, on the middle path. As a true Aristotelian, he writes:
"To use the intellect to the utmost and at the same time to keep
it in its proper subordinate place is a task that seems thus far to
have been beyond the capacity of Occidental man."

Not so much a historical, and sacramental, but a critical
Christianity is what Babbitt addresses himself to. What he most
sympathizes with in Christianity are its elements of joy and
illumination; what he most opposes is a "romantic religiosity"
mired in "the web of illusion" and "metaphysical despair."
Particularly in the Catholic Church did Babbitt find aspects to
admire, or what he singled out as its "discipline and the definite
standards that could protect society against the individual." On
the other hand, he felt that the Protestant churches were turning more and more to the doctrine of social service and thus
were "substituting for the truths of the inner life various causes
and movements and reforms and crusades."

Babbitt saw an overarching religious problem confronting
modern man. It went back to Rousseau. That religious problem,
Babbitt said, involves a major judgmental choice "between a
dualism that affirms a struggle between good and evil in the
heart of the individual and a dualism which, like that of
Rousseau, transfers the struggle to society." Insofar as the
Rousseauistic attitude has prevailed in the modern world,
according to Babbitt, spiritual disorder has become ascendant.

He was concerned with an existential as opposed to a theological evil, with those forms of evil that embody an evasion of
moral responsibility, so that they result in what he termed
spiritual indolence. To resist this form of breakdown he pre-
scribes the humanistic virtues—moderation, common sense,
and common decency. He viewed these virtues in the context of
"a positive and critical humanism" in which there is an emphasis
on the educative function: man "must be trained in the appropriate habits almost from infancy." "We need," he says, "to restore to human nature in some critical and experimental fashion
the 'old Adam' that the idealists have been so busy eliminating."
As necessary as they are, the theological virtues of faith, hope,
and charity are sequential to the humanistic as an ultimate
developmental stage in the morality of ascent and in "the paths
of Truth."

It bears repeating that Babbitt's attitude toward revealed religion was essentially one of "suspended judgment." He perceived humanism as a common ground upon which dualists,
Christians and non-Christians, could meet. No less than the
"humanistic Goethe" (as revealed in the *Conversations* with Ecker-
mann and in the critical judgments uttered in his later years),
Babbitt "would have us cease theorizing about the absolute and
learn to recognize it in its actual manifestations." Man, Babbitt
would say, needs to learn the lessons of renunciation, but the
renunciation of temperament and impulses must be "the natural
outgrowth of this life and not, as so often in religion, the violent
contradiction of it." Of Babbitt, as of Goethe, it could be said that
he avoided confusing the planes of being. "No inconsiderable
part of wisdom," writes Babbitt, "consists in just this: not to allow
the mind to dwell on questions that are unprofitable in themselves or else entirely beyond its grasp." In the Goethe who
expressed the humanistic virtues Babbitt found a mirror of himself that enabled him to trace the anatomy of his own religious
identity. What was finally disclosed was Babbitt's stress on what
he calls "instinct for a sound spiritual hygiene" and on the need
to turn away from grace to works. "The right use of grace and
similar doctrines," Babbitt states, "is to make us humble and not

to make us morbid or discouraged." Speculations about the "in-
soluble mysteries" are basically unrewarding; like Goethe, Babbitt refused "to enter into the metaphysical maze of either the
dogmatic supernaturalist or the dogmatic naturalist."

For Babbitt a "sham spirituality" signifies the death of faith.
Throughout his writings he provides a diagnostic examination
of what he judges to be religious illusions and errors emerging
from a monistic naturalism. Babbitt locates standards of what
he calls "true spirituality," the truths of humility and of the inner life, in the Orient, especially in the religion and personality
of Buddha. In Buddhism, Babbitt applauds a comparative
freedom from casuistry, obscurantism, and intolerance. The
most significant religious statement that Babbitt makes on the
subject is his long introductory essay "Buddha and the Occident," in his translation of the ancient Pāli classic of Buddhist
wisdom, *The Dhammapada,* published in 1936. This essay is
Babbitt's spiritual testament, his final witness. No understanding of his religious ethos is possible without a judicious estimation of this essay. A life-long student of Buddhism, Babbitt was
much in sympathy with the primitive (Hīnayāna) Buddhism of
Ceylon, Burma, and Siam. Austin Warren believes that Babbitt
was in fact a Buddhist and was "motivated . . . by the desire to
restate 'genuine Buddhism' in modern terms, as a religion
acceptable to those who, like himself, found metaphysics, theology, and ecclesiasticism harmful rather than salutary to the
devout life."[15] And Paul Elmer More simply states as a fact that
Babbitt was "much closer to Buddhism than would appear from
his public utterances."[16] In an essay-review, "Interpreting India
to the West," Babbitt crystallizes his concept of a Buddhism that
may be used to supplement and support our Western wisdom
when he writes, or rather testifies, his own faith:

Buddha deals with the law of control, the special law of human nature,
in a spirit as positive and dispassionate as that in which a Newton deals
with the law of gravitation. If a man wishes peace and brotherhood,

15 *New England Saints,* pp. 159–160.
16 *On Being Human,* p. 37.

he must pay the price—he must rise above the naturalistic level; and this he can do only by overcoming his moral indolence, only by applying the inner check to temperamental impulse. "All salutary conditions (*dhammā*)," says Buddha, "have their root in strenuousness."

The experience of the Far East, Babbitt believed, completes and confirms that of the Occident. "We can scarcely afford to neglect it if we hope to work out a truly ecumenical wisdom to oppose to the sinister one-sidedness of our current naturalism," he observes. The historical Buddha, Babbitt observed, was a "critical and experimental supernaturalist," a dualist and individualist who did not rest his belief on those "tremendous affirmations" of dogmatic and revealed religion that revolved around a personal God and personal immortality. Buddha can be defined as a "religious empiricist" to whom the real meaning of faith is "faith to act." Self-mastery is the most eminent aspect of this faith as meaning and as action, that is, as inner action. "Self is the lord of self. Who else can be the lord?" Buddha declares. "By oneself the evil is done, by oneself one is defiled. Purity and impurity belong to oneself, no one can purify another." What ennobles Buddhism, in Babbitt's eyes, is an emphasis on earnestness and on continual spiritual effort to subordinate the evil forces within one to an indwelling law of righteousness. Babbitt especially endorses the words that Buddha uttered at the end of his life: "Therefore, O Ananda, be ye lamps unto yourselves. Be ye refuges unto yourselves. Look to no outer refuge. Hold fast as a refuge unto the Law (*Dhamma*)." Buddhism is not a philosophical system but a "path"; one who follows this path ultimately gains insight that is marked by an increasing awareness, which precedes "right meditation" and "is at the opposite pole from the diffuse reverie that has been so encouraged by our modern return to nature." Wisdom is measured by the degree to which man has been awakened from "the dream of sense."

In Buddhism, Babbitt perceived a religion rooted in a "psychology of desire." "Immediate peace," not "immediate pleasure," is for Buddha a paramount goal. This peace is the "rest that comes through striving." It is a calm that is "without the slightest trace of languor," a "meditative tranquillity" that arises when, as Buddha says, one "has reached the other shore in two states (tranquillity and insight)." For Babbitt a saint, whether Buddhist or Christian, "is rightly meditative and in proportion to the rightness of his meditation is the depth of his peace." If Christianity was originally more emotional and nostalgic in temper than Buddhism, Babbitt states, "it is at one in its final emphasis with the older religion. In both faiths this emphasis is on the peace that passeth understanding." If, as Babbitt noted, Buddha was filled with pity, he was also very stern; in Buddha, as in Christ, love and justice are perfectly balanced so as to constitute a single virtue. The Buddhist's insistence on self-love may appear to be selfish and uncharitable, but Babbitt went on to stipulate that the teaching of true self-love accentuates the love of a higher self. This Buddhist teaching, he pointed out, is similar to the Christian concept of dying that one may live. He most admired in Buddha the importance given to the role of the intellect that is keenly discriminating and that of the higher will that is strenuous.

The security and the serenity that are at the heart of "religious comfort" have given way, Babbitt lamented, to an obsessive search for material comfort. In this shifting of emphasis he viewed the glorification of the utilitarian and sentimental facets of the humanitarian movement. Basic religious precepts are radically altered so as to satisfy this process of ethical and spiritual transvaluation. "A great religion is above all a great example," Babbitt declares; but "the example tends to grow faint in time or even to suffer alteration into something very different." More than other religious teachers, Buddha, who stands for the idea of meditation, has deep significance for the Occident. This significance is heightened by the fact that Buddha reduces the human problem to a psychology of desire and then deals with desire in terms of conflict and adjustment. Particularly in the passage from the medieval to the modern period,

Babbitt contended, the idea of meditation and the transcendent view of life have steadily declined. "Yet it is not certain," Babbitt adds, "that religion itself can survive unless men retain some sense of the wisdom that may, according to Dante, be won by sitting in quiet recollection." In Buddhism, as tested by its fruits, Babbitt saw a striking confirmation of Christianity. Buddha provides spiritual paradigms and humanistic truths that, if accepted, would augment the Christian faith by saving it, as Babbitt hoped, from a Calvinist nightmare or an Arcadian dream. Buddha's relevance to Christianity, Babbitt says, is positive and critical in the sense of reinforcing and remobilizing its intrinsic strength in a modern world. These final sentences from Babbitt's essay "Buddha and the Occident" identify the connections that he sought to establish between two great religious movements in a period that has seen the eclipse of the religious sense:

> The meditation of the Buddhist involves like that of the Christian the exercise of transcendent will; this will is not, however, associated, as it normally is in the meditation of the Christian, with that of a personal deity. Persons of positive and critical temper who yet perceive the importance of meditation may incline here as elsewhere to put less emphasis on the doctrinal divergence of Christianity and Buddhism than on their psychological agreement.

Predictably, Babbitt's Christian Platonist friend, Paul Elmer More, and his Anglo-Catholic pupil, T. S. Eliot, had other views of Buddhism. Of the two, More's response to Buddhism was more sympathetic. Unlike Babbitt, More favored Hindu mysticism and the Brahmanic theosophy of the Upanishads. By the end of his life he had accepted Christianity as the complement and the climax of the Greek tradition. The first essay in his book *The Catholic Faith* (1931) is devoted to "Buddhism and Christianity"; Babbitt himself had gone through the entire book with such "extreme care" as to prompt an extensive revision of that essay. In ways that recall Babbitt, More brought Buddhism into vital relation to Christianity; he saw both religions covering and dividing "the deeper possibilities of faith." In the history of the two religions he found similarities, as he also found in the morality of discipline taught by Buddha and by Christ. More's admiration of the Buddhist's three stages of progress in sanctity—discipline of conduct, discipline of mind, and the higher wisdom and power— is no less than Babbitt's.

But More discerned profound absences in Buddhism: it contains no creator, no providential ruler, no judge, no savior. Like Babbitt, he considered Buddhism more joyous and even tempered than Christianity, but, in contrast to the latter, More believed that "the notion of *telos* plays no part in its cosmogony or ethics." That is, in Buddhism there is "no continuity between the end and the means to the end." Though More admitted that Buddha was "the noblest of all religious teachers, saving only one," and that Buddhism, by its reticence about the soul and by its very omission of God, "was preserved from the evils of intolerance and fanaticism and spiritual anguish that have so often darkened the history of Christianity," he also stressed that Buddhism has "missed something of the positive riches of experience that Christianity at its best can bestow." In what can be construed as a magnanimous rebuttal of Babbitt's position, More concludes with these words regarding Buddha:

. . . it seems to me at times as if that great soul were searching on all the ways of the spirit for the dogma of the Incarnation, and that fact of the historic Jesus, could it have been known to him, might have saved his religion in later ages from floundering helplessly. . . . Buddhism, I think, may be accepted as a preface to the Gospel . . . and as the most convincing argument withal that truth to be clearly known waits upon revelation.

Far less magnanimous is Eliot's critique of Babbitt's Buddhism. It leaves the distinct impression that Eliot, once and for all, is dismissing a heretic who dismisses the doctrine of revelation. This critique constitutes a long introductory essay written by Eliot for a collection entitled *Revelation,* edited by John Baillie and Hugh Martin, and published in 1937. Eliot categorically declares that "the division between those who accept, and those who deny, Christian revelation I take to be the most profound division between human beings." Throughout, his critical perspective is tough and unsparing. In Babbitt he sees "the most remarkable, the most ambitious attempt to erect a secular

philosophy of life in our time." He terms Babbitt a "disbe-
liever," unique because "he attacked the foundations of secularism more deeply and more comprehensively than any other
writer of our time."

Eliot concentrates on the essay "Buddha and the Occident" to
show how Babbitt sought "to evade Christian conclusions at any
cost." The Buddhism of Babbitt, he concludes, instances a kind
of "psychological mysticism." "This is the mysticism which seeks
contact with the sources of supernatural power," writes Eliot,
"divorced from religion and theology; the mysticism which
must always be suspect, and which sometimes springs up in cults
whose aims are not far removed from those of magic." Especially interesting in Eliot's essay is his coupling of Babbitt and D. H.
Lawrence: "The point is that the will to get out from Christianity
into a religion of one's own operated in Lawrence as it operated
in Babbitt." Eliot ends his discussion of "the literature of
secularism" by remarking that the religious sentiment, which
can be satisfied only by the message of revelation, "is simply
suffering from a condition of repression painful for those in
whom it is repressed, who yearn for the fulfilment of belief,
although too ashamed of that yearning to allow it to come to
consciousness."

That Eliot is doubtlessly aware of his arbitrary yoking of
Babbitt and Lawrence in their "will against Christianity" is
suggested by the tone in which he distinguishes Babbitt ("by
nature an educated man, as well as a highly well-informed one")
from Lawrence ("a medicine man" and "a researcher into religious emotion"). But his indictment of both men as examples
of "individualistic misdirections of will" is uncompromising
insofar as both men, he claims, teach and affirm secular philosophies and are examples of "titanism," "the attempt to build a
purely human world without reliance upon grace."

Eliot's case against Lawrence's "religion of power and magic"
has been largely answered by Dr. F. R. Leavis. The case against
Babbitt, however, remains curiously unanswered, perhaps
because of the paradoxical alliance between Babbitt's Christian
friends and his liberal enemies, who propagate Eliot's thesis for

their special purposes. The fact remains that Babbitt's humanist beliefs cannot be understood without the background of his religious thinking. He was not an orthodox Christian, but he gave his spiritual witness in the very character of his writing and teaching. He had integrity. He had humility, the humility that Eliot tells us is endless. And he had standards. These qualities never failed to compass his work and thought: his judgments, which he conveyed resolutely and directly. "There appears to be evidence," he says, "that religion has existed without the accompaniment of morality." Such a statement again reminds us that, for Babbitt, the validity of religion lies in psychology rather than in history, and makes even more emphatic Babbitt's reverence for the Buddha who declares in his message of joyful deliverance, "Only one thing I announce today, as always. Sorrow and its Extinction."

To connect and unify the inner life and the outer life constituted for Babbitt a paramount spiritual need. Those who face up to the moral requisites of this need, he believed, "face unflinchingly the facts of life and these facts do not encourage a thoughtless elation." Thus Babbitt esteemed Saint Francis de Sales because this Doctor of the Church had worked out a synthesis between the demands of "this-worldliness" and those of "other-worldliness." By the same token, Babbitt frowned upon Byzantine sacred art, obviously detecting in the ikons of the Eastern Church an obscure, even passive, soteriological quality that he equated with excessive melancholy and with the loss of "one's self in a shoreless sea of revery."

In respect to sacred music, too, Babbitt had clear-cut views. He stressed the need to distinguish between the genuine "devotional music" of Christian plainsong, which inspires prayer and peace, and the "insurrectional music" of *The Requiem Mass* of Hector Berlioz, which Babbitt equated with "emotional unrestraint" and with sheer "noise and sensationalism." Spiritual romanticism, for Babbitt, was no less harmful than the romanticism that subverts the aesthetic criteria of "dignity, centrality, repose." In particular he distrusted what he termed "the expansion of infinite indeterminate desire" that he related to the neo-Platonic side of Christianity, though he was careful to praise that aspect of the Christian faith that "has dealt sternly and veraciously with the facts of human nature. It has perceived clearly how a man may move towards happiness and how on the other hand he tends to sink into despair; or what amounts to the same thing, it has seen the supreme importance of spiritual effort and the supreme danger of spiritual sloth." It is almost unnecessary to theorize how Babbitt would view the current vogue of "liberation theology," which revolves so loosely and sentimentally around a messianic materialism and the whirl of "the secular city." Such a theology of unilateral desanctification, Babbitt would say, is another blatant example of "eleutheromania," or as he writes in *The New Laokoon:* "Everybody is becoming tinged with eleutheromania, taken up with his rights rather than with his duties, more and more unwilling to accept limitations."

We must not judge Babbitt according to a systematic or dogmatic theology; his was not a concern with what Paul Tillich designates as the theology that "is the methodical explanation of the contents of the Christian faith." First and last Babbitt was a moral critic and comparatist, who saw "connections that no other mind would have perceived," as Eliot says. Babbitt practiced the wisdom of Confucius's admonition that "the man who does not take far views will have near troubles." On the first page of *Democracy and Leadership* he writes: "When studied in any degree of thoroughness, the economic problem will be found to run into the political problem, the political problem in turn into the philosophical problem, and the philosophical problem itself to be almost indissolubly bound up at last with the religious problem." These noble words help to identify Babbitt's achievement in its value and "constant aspiration toward the central unity of life." Nor must we forget that he was a teacher, a *didaskalos,* "an enlightener and enlarger." Hence to assess his religious significance in terms of a theological orthodoxy is to violate the intrinsic spiritual strength of his thought. He was not a religionist, nor a philosopher of religion, nor a teacher of theology. He was quintessentially a spiritual man, indeed, a spiritual genius, "to whom reality was the spiritual life," to recall Warren's words. He revered the interior life, as well as the ethical and moral life. He possessed an informing religious sense, not one that was vague and numinous, but analytical and judgmental. He sought for a "sense of the absolute," for the absolute of an Emerson or a Tennyson, which Babbitt defined as "a purely spiritual percep- tion of the light beyond reason, entirely disassociated from the faith in creeds and formulas."

There is some truth in R. P. Blackmur's symptomatic com- plaint that Babbitt was a preacher,[17] if by preacher we mean a humanistic and religious realist who traces causes and effects and who distinguishes between the law of the spirit and the law of the members, between the "law for man" and the "law for thing." Such a realist finds a common good in morality and affirms the meaning of the moral real and the meaning of all existence within the universal moral real. The religious sense diminishes, as Babbitt averred, when moral struggle and deliberation and choice are minimized. He vividly imagined this reductionist process in his contrast "between the spiritual athlete and the cosmic loafer, between a Saint Paul . . . and a Walt Whitman." "The greater a man's moral seriousness," he reminds us, "the more he will be concerned with doing rather than dreaming." Babbitt clearly indicated that he had no aversion to a humanist who, seeking support in something higher than reason, turns to Christian theology. "I hold that at the heart of genuine Christianity," he declares, "are certain truths which have already once saved Western civilization and, judiciously employed, may save it again." But he also claimed that for one to be fully positive and critical in the modern world, one has to deal with life more psychologically than meta- physically. He thought it possible, perhaps necessary, to con- ceive of a humanistic or even a religious psychology that

17 "Humanism and Symbolic Imagination: Notes on Re-reading Irving Babbitt," *The Lion and the Honeycomb: Essays in Solicitude and Critique* (New York, 1955), p. 153.

transcends both the dictates of a naturalistic psychology and the symbolic view of the world.

Indeed, Babbitt saw a close affinity between the elimination of the teleological element from modern life and the decline of traditional religion and the older religious controls. He never-theless believed that, from a humanistic point of view, to restore this teleological element it is more advantageous to start with observation of experience, as in early Buddhism, than with theo-logical affirmations. Warning against "dogmatic exclusiveness," he says that one could eclectically acquire humanistic and religious purpose without indulging in ultimates and absolutes. "The good life," he writes, "is not primarily something to be *known* but something to be *willed.*" And when "willed" the life-problem of avoiding "the indolence of extremes" is mitigated.

Irving Babbitt chose to speak out not as an orthodox Chris-tian but as "a psychological observer" and a "complete posi-tivist" (terms whose unintended naturalistic connotations mis-led some of his readers). In this capacity he judged "the mod-ern movement," the social benefits of which he found largely illusory and the spiritual offshoots of which made "neither for humanistic poise nor again for the peace of religion." He discriminated practically and concretely between true and false religion, as he discriminated rigorously between "the moral imagination" and "the idyllic imagination." His standards were clear and unshakeable in demarcating and avoiding "a confu-sion of categories." Any softening of standards, he never ceased to state, has a commensurate impact on spiritual life. A dire threat to religious, and humanistic, standards, Babbitt said, is man's consuming "interest in origins rather than in ends." In this connection, he especially esteemed Aristotle's dictum, *"To proton ou sperma estin alla to teleion"*—"The first thing is not seed but the perfect being."[18] These words, it should be remembered, closely follow Aristotle's other emphatic declaration, in his *Metaphysics,* that "life belongs to God." The critical centrality of his religious views must be fully comprehended if Babbitt's

18 *Metaphysics,* p. 1072^b.

moral and spiritual vision is to be saved from both the tests of religious orthodoxy and the incubus of heresy. When this reparative task has been finally accomplished, then what Boswell said of Dr. Johnson will be said of Babbitt: that he is, incontestably, a "majestic teacher of moral and religious wisdom."

Claes G. Ryn

Babbitt and the Problem
of Reality

PERHAPS THE MOST original and fruitful of the insights of
Irving Babbitt pertains to the relationship between will and
imagination. His explication of that relationship forms at once
a compelling diagnosis of the ills of the present age and a deeply
challenging statement of the prerequisites for a restoration of
Western life and letters. In Babbitt's understanding of the interaction of will and imagination lies not only an important
contribution to ethics and aesthetics but also a highly significant
ingredient for a new theory of knowledge.

The present inquiry into Babbitt's ideas will be governed by
the question: How does man achieve a grasp of reality? Differently put: What is the criterion of reality? One only hints at
Babbitt's answer by pointing to the cooperation of what he calls
the ethical will and the ethical imagination, for both these ideas
have been poorly understood by most of his commentators.
Explaining Babbitt's view of the relationship between will and
imagination in the search for reality requires bringing some
clarity to each of the two subjects while keeping the main objective in sight.

According to Babbitt, attempts by modern philosophy to
solve the problem of knowledge rest on a vain belief in abstract
rationality as the way to truth. These attempts signify a failure

to understand that in the end man will attach himself only to a standard of reality that has immediacy and concreteness, that is, one that is firmly established in experience. Thinking specifically of the failure of epistemology, Babbitt is moved to the sweeping and indiscriminate statement that "modern philosophy is bankrupt, not merely from Kant, but from Descartes." Babbitt's doctrine of the ethical and aesthetical basis of man's search for reality is, among other things, a contribution to the development of a new theory of knowledge.[1]

Probably the weakest part of Babbitt's work is his notion of reason. Except for scattered ideas pointing in a different direction, reason is usually rather vaguely assumed by Babbitt to be a pragmatic and analytic faculty. It helps man to discriminate between illusion and reality by breaking up the intuitive wholes of imagination into constituent parts and by scrutinizing the internal consistency of those parts. But reason is also seen by Babbitt as incapable of grasping what is most fundamental in human consciousness, the primordial tension between the One and the Many. It is the nature of reason to attribute reality only to what is reified and formally consistent. The paradox of dualism, of which man is nevertheless directly aware, is for Babbitt "the scandal of reason." Man's most important contact with reality, therefore, is not reason but unmediated, direct experience of life.

Like almost all his contemporaries, Babbitt never systematically considers that part of modern epistemology that is perhaps best exemplified by Benedetto Croce. Genuinely philosophical reason, Croce argues, is in fact fully compatible with man's immediate self-awareness. Far from violating the dualistic facts of actual experience by insisting on some formal consistency, philosophical reason finds reality in our concrete experience of the Whole and gives it reflective self-awareness. Croce agrees with Babbitt that life is "a oneness that is always

1 Irving Babbitt, *Rousseau and Romanticism* (Austin, Tex., 1977), p. 9. The Introduction to this book is only one of many places where Babbitt calls attention to the epistemological significance of his ethical-aesthetical ideas.

changing," but contrary to Babbitt he does not regard this intuited reality as being beyond the grasp of reason. Philosophy is the conceptual ally of experience. Reason does not have to flee from the contradictions of life, for its logic is dialectical. Students of Babbitt should take note of the many fruitful parallels between him and Croce and can learn from Croce's logic without accepting his highly questionable Hegelian monism and historical metaphysic.

The organic unity of philosophical reason and direct experience is itself a large and difficult subject, and the emphasis here must be on that side of the problem of reality that most occupies Babbitt's attention. It should be kept in mind that Babbitt's ethical-aesthetical doctrine is eminently compatible with the view of reason just described and may indeed require it as a natural supplement.[2]

I

Instead of taking ideas on authority, modern man proposes to submit them to the test of experience. Babbitt is willing to accept this challenge and to adopt what he calls "the positive and critical spirit." He also insists that what is typically meant by "experience" in the modern world is artificially restrictive. Babbitt accuses representatives of the modern project of being "incomplete positivists." They are not really attentive to the full range of human experience but arbitrarily select fragments of it or distort it through methodological reductionism. Babbitt points out that human experience, now and over the centuries, provides a vast array of evidence regarding the nature of man, including evidence of a universal moral order. This experience must be examined on its own ground.

Because he uses a poorly chosen phrase, "a more complete positivism," to describe his own respect for experience, Babbitt

2 On the need to supplement Babbitt's ethical-aesthetical ideas with a dialectical understanding of reason, see Claes G. Ryn, *Will, Imagination and Reason* (Chicago, 1986), which develops a general epistemology of the humanities and social disciplines. Croce's view of reason is presented in *Logic as the Science of the Pure Concept* (London, 1917).

might appear to endorse a more complete devotion to the gathering of empirical evidence in the ordinary modern sense. In actuality, the experience with reference to which Babbitt would judge the validity of ideas is man's direct awareness of the Whole, of the One and the Many in indissoluble interaction. Our most fundamental awareness of reality is at once synthetical and analytical. We grow in understanding of that Whole, not by accumulating "data" in the empirical sense, but by acquiring a firmer grasp of the oneness or unity of life that abides in the midst of change and diversity. Questions regarding reality are best answered by those who have let their own experience be enriched, ordered, and interpreted by that sense of the universal that emerges from the human heritage of life and letters. So-called empirical data are arbitrarily separated from this more fundamental and continuous consciousness of the Whole.

Man discovers the essence of reality in ethical action. Such action, Babbitt contends, realizes the ultimate meaning of life and is its own reward. An admirer of Plato and Aristotle, especially the latter, Babbitt is at the same time critical of the Greek tendency to equate virtue and intellectual knowledge. He sees in Christianity a deeper ethical wisdom, more fully attuned to the centrality of will and to the need for man to take on the discipline of a higher will. As a representative of the Orient rather than the more intellectualistic West, Jesus of Nazareth does not present man with a new philosophy, to be tested on abstract intellectual grounds. Jesus asks men to follow him, that is, to perform Christ-like actions. Genuine religion and morality, Babbitt argues, are most importantly an exercise of good will, a path of striving. Without in some way entering upon that path, and thus undertaking a gradual transformation of character, we will not discover the reality of the path, which is first of all a reality of practice.

As against theories that tend to make of moral virtue a problem of intellection, Babbitt stresses the human proclivity for moral procrastination, the lethargy or intractability of the will that keeps the individual from moral action. Theorizing about the nature of moral virtue will not bring the individual much closer to understanding those values, unless he also has some experience of them in concrete action. Philosophizing about the good can easily become an excuse or pretext for not doing what is always more difficult, namely, getting on with the task of good action. The crux of the ethical life, Babbitt argues, is not acquiring definitive theoretical knowledge of the good, which is beyond man, but acting on whatever ethical insight we do have. With growing strength of character and new good actions, the light of reality will grow. Theoretical doubts regarding the existence or nature of the universal good will tend to evaporate. Summarizing the contribution of the Christian teaching of the Incarnation to solving the problem of knowledge, Babbitt observes, "The final reply to all the doubts that torment the human heart is not some theory of conduct, however perfect, but the man of character." The man of good action embodies, or "incarnates," in himself the reality of the eternal.[3]

Babbitt agrees with Aristotle that truly virtuous action finds its own justification in the satisfaction of happiness, which must be carefully distinguished from passing moments of mere pleasure. In the specifically religious sphere, the result of moral striving is peace. In both cases, man comes to know concretely something of the ultimate purpose and meaning of human existence. What is meant by happiness or peace cannot be understood by anyone wholly lacking in personal experience of moral action. The happy life of the mean described in *The Nicomachean Ethics* is achieved gradually, not simply through intellectual deliberation, but primarily through ethical action that transforms character. Volumes of good ethical philosophy will mean little to their reader unless the terms used find referents in personal life and help the reader better to understand his own experience. What is true of humanistic self-under-

3 Irving Babbitt, *Democracy and Leadership* (Indianapolis, 1979), p. 197. On the ultimacy of will in Babbitt's thought, see Folke Leander, *Humanism and Naturalism* (Gothenburg, 1937), Ch. X. For a discussion of the historical concretization of what is ethically universal, see Claes G. Ryn, "History and the Moral Order," *The Ethical Dimension of Political Life*, ed. Francis J. Canavan (Durham, N.C., 1983).

standing is true also of religious self-understanding. In Babbitt's words, "Knowledge in matters religious waits upon will."[4] To submit questions of truth or falsity to the test of experience means to judge them ultimately from the point of view of life's completion in good action. The final criterion of reality is for Babbitt that special type of willing that by its very nature satisfies man's deepest yearning. This is the meaning of his statement that the epistemological problem, "though it cannot be solved abstractly or metaphysically, can be solved practically and in terms of actual conduct."[5]

As "the supreme maxim" for a modern respect for experience, Babbitt proposes the words of Jesus, "By their fruits shall ye know them." Thinkers who are hostile to all traditional authority and who blindly reject the insights common to the great religious and ethical systems of mankind will produce certain practical consequences. As their ideas are put into practice, these theorists will bring upon others and themselves a sense of life's absurdity and misery. On the other hand, persons willing to undertake some of the action called for by the older traditions, if not to accept the literal meaning of inherited dogmas, will grow in a sense of the ultimate reality and happiness of life. If absolute knowledge must forever elude man, Babbitt writes, "We may still determine on experimental grounds to what degree any particular view of life is sanctioned or repudiated by the nature of things and rate it accordingly as more or less real."[6]

It may be noted in passing that in stressing the ultimacy of the practical criterion of reality, Babbitt sometimes unduly discounts, or at least appears to discount, the contribution of reason to man's search for reality. Speaking of the path of religious striving, he says, "The end of this path and the goal of being cannot be formulated in terms of the finite intellect, any

---

4 *The Dhammapada*, translated and with an essay by Irving Babbitt (New York, 1965), p. 109.
5 *Rousseau and Romanticism*, p. 9.
6 *Democracy and Leadership*, p. 36.

more than the ocean can be put into a cup."[7] This statement
would appear to push intellectual humility to an extreme. Yet,
if reason is so utterly powerless as Babbitt here indicates, by
what faculty is he observing and articulating the shortcomings
of the "finite intellect"? In his essay on the *Dhammapada* and in
other places, Babbitt does formulate the nature of the religious
"path and goal of being." Does he then not have at his disposal
a reason more powerful and more comprehensive than the
"finite intellect" mentioned in the quotation? All the arguments
and concepts presented in his various books—the practical
criterion of reality, the higher and the lower will, the tension
between the One and the Many, etc.—assume an intellect capable of significant observation. Babbitt is using not only the sort
of pragmatic intellect of which he takes account but also a more
truly philosophical reason, even though he is not reflectively
aware of its existence.

Since Babbitt regards ethical action as the final answer to
questions of reality, it is necessary to examine his idea of the
higher will or "inner check," a subject poorly understood by
most of his interpreters. Babbitt's doctrine is summed up in
these words: "I do not hesitate to affirm that what is specifically human in man and ultimately divine is a certain quality of
will, a will that is felt in its relation to his ordinary self as a will
to refrain." In most of Babbitt's work the main emphasis is on
defining the higher will in its humanistic manifestation. In
Democracy and Leadership, he explains that his "interest in the
higher will and the power of veto it exercises over man's expansive desires is humanistic rather than religious."[8] It is helpful to compare Babbitt's ideas regarding the humanistic role of
the higher will with the traditional doctrine of natural law. The
latter recognizes a standard of good intrinsic to human life to
which man has access independently of special revelation. But
while the tradition of natural law identifies what is universal and
normative with the operation of reason, Babbitt associates the

7 *Rousseau and Romanticism,* p. 125.
8 *Democracy and Leadership,* p. 28.

normative with will. In the ethical life, the authority to which man ultimately defers is not a set of conceptual propositions but a special power of will that finally transcends efforts at exhaustive intellectual definition.

In the United States, attempts to understand Babbitt's idea of a self-validating higher will have frequently centered on his view of religion. Hence it is appropriate to elucidate his meaning with reference to the latter subject. Because Babbitt tries to deal with religious truth in a positive and critical manner, without relying on dogma, and because, like the doctrine of natural law, he ascribes a certain moral autonomy to the humanistic level of life, his critics have accused him of deprecating religion and the transcendent.[9] Such interpretations miss the point of Babbitt's approach to ethical questions. He explicitly states, "It is an error to hold that humanism can take the place of religion. Religion indeed may more readily dispense with humanism than humanism with religion. Humanism gains greatly by having a religious background . . . whereas religion, for the man who has actually renounced the world, may very conceivably be all in all."[10]

Babbitt also spends much time explicating the specifically religious spirit of otherworldliness. What he questions is not the reality of the divine but the necessity, and the prudence in modern intellectual circumstances, of tying it closely to inherited creeds or dogmas. Those who complain that Babbitt does not embrace a particular theology ignore the difference between revelation and philosophic-scientific observation,

---

9 See, for example, Allen Tate, "The Fallacy of Humanism," in *The Critique of Humanism*, ed. C. Hartley Grattan (New York, 1930). A work of polemics rather than scholarship, this article misrepresents Babbitt's position, as well as that of Paul Elmer More. More sympathetic to Babbitt in both tone and substance, but also marked by failure to understand Babbitt's idea of the higher will, is T. S. Eliot, "The Humanism of Irving Babbitt," in *Selected Essays* (New York, 1932). On this controversy and the meaning of the higher will, see Claes G. Ryn, "The Humanism of Irving Babbitt Revisited," *Modern Age*, Vol. 21 (Summer 1977).

10 Irving Babbitt, "Humanism: An Essay at Definition," in *Humanism and America*, ed. Norman Foerster (Port Washington, N.Y., 1967; first published in 1930), pp. 43–44. Similar statements are made by Babbitt elsewhere, e.g., *Rousseau and Romanticism*, p. 287. It is not possible here to go into Babbitt's understanding of the relationship between humanism and specifically religious life. For a discussion of that subject, which builds in part on Babbitt, see Claes G. Ryn, "The Things of Caesar," *Thought*, Vol. 55 (December 1980).

between devotional literature and scholarship. Although a sharp, definitive distinction cannot be drawn between them, special criteria of knowledge obtain for the scholar. The truth of religion, Babbitt believes, does not have to be taken on doctrinal authority; it can be judged critically, by its fruits. If it were necessary, to speak meaningfully about religion, first to adopt a particular formal creed—say, that of Christianity—all real discussion with Jews, Buddhists, Hindus, and others would have to await their conversion to that creed. The obstacle to serious debate would be even greater, for Christians themselves would have to reach agreement on the precise meaning of the creed. But religious dogmas, Babbitt points out, are in part an attempt to express what is also a living reality of practice and intuition. In matters of religion, as in matters of humanism, a vast body of historical experience is available to the scholar that provides the basis for an ecumenical knowledge and wisdom.

Religious denominations claiming a privileged insight beyond what can be verified in mankind's actual experience have no reason to feel threatened by such philosophic-scientific examination of the spiritual evidence, for they can add to the latter their own revelatory vision. Babbitt freely admits that theological dogmas may contain truth beyond what can be established critically on the basis of experience. "Many other things are true, no doubt, in addition to what one may affirm positively, and 'extra-beliefs' are in any case inevitable."[11] Babbitt recognizes the possible value of dogmas and creeds in bringing forth the fruits of religion. Man's religious symbols sometimes convey a deep sense of the mystery beyond themselves, and, as material for the ethical imagination, they may inspire right conduct. But religious symbols can also succumb to fundamentalistic reification. Formalistic and literalistic hardening is a sign that they are losing contact with reality.[12]

Babbitt raises the important question, "whether one's

---

11 *Democracy and Leadership,* pp. 250–251.
12 See the similar argument of Eric Voegelin, *The Ecumenic Age* (Baton Rouge, La., 1974).

religiousness is to be measured by the degree to which one brings forth the 'fruits of the spirit' or by one's theological affirmations."[13] Submitting to an external religious authority is not necessarily an act of devotion. It may express a flaw of character in an individual of unstable and relativistic romantic temperament. Inner uncertainty and flux crave outer certainty and order. Babbitt speaks of the affinity of the jellyfish for the rock. Seemingly pious adherence to external norms may in fact signify an escape from what is more difficult, the actual improvement of character. Behind the reverential pose there is no genuine conversion, but much chronic self-pity and half-heartedness. Professions of sinfulness can be a delicious enjoyment of what, with our lips, we feign to deplore. At the extreme, "faith" becomes everything, "works" nothing.

Peter Viereck, a thinker deeply influenced by Babbitt, says of the "pious intolerance" of certain modern proponents of religious orthodoxy that it can be seen as an attempt by persons who are still at bottom relativists "to shout down that nagging inner voice of doubt."[14] An individual who is more secure in his own character will not feel quite the same need to submit formalistically to external authority. Obviously, Babbitt's concern is not to do away with authority; the importance of sound leadership is a central theme in his work. What he criticizes is doctrinal and personal rigidity born of neglect of the primacy of ethical effort. He offers the educated guess that Buddhism with its nondogmatic religiosity has had as many saints as Christianity. He adds that it has been "less marred than Christianity by intolerance and fanaticism."[15] An ethically maturing person may well derive a heightened sense of reality from the rich religious traditions of mankind or of a particular church, but he is able to do so because their symbols and practices find

13 Irving Babbitt, *On Being Creative* (New York, 1968), p. xxxiii.
14 Peter Viereck, *Shame and Glory of the Intellectuals* (New York, 1965), p. 46. Viereck has in mind, among others, the clerical-minded T. S. Eliot, who is seen as having within himself also a romantic modernist. See *Rousseau and Romanticism*, p. 205.
15 *On Being Creative*, p. xxxiv.

referents in actual experience and can expand and deepen that experience.

A person of fundamentalist inclination may feel compelled to say that in religious and moral matters we can defer only to God, never to man, not even to what Babbitt calls man's higher will. That kind of reaction to Babbitt is indicative of misunderstanding his argument or failing to view it in its own terms. To be able to defer to the authority of God, man must somehow be aware of that authority. To exist for man as a living, concrete reality, God's authority must have entered human consciousness. To that extent it is part of man's self-awareness. It is to indicate the universal authority of that power within human experience that Babbitt calls it man's higher self or higher will. If that wording is objected to because it appears to build up man at the expense of God, the effect of the complaint is to draw attention away from the experiential facts themselves and to substitute statements of faith for philosophical inquiry. Babbitt is less interested in how to name the presence of the good than in accurately describing its observable influence on man. What others, relying on theological assumptions, might prefer to call the work of divine grace in man, Babbitt views ecumenically and nondogmatically as the exercise of the higher will.

Many modern Westerners would reject Christianity because inherited creeds have no authority for them. According to Babbitt, these Westerners must, if they are to be true to "the positive and critical spirit," still consider the experiential evidence. In his explication of the prerequisites for bringing forth the "fruits of the spirit," Babbitt prepares the way not only for a modern recovery of religious and ethical truth but for a recovery that is as free as possible of aesthetic posturing and of secret reservations and doubts.[16]

---

16 For a more detailed analysis of Babbitt's idea of a higher will, see Folke Leander's monograph, *The Inner Check* (London, 1974), and Claes G. Ryn, *Democracy and the Ethical Life* (Baton Rouge, La., 1978), especially Part Two.

II

To explain the relationship Babbitt sees between will and imagination, it is necessary to deal briefly with will in general (ethical or unethical) as the energy carrying all human activity, whether practical, philosophical, or aesthetical. Many words— desire, wish, aspiration, impulse, interest, inclination, passion, etc.—denote the fundamental, impelling power of will without which the life of human society and culture would cease. Will is the generic, categorial name for that infinity and variety of impulse that orients the individual to particular tasks. Whatever a person's dominant disposition at a particular time, it is a manifestation of will. This is true also of theoretical, contemplative activity. Man is no less active when he is thinking than when he is acting practically. Philosophizing, too, must be maintained through the intent of will. When the desire to obtain philosophical knowledge is no longer strongest in a person, it is followed by either practical action or intuition (imagination). Which activity takes the place of philosophizing depends on the desire now dominant. At some moments we wish merely to imagine something, that is, to become aesthetically active. In the latter case a desire is not enacted in practice but inspires imagination. We may become absorbed in a daydream. An aesthetically inclined and gifted person may forget the original practical stimulus and enjoy a poetic vision. Whatever the kind of activity taking hold of man, be it practical or contemplative, it must be sustained by some desire, by will.[17]

To understand Babbitt, it is important to realize that in one sense will and imagination are the same. A desire, in reaching the human consciousness, is no longer some blind, practical urge. Even a seemingly simple impulse to quench our thirst immediately translates itself into imagination. It becomes, for example, the intuition of clear, cool water passing down the throat. Without articulating itself in concrete images, the desire

17 For a detailed explication of the voluntaristic basis of all human activity, see Benedetto Croce, *The Philosophy of the Practical* (New York, 1967). This edition is a reprint of the partly unreliable English translation of 1913.

to drink is unaware of itself, indefinite, and powerless to move the individual. The intuition is potentially highly complex, for the imagined act of drinking must include a sense of the larger situation of life in which it is taking place. Particular short-range impulses of desire emanate from a broader disposition of character. What is expressed in each intuitive transfiguration of desire is also a more comprehensive vision of life's possibilities. Different personalities will be attracted to different possibilities. Babbitt explains that men develop such imagination as is pleasing to their underlying orientations of character.

If will decides the direction of human activity, Babbitt also emphasizes that the human will is dualistic, forever torn between higher and lower potentialities. Both of these poles of man's being express themselves in imagination. Transfigured into more or less poetic intuition, the higher or lower desires acquire the power that comes with concreteness, sensual texture, immediacy. As intuitions they are not realized in practice, but, as living visions of what life could be, they stir the human self, inviting practical action consonant with themselves. It has often been noted in older Western philosophy that what is highest in man cannot by itself withstand strong contrary passions. Plato stresses the need for a power of "spiritedness" (*thymos*) to enforce the authority of reason. Babbitt finds the highest moral authority not in intellect but in will of a special quality. That will is never present to man in its fullness. It is a potentiality for good to be progressively realized in continuous tension with an opposite quality of will. To become more fully realized, the ethical will needs the power of imagination to give it concreteness and to draw the human will more deeply into its own potentiality of goodness. In the perpetual struggle between higher and lower possibilities of existence, Babbitt argues, "the imagination holds the balance of power." In this sense he agrees with Napoleon that "imagination governs mankind."[18] To prevail, the ethical will must express its purposes through the magnetic imagery of intuition.

18 *Democracy and Leadership,* p. 32.

Corresponding qualities of character and imagination tend to beget and reinforce each other. An individual caught up in a life of pleasure-seeking is predisposed to be responsive to works of poetry that are carried by a similar sense of life's possibilities. As his personality is absorbed into poetic vision of new hedonistic thrills, his will finds satisfaction in it and deepens in its commitment. Moments of aesthetic enjoyment tend to call forth corresponding attempts at practical realization of desire. Such transition to practical action is never automatic—man is free to reject even strong appeals of desire—but if it takes place, it is not unexpected. The will that now proceeds to practical action belongs to the same disposition of character that previously found aesthetic enjoyment in the vision of a hedonistic state.

A person more under the influence of the higher will has a different sense of what brings genuine satisfaction. This person may well be enticed by a powerful poetic statement of a hedonistic existence; it richly embellishes and supports his own moments of hedonistic flight from aristocratic character. But, by virtue of his predominant orientation of personality, the hedonistic vision is likely also to create uneasiness. He senses in it the expression of an ignoble, incomplete, and ultimately miserable state of soul, one in which he has sometimes participated.

For a person in whom will of an immoral type is strongly entrenched and in whom imagination attuned to that will is continuously reinforcing the same orientation of character, it may be quite difficult to change. Even a cultured individual of predominantly sound character will remain to some extent susceptible to the stirrings of his lower will, especially if it finds expression in vibrant, luxuriant poetic vision. Plato feared the influence of wrongly inspired poets on souls still lacking in ethical maturity. Babbitt suggests that in the relatively good man, too, the imagination can become the ally of secret drives, which, in his better moments, he would not indulge. If a person lets himself be drawn into intuitions that play upon and expand his more ignoble self, the imagination will help him conceal his moral qualms. These become portrayed, perhaps, as symptoms of a ridiculous and narrow-minded "bourgeois" puritanism. The now dominant desire, by contrast, is depicted as the manifestation of a higher freedom, above such petty notions of responsibility. A powerfully endowed imagination may paint even diabolical drives in alluring images. Were it not for man's ability to fashion the potentialities of his own lower self in aesthetically enthralling ways, that self would have little power to influence men of culture. The more creative a person's intuition, the greater its influence, for good or evil.

It is pertinent here to explain in what sense the higher will can be described as an "inner check." When ignoble hedonistic intuition is pulling an individual into itself or into practical action, he may be suddenly stopped by moral uneasiness. What Babbitt calls the inner check is the transcendent good breaking into consciousness by arresting incipient activity. It affords man an opportunity to reconstitute his intentions. What begins as a negative act, as moral censuring of a present intention, may in the next moment assert itself positively. In a person of some habitual responsiveness to the higher will, the latter may be given the opportunity to articulate itself in imagination, for example, in the intuition of the ultimate misery of the hedonistic life as the defeat of the promise of happiness. At best, this means the purging of the previously dominant lower imagination and with it the sustaining lower will.

In most men the interplay of will and imagination does not often result in intuitions of a particularly poetic type. The imagination usually works in spurts and at the mercy of pressing practical needs. In the poetically inclined and gifted person, on the other hand, the imagination may detach itself from service to impulses of the moment and swell into an elaborate, finely harmonized vision of life. In art, intuition synthesizes possibilities of human existence according to the aesthetic requirement of beauty. Still, it must not be overlooked that, even in the aesthetic intensification of art, intuition is at the same time will. It emanates from an underlying disposition of character. The work of art is the expression of a personality whose sense of reality is the result of innumerable acts of will in the past that have led the artist to explore some possibilities of experience and neglect many others. The disposition of character and sensibility that has been built up over the years now selects the material for the aesthetic creation. By virtue of his past willing, the artist is particularly sensitive to some potentialities of human life, less sensitive to others. We know the will by its fruits in imagination.

Babbitt insists that, although art must have a special aesthetic integrity and coherence to be truly itself, what is poetically expressed can differ greatly in value. Art can be more or less profound or truthful in its statement of life's possibilities—truthful not in an intellectual sense but in an intuitive sense. Art ranges from works that capture with depth and fullness the essence of human existence, with its anchor in a universal moral order, to works of a trivial and superficial type or of positively distorting vision. Some richly poetic works exclude or disfigure elements of reality. For instance, it is not uncommon for man to crave refuge from everything mundane and uncomfortable. The individual sometimes allows himself to be intoxicated by his imagination. He loses himself in *das Fabelhafte*. Intuitions that might disturb the escapist vision of a pleasant, rosy existence are not allowed to enter the poetic synthesis. The will at the root of the intuitive creation excludes what is not pleasing to it. Most works of art reflect some such more or less deliberate contraction or distortion of reality, betraying the bias and selectivity of the will that created it. Truly great works of art, by contrast, are open to all of what life may contain. This requires a will permitting contemplation of the more disturbing and painful dimensions of experience, as well as the potentialities for pleasure and happiness.

A person used to finding the meaning of existence in passing pleasures will tend to express in his art possibilities of experience consonant with that sense of what life has to offer. Insofar as he has any intuition of moral responsibility and allows it to enter his poetic vision, he is likely to express it according

to his accustomed hedonistic sensibilities, hence in some cynical-
ly distorted form. The resulting poem will not convey man's
actual moral predicament. The poem will lack what Babbitt calls
"centrality." Although the hedonistic intuition may be aesthetically enthralling, it has no depth of vision. To the extent that
the poem does not build up an entirely illusory intuition of life,
it offers merely fragmentary vision.

If, on the other hand, the hedonistically inclined poet permits
the sudden intuition of the ethical will to expand and deepen so
as to come into its own, which assumes that an orientation of
will hospitable to that new quality of imagination is asserting
itself, his aesthetic vision will undergo a transformation. A different sense of what life may contain begins to arrange the
material of intuition. Only an imagination that is sensitive to
possibilities of experience in their relation to what is ultimately
real can express the essence of the human condition. This does
not mean that all men of good character can also write and
appreciate poetry. It does mean that the most penetrating
imagination can emanate only from a human soul attuned to
the real ethical opportunities and dangers of existence.

The unwillingness of most modern aestheticians to consider
the ethical content of art leads Babbitt to stress that question in
his own work. Observers insufficiently attentive to Babbitt's
arguments have concluded that for him the only value to be
expressed in art is ethical. One interpreter generally sympathetic to Babbitt has suggested that according to Babbitt literature
is "ethics 'touched by emotion' ."[19] This is a misunderstanding.
Babbitt regards literature not as ethics but as imagination, and
as such it must meet the aesthetic criteria of all genuine poetry.
Also, poetry cannot be confined to ethical intuition. With its
characteristic freshness, art should express a wide range of
possible experience. In Babbitt's words, "Art of course cannot
thrive solely, or indeed primarily, on the higher intuitions; it

19 Austin Warren, *New England Saints* (Ann Arbor, Mich., 1956), p. 154. The phrase
quoted by Warren is from Matthew Arnold.

requires the keenest intuitions of sense." What is distinctive about Babbitt's aesthetics is his view that "if art is to have humane purpose, these intuitions of sense must come under the control of the higher intuitions."[20] This does not mean that great art somehow dismisses or ignores the variety of human experience. What distinguishes great art is that it intuits this multiplicity in its most significant aspect, that is, in its bearing on what ultimately completes human existence. Without this sense of proportion, art must present more or less unreal and twisted visions of life. Deeply pessimistic, cynical, or utopian views of the world reveal in their own way the self-indulgent, confining orientation of the will that carries them. Poetry that is not sensitive to the real terms of life may still capture acutely and vividly some elements of existence. It may give fine expression to feelings of absurdity and despair. The ethical imagination is certainly not unfamiliar with such states. But in the ethical imagination bursts of fragmentary insight found in lesser works of intuition are absorbed into a more comprehensive vision that deepens and completes the intuition of the Whole that they render only imperfectly. Feelings of absurdity and despair are affirmed and expressed by the higher imagination, but through it they are seen more deeply and clearly as the manifestations of life lacking ethical order. The ethical imagination synthesizes the vast and varied potentialities of human experience by creatively subsuming and arranging them under the intuition of that power in the world that makes for happiness.

Because of his insistence that art is more or less profound in proportion as it penetrates to the ethical core of existence, Babbitt has often been accused of favoring moralistic or didactic art. Typically, this charge has been made without citing specific evidence. Insofar as it does not simply rest on willful ignorance of Babbitt's actual arguments, the charge shows an inability to grasp the subtleties of his reasoning. Babbitt's view that great art must have "centrality" is in fact indistinguishable from his

20 Irving Babbitt, *The New Laokoon* (Boston, 1910), p. 227.

emphatic rejection of didacticism. He writes, "It is in general easy to be didactic, hard to achieve ethical insight."[21] The mark of genuinely ethical art, Babbitt argues, is that it is free from preaching. "Sophocles is more ethical than Euripides for the simple reason that he views life with more imaginative whole-ness. At the same time he is much less given to preaching than Euripides."[22]

Equally unwarranted is the accusation that Babbitt is a "doctrinaire neoclassicist" in aesthetics.[23] Babbitt does discern an element of truth in the classical idea of imitation: Art should express the universal. But he also endorses the modern idea of the creative imagination. Great art freshly expresses the univer-sal. Babbitt rejects the Greek conception of the imagination as an essentially passive faculty: "In its failure to bring out with sufficient explictness [the] *creative* role of the imagination and in the stubborn intellectualism that this failure implies is to be found, if anywhere, the weak point in the cuirass of Greek philosophy."[24] Babbitt often criticizes, and sometimes ridicules, neoclassicist and formalist notions of art. He warns that "a purely traditional humanism is always in danger of falling into a rut of pseudo-classic formalism."[25] Even sympathetic inter-preters of Babbitt have simplified his notion of ethical imagina-tion. Neo-Thomist Louis Mercier, for instance, equates it with the *intellectus* of scholasticism.[26] Although *intellectus* may be understood as having a strong intuitive element, the parallel drawn by Mercier is bound to be misleading. Babbitt goes to great lengths to show that while the ethical imagination grasps the universal, it does not do so in an intellective, conceptual manner. Artistic intuition and thought are different modes of

21 *Rousseau and Romanticism*, p. 272.

22 *Rousseau and Romanticism*, p. 164.

23 The charge is made by G. N. G. Orsini in *Benedetto Croce: Philosopher of Art and Literary Critic* (Carbondale, Ill., 1961), p. 219.

24 *Rousseau and Romanticism*, p. 308n.

25 *Democracy and Leadership*, p. 57.

26 See Louis Mercier, *The Challenge of Humanism* (New York, 1933), especially pp. 161–170, and *American Humanism and the New Age* (Milwaukee, Wis., 1948).

knowing life. The wisdom contained in great art does not result from reason controlling the imagination but is intrinsic to
the most penetrating imagination. This wisdom is intuited
universality. Genuine art, Babbitt insists, is free from "clogging
intellectualism."[27]

What has been superficially interpreted as aesthetic moralism
or didacticism in Babbitt is in fact his opposition to art that
distorts life and loses its fullness. He knows certainly as well as
his critics that art has its own aesthetic needs, which are different from those of moral action and philosophy. He is fully aware
that art discovers new and sometimes unexpected potentialities
of existence and thus liberates man from ever-threatening rou-
tinization and entropy. But primary among the things that the
highest form of imagination creatively expresses is the ethical
purpose at the core of human life, thwarted or realized. Babbitt
writes: "To assert that the creativeness of the imagination is
incompatible with centrality or, what amounts to the same
thing, with purpose, is to assert that the creativeness of the
imagination is incompatible with reality or at least such reality
as man may attain."[28] The aestheticism of *l'art pour l'art* detaches
art from that deeper stratum of order and direction in life and
leaves the imagination "more or less free to wander wild in
some 'empire of chimeras'."[29]

It is possible to turn to the literary credo of Peter Viereck for
a succinct expression of what is also Babbitt's aesthetic theory.
Viereck rejects both "soap-box poetry" and formalistic virtuosi-
ty. "Why confine poetry to this false choice between Agitprop
and furniture polish? We have a third alternative: not the moral
preachiness of didacticism, but the moral insight of lyrical humanity." Poetry without ethical center is poetry without gen-

---

27 *Rousseau and Romanticism*, p. 170. Man's past conceptual reflection on life does of
course contribute something to the structure of a poetic vision, but ideas are absorbed
into art not in a conceptual but in an aesthetically transfigured form.

28 *Rousseau and Romanticism*, p. 203.

29 *Democracy and Leadership*, p. 171. On Babbitt's idea of the imagination and on
various misunderstandings of that idea, see Folke Leander, "Irving Babbitt and the
Aestheticians," *Modern Age*, Vol. 6, No. 4 (1960).

uine humanity. Devotees of aestheticism do not understand, Viereck writes, that "you will capture beauty only by seeking more than beauty." Beauty that does not express our essential humanity tends to lose also its beauty. "What dehumanizes, de-lyricizes."[30]

A poetic vision, whether created or recreated by us, draws our whole personality into itself. If we have some moral character, a part of our experience of the poem is the reaction of our higher will to the intuition of life presented in it. To the extent that the intuition ignores or violates the concerns of the higher will and is censured by the moral uneasiness of our participating self, a dissonance mars the aesthetic vision. If, by contrast, the poem successfully renders the presence of the higher will in the world, the intuition expresses our deepest humanity and pulsates in harmony with reality itself. For a mature literary critic to take account of these reactions of his aesthetically participating self has nothing to do with narrow-minded moralistic censorship. The critic is providing a statement regarding the imaginative depth of the poem.

Irving Babbitt has long been vilified by the aestheticians. Yet, in one of the intellectual ironies of this century, his aesthetic position was belatedly confirmed by the philosophical authority who more than perhaps anybody else in this century has contributed to a neglect of the moral substance of art—Benedetto Croce. Possibly under the influence of Babbitt, whose *The New Laokoon* (1910) he reviewed favorably, Croce substantially revised the views he had expressed in his *Aesthetic* (1902). Starting about 1917, he increasingly stresses the universal content of imagination as such: "In every poetic accent, in every imaginative creation, there lies all human destiny—all the hopes, the illusions, the sorrows and joys, the greatness and the wretchedness of humanity, the entire drama of Reality. . . . It is therefore unthinkable that artistic representation may ever affirm the mere particular, the abstract individual, the finite in its finite-

30 Peter Viereck, *The Unadjusted Man*, (Boston, 1956), pp. 288-289.

ness." Even more significant in the present context, Croce
accepts Babbitt's idea that there are degrees of imaginative
profundity and that art achieves greatness in proportion as it
expresses the ethical essence of human existence. In great art,
Croce argues in 1917, the whole of the human spirit is intuited;
such art has *totalità*. That "totality" includes man's ethical nature. Stating now what had long been Babbitt's view, Croce
writes: "If the moral force is, as it certainly is, a cosmic force
and queen of the world . . . it dominates by its own power; and
art is the more perfect, the more clearly it reflects and expresses
the development of reality; the more it is art, the better it shows
the morality inherent in the nature of things."[31] It is hardly
plausible to suspect Croce of doctrinaire neoclassicism, moralism, or didacticism. Like Babbitt, he is reacting against poetry
lacking proportion, depth, and fullness.

III

If Irving Babbitt does not sufficiently explore the logical dimension of knowledge including the epistemological basis of his own
concepts, he has much of importance to say about the ethical-
aesthetic aspect of the problem of reality. For him the human
personality is turned toward reality primarily through the
interplay of ethical will and the type of imagination that it
begets. Conversely, the unethical will and its corresponding
imagination draw man into unreality. Were it not for the possibly poetic quality of the lower imagination, it would have little
power to influence civilized men. To reorient the will of modern
man, Babbitt teaches, it is necessary to expose his decadent,
escapist imagination.

Babbitt's ethical-aesthetic doctrine suggests that epistemology
as ordinarily conceived in the modern world must be thoroughly revised. Unfortunately, Babbitt's conception of reason is not
integrated with his understanding of the ultimate criterion of

---

31 Benedetto Croce, *Nuovi saggi di estetica* (Bari, Italy, 1920), pp. 126, 131. The latter
quotation is from the essay "The Character of Totality" first published in 1917.

reality. The latter part of his work requires a logical supplement. For reason to know reality and have human relevance, it must be able to align itself with the light that streams forth from ethical-aesthetic activity. And so it can, according to Croce. Unlike the pragmatic and analytic intellect recognized by Babbitt, truly philosophical reason gives reflective self-awareness to the universal as it manifests itself in concrete experience.[32] Is that not the same reason that formulated Babbitt's various ideas about life and letters? Justified reservations about Croce in some areas do not preclude learning from his logic.

It is not possible here to delve into the ways in which reason and intuition converge and diverge. It might lead to misunderstanding, however, not to bring up the distinction between historical reality and the sense of reality conveyed by art. According to Croce, the office of philosophy is to take account of experience in its simultaneously universal and historical aspect. The specifically philosophical criterion of reality is the direct perception of the difference between will realized in practical action and will remaining in the form of unrealized desire, more or less transfigured into imagination.[33] To exemplify, philosophical reason records in existential judgments what the ethical or unethical will has wrought historically. The events depicted in poetic intuition are identified by reason as not belonging to the historical world. At the same time, philosophy registers poetic intuition as a historically existing activity creating images of that nonhistorical type.

In Babbitt's view, the question of reality is finally settled on nonintellectual grounds. Most fundamentally, reality becomes known through the exercise of the higher will, which brings forth both practical action and intuition. The ethical imagination in art does not seek historical truth, but in its own nonconceptual manner it expresses the core of reality. Babbitt's ethical-

32 The distinction between pragmatic and philosophical reason is developed at length in Croce, *Logic.*

33 For a brief but penetrating explication of the philosophical criterion of reality, see Croce, *Philosophy of the Practical,* Ch. VI.

aesthetic doctrine discloses the impotence of formal intellectual brilliance divorced from ethical insight. Epistemology can learn from Babbitt that the philosopher who wants to know reality must partake of the character of the good man and of the intuition of the great poet.

Folke Leander

Irving Babbitt and
Benedetto Croce

IT IS INDEED a strange fact that so few have succeeded in fully understanding the philosophical basis of Irving Babbitt's and Paul Elmer More's achievement as critics of literature and life. In 1923, their closest disciple, Stuart P. Sherman, wrote to Frank Jewett Mather:

I have agreed with More and Babbitt at a great many points. But I have never embraced with any completeness More's metaphysical doctrines: I don't understand them. . . . In their ultimate position, they are both dogmatic and mystical, to an extent which makes it impossible for one to understand or follow them, to say nothing of expounding them. That is precisely why they are not exerting the influence which their own doctrines—some of which I sharply dissent from—are entitled to exert. Whatever small service I may perform in defending what we all agree should be defended, must [lie] in finding a rational and discussable basis—at points where they refuse to discuss, and Babbitt erects his *chevaux-de-frise* of arbitrary "definitions" warranted to eviscerate every gizzard and break every neck born into this disastrous world since Aristotle; while More retreats into a blinding white mist of Platonism, where God himself would think twice before pursuing.[1]

1 Jacob Zeitlin and Homer Woodbridge, *Life and Letters of Stuart P. Sherman* (Freeport, N.Y., 1929; reprinted in 1971), Vol. 2, pp. 548–549.

One may disregard the tone—the letter was written in a moment of personal irritation—and yet retain the admission: Babbitt's and More's most distinguished disciple in the field of
literary criticism simply did not understand their philosophical
background.

Ten years later, in 1933, another distinguished pupil of
Babbitt's, T. S. Eliot, wrote in the *Criterion:*

A regrettable error, for which I think Babbitt himself was partly
responsible, has led, within the last ten years or so, to people looking
into his doctrine for something which is not there: the search has been
unfortunate both for those who thought they found it and those who
have repudiated his views because they did not find it. His mind was
in a sense profoundly philosophical. . . . But of philosophical technique
he had none; and in his writings you will find no coherent system, but
some apparently important inconsistencies.[2]

Now if this were true of Babbitt, it would also hold of More;
and the *Shelburne Essays* as well as *The Greek Tradition* would be
ultimately meaningless works that may justly be neglected.
Confusion and mystification would be the central inspiration in
what both of them wrote. Such a view simply will not do: They
may have been wrong, but they must have meant something
definite.

Steps towards a better appreciation especially of Babbitt's
philosophy were taken when Louis J.-A. Mercier published *The
Challenge of Humanism* (1933) and *American Humanism and the New
Age* (1948). And there were other students who also contributed
to the discussion. Yet much work remains to be done: the clouds
have only partially been dispelled, and much of the "white
mist," of which Sherman spoke, is still there.[3] In the thirties,
Babbitt and More attracted much attention and many followers.
But soon their influence began to wane, the main cause being

2 T. S. Eliot, *The Criterion* (October 1933).
3 Dom Oliver Grosselin, *The Intuitive Voluntarism of Irving Babbitt* (Latrobe, Pa.: St.
Vincent Arch-Abbey, 1951) is far better than earlier books on Babbitt. But Babbitt's
"intuitionism" in epistemology does not make sense as presented by Grosselin. And
several other objections may be made. (See following notes.)

the irritating fact that the public failed to understand the peculiar and obscurely expressed philosophy that was the very basis of their criticism of life and letters. The general feeling on the subject is no doubt that expressed by Herbert J. Muller in his book on *Science and Criticism* (1946): The New Humanism is "based on nothing," it has "no perceptible foundation in heaven or on earth."[4]

Now this is all wrong. Babbitt's and More's work was not "based on nothing"; they knew perfectly well what they meant, and they meant something quite intelligible. The situation in American criticism is simply scandalous: two truly great men have not managed to make themselves understood by a younger generation and are openly accused of talking sheer nonsense!

In the following pages I shall explain at some length Babbitt's and More's ethical doctrine (which is the central and really difficult part of their thought) and then briefly indicate its application in esthetics and in the theory of literary criticism.[5]

I

The most peculiar characteristic of Babbitt's and More's ethical view of life is the pronounced emphasis laid upon the fact that man's conscience is a restrictive force. We usually imagine the voice of our conscience as positively ordering or prompting us to act in a certain way. Babbitt and More, on the other hand, describe conscience as an inner protest, an "inner check." When we do not notice any such protest we can have a kind of conviction of being on the right way—but we had better not be too sure. Perhaps after all there was some protestation, although, being impatient and in a hurry, we did not observe it but rushed along and acted rashly. The modus operandi of the conscience as a restraining force can be explained by a metaphor that will at the same time illustrate Babbitt's and More's

---

4 H. J. Muller, *Science and Criticism* (New Haven, 1946), p. 6.

5 Perhaps I should add that I have chosen to focus my exposition on a doctrine on which Babbitt and More essentially agree.

idea of logical thought as having a subordinate function in man's ethical life.

We can compare the conscience with a customs house and the various impulses to act with travelers who are to pass through. At the customs house there is an officer (the sense of right and wrong) and also a subordinate official (reason). The former has been given the task of deciding who is to be stopped and who is to be let through; the latter has to open the bags and cases of the passengers and spread about the contents before the eyes of his superior. In other words we can say that when our impulses are checked, reason has to figure out their purpose and also the consequences of their passing into action as far as these can be anticipated. The task of reason is not to value the impulses but to analyze the actual situation; it does this by getting a survey of all relevant knowledge that at the moment of deliberation is at the command of the person about to act. When the subordinate official has spread around all the passengers' luggage for inspection, the officer has to pronounce his decision: "Stop" or "Pass." This is an alogical act of valuation, meaning: "I approve" or "I disapprove"—although the "I" or self that in this case approves or disapproves is supposed to be identical in all human beings, as it is in Kant's philosophy, and not subject to individual variations.

Attention should be given to the fact that our moral sense works as a restraining power: Even if an impulse is allowed to pass into action, this never takes place before it has been stopped long enough to be submitted to control. All positive energies come from our impulses. Conscience *allows* some of our impulses to develop into overt action, which means sanction or approval, but they have their own positive force.

It should also be noticed that there is a distinction between the two functions: that of analyzing the actual situation and that of valuing. In obtaining knowledge we perceive reality hitherto existing; in willing we create new reality. In obtaining knowledge we try to discover the truth; valuing in the sense of choosing is a different activity from finding out what is true or false and is subject to another alternative: right or wrong.

The daimon of Socrates protested and warned him when he was on the wrong path but never positively told him what to do. He had to examine himself thoroughly before he found any positive line of conduct, his daimon working as an eliminating power. In the same way we all have to find the acceptable action in every case by a process of elimination. Conscience speaks by protesting, and when at last it protests no longer, this means an approval of the only remaining impulse to act.

All this can also be illustrated by an analysis of what goes on in another part of the human mind, i.e., in man's aesthetic activity. Every artist has his own sense of beauty as a guide in his creative work. Within him there is something to tell him: "No, not like that—not like that—that's it!" His sense of beauty finds its way by a series of eliminations, a series of aesthetic "inner checks." Do these "inner checks" act at random? Does the artist decide arbitrarily when his sense of beauty should protest? No, evidently not. Every artist has surrendered his freedom and made himself the slave of his own sense of beauty, and in the very act of asserting his "freedom" he would no longer be an artist. If he follows the directions of his sense of beauty step by step, a work of art will gradually emerge. When this creative process began, he had no idea of the final result but only followed by steps the inner guide that directed him, exactly the way a rider guides his horse: by using the reins. It almost seems that the artist had a deity above him, who knew the result beforehand and only leads him towards it. But the "spirit" that leads him is no transcendent personal being but his very self, his own sense of beauty. Our sense of beauty can be compared to a compass needle, which first has to oscillate in various directions before it finally comes to a halt. The oscillations must be eliminated before we can entirely depend upon our compass to find our way. In the same way the creative artist must patiently allow his sense of beauty plenty of time to achieve something and must not hurry along too quickly. By listening humbly he must find out the reactions of his own sense of beauty, and he must not let his own self-will take the lead.

If we examine our sense of truth, the same description will be

applicable. The scientist can also be in a hurry and allow himself to be rushed along by his self-will without listening to the
protests of his sense of truth. In this case we can also talk about
an "inner guide," which, by performing the function of a rein,
leads him aright. It leads him by way of eliminations and
protestations: "This is untrue—this is wishful thinking—this is a
premature conclusion," and so on; and only when he can no
longer perceive any protests from his sense of truth will the
thinker (provisionally at first, and with great care) accept any
result.

These comparisons may explain Babbitt's and More's notion
of conscience as a restraining principle.[6] But—after all this—the
reader will probably ask: "What are the advantages of looking
upon conscience in the way just described? Where does all this
get us? What are the consequences?" In asking these questions
we approach the application of this idea in Babbitt's and More's
criticism.

We can approach the subject by inquiring into what characterizes a fanatic. Now, is he not a person who is too quick and
uncritical in concluding what his duty or God's will demands of
him, while at the same time his vanity and will to power have
treacherously usurped the place of his real conscience? He con-
fuses the voice of God with that of his own pride, the demands
of duty with those of his own will to power. If he penetrated
deeper into his own self he would find that his real conscience
demanded entirely different things of him. But he is not patient
enough, he lacks humility before the spirit. Ethical doctrines that
describe conscience as a positive propellant and, accordingly, do
not stress the humble searching that must precede the final
(although guarded) positivity, by this neglect of theirs encourage
the premature positivity that characterizes fanaticism.

Probably clear-cut, cynical egoists have not done half so much
harm in the world as those egoists who are at the same time

---

6 Grosselin (p. 38) says that "the higher will is restraintive of individuality without
itself determining the limits of restraint." This is a misunderstanding. Babbitt maintains
that man "has his standard within him—living, flexible, intuitive." (This passage is
quoted by Grosselin himself on p. 58.)

radiant "idealists." Among Jacobins, Nazis, and Communists it is not at all difficult to find specimens of the latter kind of human being. Their "premature positivity" is explained by the fact that their self-assertion, unbridled by their *real* conscience, is permitted to assume an idealism that makes individuals and groups feel like inspired heroes. In the disguise of exalted ideals their own will to power is visited upon suffering fellow creatures.

A more harmless version of the same spirit can be traced in our romantic individualists. Of course the following well-known words in Ibsen's *Brand,* "What thou art, be fully and wholly and not partly and by pieces," permit of a noble interpretation. However, there is an element of truth in the following reflection of Strindberg's: "Brand was a pietist, a fanatic, who was so bold as to believe that he was right in contrast to the whole world, and John [the name Strindberg has given himself in his autobiography] felt he had something in common with this terrible egoist, who was wrong into the bargain. No half-heartedness, just go ahead, break and pull down all that is in your way, for you alone are right."

According to Babbitt and More, romantic individualism, however great its value and justification, from the very outset contained a considerable element of premature positivity, against which we must all be on our guard. The romanticist has been too ready to approve of many impulses and feelings as "divine," which to a sober observer seem to possess entirely opposite qualities. In spite of all his beautiful talk about "spirituality" and "soul," the romanticist has suffered from a constant lack of humility before the spirit within him. He has been much too quick in accepting as heavenly inspiration, under the names of idealism and spirituality, various impulses that really have never been sanctioned by the spirit within him.

Thus, the doctrine of "the inner check" in American Humanism is aimed especially at the romantic mentality in its various aspects. To the romantics it says: "Humble yourselves, not before outer conventions and laws (as these are often perverted by human wickedness), but before the spirit within you! You have been too rash in constructing your 'idealisms.' More ethical seriousness and more penetrating self-criticism will alone subdue romantic tendencies in all of us."

Babbitt thinks his own description of the function of conscience is better than Kant's, inasmuch as the latter's categorical imperative "is primarily a freedom to do, and not, like that of the ethical will, a freedom to refrain from doing."[7] We now easily understand the meaning of this judgment. It has often been stated, and certainly not without justification, that the Germans have too readily identified the promptings of duty with those of the state or of the autocrat—a true specimen of "premature positivity." It is also very interesting to study the transformation of the categorical imperative that took place under the hands of certain romantics, Fichte being the intermediary link. Against all utilitarianism and hedonistic materialism Kant had formulated his doctrine of "duty for duty's sake." Fichte changed this into a panegyric upon the heroical life of the warrior who does not seek wealth and comfort but who gives his life for his nation, disdaining material prosperity. Some romantic poets developed this into a kind of militaristic mysticism, into an idea of war as an extraordinarily grand and inspiring spectacle. A cruder version of these thoughts was propounded by Nietzsche.[8] It is obvious that what Fichte and his generation accepted as conscience, idealism, and categorical imperative were too polluted by national and individual lust for power, by the love of adventure and fighting. When "duty for duty's sake" could be changed into "war for war's sake," we can be sure that men were too rash in interpreting the promptings of their conscience.

By their doctrine of a *frein vital* that is to control our *élan vital*, Babbitt and More only want to formulate what has always been

---

7 *Democracy and Leadership* (Boston, 1924), p. 226.

8 "Der freigewordene Mensch tritt mit Füssen auf die verächtliche Art von Wohlbefinden, von dem Krämer, Christen, Kühe, Weiber, Engländer und andere Demokraten träumen. Der freie Mensch ist Krieger." Götzen-Dämmerung, § 38. The Fichtean aspect of romanticism has been admirably treated in Fredrik Böök's *Esaias Tegnér*, I (1917).

the essence of the classical spirit: moderation and restraint. Passion is something expansive that sweeps through man like a gale and blows him along with it. It blinds him and throws him into excesses and calamities; its achievements can be illustrated by the words *hybris—atē—nemesis.* "Reason" was supposed to bridle man's various forces. Plato and Aristotle described the whole cosmos as being constructed according to this formula: dynamic, rebellious matter, subdued and shaped by molding forces. In this sense their view of man and the world was dualistic. The higher principle in both man and the world was supposed to act in a molding, shaping, subduing manner—in short, restrictively—upon an independent and original material that is expansive, insubordinate, and rebellious against all order.

To step from this dualism into some kind of pantheism is, according to Babbitt and More, to fall into vicious confusion. This step is taken as soon as it is asserted by a thinker that not only the restrictive but also the expansive principle is an emanation from the deity. It is assumed that the Spirit of the Universe or of Life manifests itself just as much in the torrent of passion as in the restraining force of reason. The cosmic process is the self-realization of the Oversoul, in which both factors are necessary: the streaming forth as well as the holding back, the change as well as the restoration of stability. They are at the same time identical and opposed, and thus we get a *coincidentia oppositorum.* The flux of manifoldness and change must be present at every moment; but the striving toward synthesis and order, toward the reestablishment of original divine unity is the contrary and complementary aspect of the cosmic process. Both forces are at bottom equally divine as they are both needed in the self-realization of Life. And a careful analysis of evil shows that in reality it is nonexistent. The problem of evil turns out to be a sham problem, for in everything pantheists only find the divine spirit at work, and what we call evil is only the aspect of the divine spirit that we have not been able to appreciate. The World-Spirit is constantly splitting up into innumerable individual centers of life, and at the same time we find in these centers an attempt to achieve synthesis and to restore unity. Expansion and contraction are dialectically united in an all-embracing divine reality.

This type of pantheistic idealism can be followed from Plotinus throughout the writings of Fichte, Schelling, and Hegel down to Bergson and Croce. Rather than openly contradict dualism, pantheistic idealism wants to incorporate it into an all-embracing monism. Babbitt and More reject this type of metaphysics. To start with, it has never been proved and remains a dogmatic assertion. What we find by experience does not get us beyond dualism. And then, Babbitt and More want to show us that this type of metaphysical abstraction has had a bad effect upon those who have believed in it. In spite of all verbal concessions in favor of dualism, it tends to undermine the moral law and to deify the instincts. When the deity is primarily conceived as expansive and only secondarily as restrictive—that is how all romantic philosophy looks upon the pulsations of the universe—how will man's view of his own nature be modified by such a belief? The risk involved in telling people that their instincts are divine seems evident. Egoism, individual or national, does not need any such extra stimulation to break forth. Even if we afterwards add a qualification that God is also present in our higher spiritual functions, the previous admission will in practice have insidious effects. The immense spread of pantheistic sensibility during the last two centuries has also resulted in the idolizing of individual and collective passions.

In Socrates' restraining daimon, in Plato's Demiurge giving shape to rebellious matter, Babbitt and More find an expression of what the classical Greeks held to be most divine in human experience. In the Hellenistic world, on the other hand—the world of mystery religions, of hermeticism and gnosticism—an emotional type of human being appears who in many respects reminds us of the romantics of the modern period. The Hellenistic age was characterized by the fact that men were tired of seeking the truth and meaning of life by way of rational inquiry and now looked for them in emotional experience instead. The thoughts of the Greek enlightenment had implacably destroyed not only the ancient Olympic religion but also—through the achievements of Protagoras, Callicles, and their kind—the high-er values that made life worth living. Humanity got tired of thinking, which to them only seemed to cause destruction, and were more and more willing to find the meaning of life in other ways, especially by looking for communion with the divine spirit in strongly emotional experiences. What was most divine in the experience of Hellenistic man? Revelations and visions, full of feeling, tender emotions that gushed into his soul from Pleroma, from the divine Fullness. Emotions are expansive and not restrictive. And so Pleroma, the plentitude of all tender feelings, the One from which everything emanates, was described as an expansive principle—as the heart of the world, from which divine life gushes forth. The philosophy of Plotinus formulates the attitude of Hellenistic man as perfectly as Plato's formulates that of the classical Greek.

II

Anyone searching for parallels of some of the lines of thought underlying the New Humanism could not possibly undertake a more fruitful task than that of acquiring a thorough knowledge of Benedetto Croce's philosophy. For this philosophy is the most keenly formulated vindication of the idea of eternal values that twentieth-century thought has produced.

Like the Neohumanists, Croce defends the idea of certain mental functions, which are identical in all human beings although the individuals and situations vary in an inexhaustible flux of multiplicity. Moral customs vary, but the capacity of attempting civilized life is the same in everybody. Our senses of beauty and truth are also supposed to be identical everywhere as *functions*, however the *contents* may vary. All men have a capacity for intuitive understanding of one another, and in so far as they achieve this, they will realize that in the depths of their souls the same spirit is active, although the confusing multiplicity of changing situations often overwhelms them and makes them listen to the arguments of relativism. Croce, as well as the American humanists, regards the subject valuing ethically as a superindividual subject or, what amounts to the same thing, as a kind of subjectivity that acts in the same way in all men; the better we manage to understand one another, the better we understand this. The valuation that we can perceive in the protests of conscience emanates from the spirituality common to all human beings.

If we want to describe the process illustrated by the above metaphor of the customs house in Croce's terminology, the term "ethical synthesis *a priori*" will have to be introduced. While man is busily driven forward by his passions, something entirely new occurs in his mind; he sees things in a new light; his conscience "pricks him," as the saying goes. This is the very start of the ethical synthesis a priori; the beginning of something that is new in relation to what had filled consciousness before. The deeds we are about to perform, the ends we have in view, are suddenly regarded from an entirely new point of view that can be formulated in the question: "Is this right?" The immediate consequence is that we hesitate for a moment in order to look into our impulses and motives. Other impulses also turn up and are examined with regard to possible consequences. When we have at last found a line of action, against which there is no protest from our moral sense, we act accordingly. When our inward deliberation results in decision and action, the ethical synthesis a priori is completed, which means that our whole personality is unified and that the ensuing action is ethically inspired. There would be no ethical synthesis, if the first impulse was not stopped and held back long enough for deliberation to take place. To concentrate our personality is exactly the same thing as to collect our instantaneous impulses into deliberation under the presidency of our sense of right and wrong. They must be held back just as restive horses are reined by the driver so that man can act with the most extensive survey possible of the consequences within his reach. The governing power is identical to the ethical principle, the sense of right, the moral sense, or whatever term we prefer. Like a ripe fruit falling from the tree, that action issues forth from our deliberation, against which our sense of right does not protest.

Mere "vitality" is, according to Croce, the willing of a "particular end"; the ethical will is the will to "the rational end" (*il
fine razionale*), to the good of the whole, to the higher development of life, of the Spirit. The particular end is finite: The power
and pleasure of the individual or of some special group is made
an end in itself. The "rational end" is infinite. And there is no
gradual transition from any separate interest as primary to the
rational end as primary, but only an abrupt step. *Finiti et infiniti
nulla proportio.* It is an either-or with no in-betweens. But at the
same time Croce points out that every ethical act is also a vital
act: "How can anyone will the rational end without willing it as
his particular end at the same time?"[9] In other words, the ethical
valuation must be incarnated in the impulses, it must seek its
abode among them, unify itself with them.

These last thoughts also appear in American Humanism:
nobody (not even a Socrates, a Christ, a Buddha) has ever
performed a deed without finding pleasure in it. The activity of
the inner check, which is attended by some degree of pain,
precedes the positive actions. All acts have their origin in positive impulses—in an ethical person such impulses as are not
disapproved of by his moral sense; they are impulses that are
not considered shameful. As far as they develop successfully and
reach their goals, the result is pleasure. As far as outer obstacles
stop and frustrate the development of man's impulsive life, the
result is pain. As an ethically inspired human being naturally
wants to achieve success in all his doings, it has already been
implied that he seeks pleasure in all his actions. The difference
between him and the practical hedonist is "only" that the
former refuses all shameful pleasure—what they have in common is that they both seek the greatest amount of pleasure
possible. With this in mind, it will be possible for the reader to
understand the chapter titled "The Dualism of Plato" in Paul
Elmer More's *Platonism* (1917)—the most difficult chapter of one
of the most difficult books ever written. It will also be possible
to understand an abstruse passage in More's "Definitions of

9 *Estetica,* 6th ed., p. 63.

Dualism," from which I shall quote. Let us premise that the word *morality* means an ethical disposition, and *virtue* and *vice* mean skill and lack of skill, respectively. The passage runs as follows:

The morality or immorality of an agent is determined by the exercise or quiescence of the inner check. The rightness or wrongness, virtue or vice, of a particular act is determined by the final result in pleasure or pain to the agent as an individual existing amid certain circumstances—that is to say, by the harmonious increase of life or the contrary. If the inner check permits full attention on the part of the agent, he will to the best of his experience choose the act which shall result finally in pleasure, and which is therefore right and virtuous. At any moment, even with full attention, he may be mistaken in his opinion and thus be moral while acting wrongly and viciously. . . .[10]

Let us continue the comparisons with Croce. The view of human nature held by American Humanism can be illustrated by the following diagram:

1. ethical intuition
2. reason   3. imagination
4. positive impulses

Reason and imagination are no propellants; they are instrumental and can be used either by the lower will or by the higher will. Babbitt and More accept the maxim: *voluntas superior intellectu.* So does Croce, and the diagram can also be used to illustrate his view of human nature. And to analyze a number of problems that have been left unsolved by the Neohumanists there is hardly anything that will help us better than a thorough understanding of the Italian philosopher.

According to Croce the moral sense is a *will,* thus something different from reason if by this latter term we mean the mental function at work in the knowledge-getting process. To know reality is one thing, to create new reality another; the former function is called perception of reality (or simply knowing), the latter volition or will. But is not an act of knowing itself a new

10 *The Drift of Romanticism* (Shelburne Essays, Vol. 8, Boston and New York, 1913), pp. 276–277.

creation, a new reality added to that previously existing? Yes, it is, and every knowledge-getting act is at the same time always an act of willing. That thought is the instrument of the will means that acts of knowing are simultaneously acts of willing. This may seem a bit confused but Croce's trend of thought can easily be explained by an illustration.

Let us take a man climbing a mountain. He climbs for a while (mainly volition), then he stops to look for his way (mainly perception of reality), then he starts climbing again, and so on. Of course his perceptive function is not inactive for a single moment, not even when his physical exertions reach their climax; if his perceptive faculty fell asleep, he would faint. Thus, perception of reality also takes place during the phases of climbing that I have called "mainly volition." But on the other hand volition does not disappear when our mountaineer stops to take his bearings and get a survey of his position. He *wants* to get a survey, and without this will to know, his rational activity (perceiving reality) would cease to exist. Consequently we find that there is no perception of reality that is not volition at the same time. But, under these circumstances, how can we make any distinction between rational and volitional activity? Croce replies that we can, for knowledge (perception of reality) is knowledge because it is true, because it has a certain kind of validity, because it is subject to the law of logic. To will knowledge is to will an achievement with this special kind of validity. The willing of a product that is valid theoretically is something quite different from the willing of a practical achievement. By willing we create new reality: a theoretical achievement or a practical achievement that did not exist before. The function of the will is to create new reality, that of reason to know present reality; our perceptive function is set into operation and urged on by the will.

We have now seen that in one sense Croce as well as the American humanists regard reason and, in an analogous way, imagination as passive and merely instrumental faculties that cannot urge man forward. If man had no ethical intuition, these faculties would be helpless in the hands of the passions and only the instruments of the latter. Of course it is true that anyone seeking truth (and this is something the clear-cut egoist must also do to a certain extent to reach his goal) has to submit to the "inner checks" inherent in the inquiring after truth. And in a parallel fashion, our clear-cut egoist would have to submit to the "inner checks" of his artistic faculty, insofar as he wants to create something beautiful (e.g., to say something witty or expressive). But now we also see that these aesthetical and logical "inner checks" do not at all get us beyond our lower will, which uses them only for controlling itself to gain its logical and aesthetical ends. There are only two active forces at work in human nature: the lower will and the higher. This will enable us to understand why Babbitt and More put a unique emphasis upon conscience as the only real "inner check": the analogous phenomena in man's rational and aesthetical life are at bottom only manifestations of the self-control of the lower will.[11]

It is a pity that Babbitt and More never studied Croce's philosophy closely enough to enable them to discover how much it has in common with their own view of human life. Then they would also have been able to point out exactly where Croce went astray, i.e., in his acceptance of the pantheism of Plotinus and Hegel. This is the *fons et origo* of all in Croce's philosophy that, from a humanistic point of view, must be considered as illusion and confusion. Probably the most objectionable feature in Croce's philosophy is his defence of Machiavellian politics, which produced disastrous effects in Italy, inasmuch as the way was paved for Mussolini's Fascism. But such disasters are inevitable if the lust for power is regarded as a direct emanation from the Godhead and, in accordance with Hegel, the real is identified with the good.[12] In the technical aspects of Croce's *filosofia dello spirito* this confusion is reflected in the fact that the

11 The "higher will," then, cannot be equated with William James' "mental effort." This was my mistake in *Humanism and Naturalism* (Gothenburg, 1937).

12 See *Philosophie des Rechts* (*Sämtliche Werke,* 7, 1928, p. 33): "Was vernünftig ist, das ist wirklich; und was wirklich ist, das ist vernünftig. In dieser Überzeugung steht jedes unbefangene Bewusstsein, wie die Philosophie, und hiervon geht diese ebenso in Betrachtung des geistigen Universums aus, als des natürlichen."

Platonic triad of *verum—bonum—bellum* is vitiated by the addition of *utile* (meaning: what everyone finds useful for himself or his group). The gratification of the instincts is put on a par with what was previously looked upon as spiritual values. Even Croce has been influenced by the optimistic revaluation of human instincts that has prevailed since the days of Rousseau.

To Babbitt and More the instincts or impulses are not an "economical-political form of the spirit," on a par with the rest; they are not spirit at all but the natural man, the "material" aspect of his dual nature. But even if this pantheistic element is rejected, there remains in Croce's philosophy a tremendous lot of thoughts of great interest to the humanist. All those who do not believe that the last word has yet been uttered in the debate on values and who do believe that Plato's idea of goodness-truth-beauty will mean something to future generations as well—all those ought to undertake a careful study of Croce who has, in a better way than anyone else, formulated the idealistic theory of value. We have looked at his moral philosophy. His aesthetics are of great value even if they have to be supplemented by the humanistic idea of an "ethical imagination." And his logic contains lines of thought that the followers of Babbitt and More would easily profit by studying. For reason is a word used by the two Neohumanists without an adequate analysis of its various meanings. One example would suffice to show this. The higher will is supposed to be superrational, and undoubtedly it is, in one sense of that word: in the sense that it is an alogical act of volition and not an act of perception. But what is alogical can nevertheless be made the *object* of knowledge: There is knowledge *about* the instincts, knowledge *about* man's aesthetic activity, knowledge *about* his ethical will. And then we can also reflect upon our rational life and its history, and, in this case only, the object of our reflection is logical activity. We philosophize when we carry out this study of human activities. Reason as our philosophical-historical organ of knowledge—Croce shows us—is something quite different from the rational organ of natural science, our pragmatic "understanding." Our understanding thinks in terms of causality and cannot grasp the idea of freedom; in relation to the understanding, the higher will remains superrational, in every sense of the term. Reason does not think in terms of causality but in terms of liberty, and reason cannot admit of anything as superrational in the sense that it cannot be made the object of rational knowledge. Every sentence in More's "Definitions of Dualism" claims to be true, i.e., logically valid; his ethical experience was alogical but his describing his experience was a rational activity.[13]

If the New Humanism is undeveloped in the field of logic, it is, on the other hand, much more elaborate in the sphere of ethics. Here, Croce's philosophy in comparison seems somewhat scanty. Croce's formula has already been quoted: To will ethically is to will *il fine razionale,* i.e., to will the good of the whole (*il Tutto*), the development of the Spirit in higher and higher manifestations. Accordingly, he can also say that the ethical will is "the spirit that wills itself" (*lo spirito che vuole se stesso*). In the next part of this essay I am going to show how these thoughts are developed in the New Humanism. But the greater abundance of thought in Babbitt and More must not be allowed to obscure their fundamental agreement with Croce. Especially Babbitt's moral philosophy is, as we shall discover, complicated by his distinction between two styles of life, one "humanistic"

---

13 The very fact that More has a *concept* of the "inner check" proves that in one sense it is not superrational. Yet in another sense it is, for we cannot know in advance what the reactions of our moral sense will turn out to be in various situations which are yet unforseen, and so the higher will contains an infinity (of potential reactions) that transcends a finite intellect. It "can be apprehended only with the aid of the imagination. . . . This realm of insight cannot be finally formulated for the simple reason that it is anterior to formulae. It must therefore from the point of view of an intellect it transcends seem infinite. . . ." (*Rousseau and Romanticism,* Boston, 1919, p. 201).

How do I know the higher will, as it works in other people? By entering into them imaginatively and feeling the higher will as it would work in their situations, sensing what is right and wrong in their situations. When doing so, what I really feel might seem to be the reactions of my own higher will to the situations imagined; but since the higher will is the same in everybody, it is also the reactions of their higher wills that I feel. Thus I "apprehend with the aid of the imagination" the potential and actual reactions of the sense of right and wrong to various situations.

Grosselin (pp. 55 ff.) fails to deal adequately with this doctrine. It should not be called "intuitive voluntarism" for in our knowledge of the higher will (in ourselves and others) both intuitive sensing (of the reactions of the higher will) and imagination *and reason* are involved. Volitive reactions *as known* belong to the field of rational knowledge.

and one "religious." By the religious way of life he means saintliness. Conscience leads some men to a very strict way of life, some to a less strict way. But this complication does not mean that the central idea of his doctrine differs from Croce's. For on both levels of life "the spirit that wills itself" is operative; on both levels man is in the service of *il Tutto*. Conscience calls some of us to a very difficult service and some of us to a less difficult service; conscience works on two different levels, "categorically" severed from each other. But although this idea of two levels lies outside the domain of Croce's philosophy, it does not exclude a central agreement.

III

In Babbitt's description of the "humanistic level" we find the term "to will civilization," which can be explained as follows. Within all of us there is an intuition of what human life ought to be like and especially what our own lives ought to be like. This intuition man has tried to grasp, to keep, and to formulate in his ideals of life, society, and law. In the choice between different possibilities—various ideals of life, society, and law— this intuition has been the norm, i.e., the valuing function. Behind all specific formulations there is the sense of right that sanctions and approves of them. The formulations chosen are considered acceptable, sometimes for a considerable length of time, sometimes for only a short period; but sooner or later the historical situation changes, new problems arise, the ancient formulations are no longer the adequate vehicle of expression for the idealistic intuition of awakening spirits, and a new search begins in the dimension of human ideals.

Let us look at the terms mentioned. *Intuition*—what does this mean? The combination of this term with the word *formulate* will help us to a better understanding; for it is evident that what we are trying to formulate is not yet formulated, although it is not entirely unknown. The ideal of civilization cannot be formulated into a code once and for all; it contains much more than can ever be grasped in our formulas, which are all temporary and provisional. Man is constantly trying to make clear his idea of what ought to be and will continue to do so as long as history goes on. The word *ought* means that the sense of right is a valuing activity, by which various ideals are judged, as all specific impulses are judged by the same moral sense.

The ideals of life, law, and society created by humanity are of course usually more or less contaminated by the desires of the natural man, distorted and polluted by individual or collective egoism. The higher intuition has been obscured by what is only too human. This means that the moral sense as a selective principle has not been strong enough to hold back all such tendencies. But another factor must also be taken into account if we want to understand the different ideals embraced by different ages and peoples. That is the diversity of the situations in which human beings have relied upon their ethical intuition. We can easily see that some ethical problems can only be of current interest during some special historical period. Life has to face some difficulties during one period, others during the next. And man, who within him has his confused idea of what life ought to be, of course gets this intuition of his to grapple with the difficulties of the present. From his higher intuition he tries to derive all that has any special relation to what he has to cope with in his present situation. Naturally he has inherited the ideals of previous generations, the sum of their attempts at a distinct perception of what ought to be, but these ideals are found to satisfy the needs of the present no longer and so are subject to revision.

But what has been real ethical vision in some age or with some peoples cannot be incompatible with the ethical vision of other peoples. Human beings in all countries and in all ages have at bottom been moving toward the same goal; at bottom they have had the same intuition of what human life ought to be. Thus, life is not only a struggle for existence, as materialistic historians want us to believe. What has urged humanity on from the level of Bushmen and Hottentots has not been only our lower motives and desires. In spite of all its blindness and illusions humanity has also had a compass showing it the way toward civilized life—the same compass that is at work in us all when we approve and disapprove under the guidance of our moral sense.

However, Babbitt formulated his thoughts so badly that not even an intelligent disciple of his like T. S. Eliot has quite understood them. "What is the higher will to *will?*" Eliot asks,[14] and he finds the reply of "civilization." But this, he says, is something very vague. "It is, in fact, merely a frame to be filled with definite objects, not a definite object itself. I do not believe that I can sit down for three minutes to will civilization without my mind wandering to something else." Eliot has not understood that instead of being a refutation of Babbitt's ideas, this is in reality a confirmation of it. The universal will to civilization is embodied in a series of particular impulses that are all united by the fact that by them the person acting is trying to create civilized conditions. A scientist cannot sit down for three minutes and will the truth, and an artist cannot sit down for three minutes and will beauty.[15]

According to the New Humanism, the higher will primarily wills civilization—but only primarily, for it makes some persons achieve something much higher, saintliness. The majority of men are urged by their conscience to live together in a civilized manner; but in a small number of them conscience makes heavier demands than that, for the ways of life worked out by Christ and Buddha and their strict followers cannot be looked upon as the results of a "will to civilization." In them conscience is a "will to saintliness."

How are we, on an undogmatic basis, to understand this notion of two levels of life? How shall we be able to look upon these historical facts in a critical and unprejudiced spirit that—on a dogmatic basis—have been the cause of so much dispute between Catholic and Protestant theologians? Catholic tradition

14 *Selected Essays 1917-1932* (London, 1932), p. 426.

15 After all such misunderstandings it is a pleasure to turn to Chapter XV in Walter Lippmann's *The Principles of the Good Society* (New York, 1937)—Lippmann is another thinker who has been influenced by Babbitt and More—where one finds a clearer and better exposition of the idea of a "will to civilization" than the leading Neohumanists ever wrote.

has distinguished between "two ways to salvation, a good one and a better one." In the latter we find *religiosi* (monks and priests). The Catholics base their arguments upon Christ's words to the young man who said he had kept the Commandments: "If thou wilt be perfect, go and sell all that thou hast, and give it to the poor." Protestant theologians naturally reject the idea of two ways to salvation. But when, basing their arguments upon Kant's moral philosophy, they sometimes assert that the sense of duty must be the same in everybody, they have broached a subject that can also be discussed by an undogmatic philosopher.

As a matter of fact, no such conclusions can be drawn from the basic idea of Kant's ethics. Kant's doctrine means that I should judge myself neither more severely nor more leniently than I would judge anyone else in the same situation. The demands made by my unruly ego ought to be cut down to the minimum I would approve of in everyone else in the same position. This will also mean that I will award myself the same amount of temporal pleasure that I would award everybody else. According to Kant, this is the ethical view of human actions. But supposing somebody voluntarily renounced even the temporal pleasure he can claim according to the law of justice? Then he has actually got beyond the demands of the categorical imperative as regards rigor toward himself. Kant's moral philosophy is an attempt to formulate the morality valid on the humanistic level but does not deal at all with the religious level. Kant's principle is *suum cuique,* or the law of justice; but this implicates *meum mihi,* which certainly does not agree with the spirit of the Gospel. The humanistic intention in Kant's ethics is to subdue the desire for pleasure and power in the individual to the demands of social order; the saint sacrifices even more.

The idea of saintliness was not discovered by the Greeks; it was first introduced into the Occident by Christianity. The fact that Plato's greatest works are titled *The Republic* and *The Laws,* and that Aristotle's ethics were a part of his political philosophy, shows the close connection existing between social and ethical (i.e., humanistic) thought. Their endeavors were inspired by the same humanistic will to civilization that in vastly different sur-roundings had created the Jewish law. Christ did not preach the abolishment of the law but he did preach the giving beyond the demands of the law—a kind of giving that from a legal point of view is spontaneous and unmotivated. The Prodigal Son was overwhelmed with benefits that he did not deserve, but this was not an act of injustice against his brothers. The laborers in the vineyard were given all that was due them according to the law of justice, but some were given more than they deserved. The humanistic social order, created by the will to civilization, is not violated but transcended by the will to saintliness.

But somebody may ask whether Babbitt means that man has two consciences. No, only one. But while conscience calls most of us to attempt civilized life (and an infinite progress towards this goal is possible), it calls a few to attempt a much more rigorous way of life. Civilized life is good, but saintliness is better. As we have seen, an infinite progress is possible toward the goal of humanism: constantly improved theory and practice as regards civilized life. Aspirations toward saintliness are in another direction: They involve a leap from one level of life, strictly limited, to another. The end of the humanist is different from that of the saint, and one can move along as far as one likes in the former direction without reaching the latter. But although *eros* (the love of humanistic justice) and *agape* are sharply distinguished from each other, they should be looked upon as respectively a weaker and a stronger manifestation of the same higher will; the same power that subdues the ego under the law of justice can have a much stronger effect and manifest itself in a spontaneous giving of more than justice demands.[16]

16 See Babbitt's *The Dhammapada* (New York, 1936), p. 100. "The numerous persons who have seen in the original teaching of Buddha only the ethical element have been guilty of grave misapprehension. The path to religion leads through morality—on this point Buddha is most explicit; but as one approaches the goal one enters into an entirely different element: the saint who has attained the Nirvanic calm is, we are told repeatedly, 'beyond good and evil.' " He is beyond good and evil in the humanistic sense.

Grosselin (pp. 76 ff.) disregards the fact that religion, as conceived by Babbitt, is in itself (not only as combined with humanism) a union with other men. Humanism is a definite

IV

Only when Babbitt's and More's ethics have been explained will it be possible to understand their aesthetics, which are concerned with the relation between the ethical and the aesthetic aspects of experience. Perhaps the subject may best be approached by explaining what will seem unsatisfactory in Croce's aesthetics from the humanistic point of view.

In the first place Croce underestimates, or at least tends to obscure, the extent to which the artist (romantic or classical) is actually a teacher of his public. He tells us, it is true, that art is a "theoretical" activity; but he tends to shy away from explicit admission that the artist teaches us something, although not in the same way as a philosopher, historian, or scientist teaches. If the question is raised *what* art (whether classical or romantic) teaches, the humanist will answer: "possibilities of experience." Now Croce also tells us that art is concerned with "the possible," but this is left as a formula of which no further use is made. He does not make it clear to his readers that art is the envisaging of possible modes of experience, of values that life may contain, and that the artist is trying to convey to his public discoveries in this field. Artistic imagination, as described in his aesthetics, appears rather as a useless although inevitable luxury, without consequences or contextual or instrumental function in the development of experience.

In the second place, by obscuring the teaching function of art, Croce manages to escape the problem of the *value* and *truth* of the things taught by artists. He seldom touches upon the fact that poetry has "the function of humanizing the heart and aiding us towards a larger and more profound vision of the real nature of things" (*virtú a ingentilire il cuore e a intuire piú*

---

degree of union with other men, namely civilized worldly life. Saintliness is as close a union with other men as is compatible with existence as a human being. Personal needs and desires are the separating element. "Dying to the world" means finding out experimentally which needs are unnecessary and which are indispensable. Thus the separating element is suppressed and the saint comes as close to spiritual union with other men as is compatible with bodily existence.

largamente e più profondamente la realtà delle cose).[17] And then, without raising the problem, he goes on to assume as self-evident
that all art fulfills this function in the same degree. But this is the
very point where the facts will not fit into the Crocean aesthetic.
As Babbitt has shown very convincingly in *Rousseau and
Romanticism* (1919), there are two types of imagination, only one
of which—the classical type—aims at "seeing life steadily and
seeing it whole." Babbitt's terminology, when explaining these
matters in *Rousseau and Romanticism* and elsewhere, is not
altogether perspicacious and calls for a word of comment.
Especially the phrase "imitate the universal" must have puzzled
many readers. He seems to use it alternately in two senses:

1. The poet should, in the Aristotelian sense, imitate the
universal, i.e., picture life as governed by ethical laws; and
2. Morality means imitating the universal.

But these two senses can be shown to be closely connected.

What is this universal that should be imitated? Consider the
exclamation "Such is life," elicited by a drama or a novel! *Such*
refers to the particular events we have been witnessing, *life* on
the other hand is a universal, and we feel the presence of the
universal in the particular events. Life, as a universal, is a general
structure or pattern, and within this structure we must discriminate between various levels of universality. There are
all-pervasive "categorical" factors without which human life
cannot exist, e.g., the law of *hybris* and *nemesis*. Then there are
other elements that although perhaps not in the same sense
all-pervasive, are nevertheless pervasive in the experience of the
artist and his public, e.g., the temperamental difference between
man and woman. So much for the first sense in which Babbitt
uses the expression. But evidently the universal, which the poet
intuits, contains an idea of what man should be; you cannot
have a vision of life as governed by the law of *hybris* and *nemesis*

17 *Ethica e politica* (Bari, Italy, 1931), p. 196.

without at the same time having the idea of *sophrosyne* as the proper attitude for man. Hence the second sense in which man should imitate the universal. The universal is the ethical law governing life.

Classical poetry gives us the "illusion of a higher reality"; it is perception with the help of fiction of a "supersensuous order"; it is the glimpsing through a veil of illusion of a higher will that "cannot be finally formulated for the simple reason that it is anterior to formulae" inasmuch as all formulas are temporary and provisional.[18] Classical poetry, then, produces in a high degree the effect of which Croce speaks: that of "aiding us towards a larger and more profound vision of the real nature of things."

What about romantic poetry? According to American Humanism, poetry is a criticism of life and shows us possibilities of experience, values that life may contain. Human beings are more or less distorted, narrow-minded, and mechanized by dull routine. To be imaginative, on the other hand, means precisely to develop a sense of possibilities. Artistic experience is a means of escaping from the limitations and contortions debarring us from integral experience. Many of these contortions we have in common with our group, our class, our nation, even our age. Artists show us possible ways out of the curtailment, conflict, starvation, and restriction inherent in ordinary unimaginative experience. Thus we may say that every artistic experience means at least a partial integration of personality. Hence the sense of liberation, the feeling of exquisite intelligibility and clarity we have in the presence of an object that is experienced with aesthetic intensity. It is felt like a discovery of realities to which we have hitherto been blind. And returning to ordinary practical life, we are able to see things in life that we did not see quite so clearly before. After an artistic experience, we are not quite the same as we were before. Among romantic and naturalistic artists we should try to make use of the partial insight, the elements of true integration that they may contribute, when

18 *Rousseau and Romanticism*, p. 19, p. 201.

critically studied. But such artists are on the whole too disinte-grated to give us more than partial aid towards integration. They are often useful as critics of conventional narrowness. But the opening up to possibilities is only a first step toward full personal integration. After the opening of our minds we should be able to close them again, and the various possibilities of experience should be submitted to searching criticism.

Only those poets deserve to rank as classical who have been able not only to transcend conventional narrowness but to work their way to an integral view of life—seeing life steadily and seeing it whole—without loss of essential elements of human experience. Since no human life can be complete without moral inspiration, the integrated personality at bottom turns out to be identical with the truly moral personality. And life as viewed by an integrated personality in any age is life considered from the classical point of view. Humanistic morality, of course not held merely as we adopt some recent theory of life but as having by long experience become part and parcel of a man's view of life, is the key to classical art.

In one sense personal integration is the same thing in what-ever age and historical milieu it may be achieved. The results will nevertheless seem very different, since they vary according to the elements of experience that are to be reconciled and integrated; and these, of course, can never be the same in different epochs. We might say that personal integration is everywhere the same thing formally, though its contents will be infinitely various. If we call the results of personal integration common sense, normality, or centrality, these words do not refer to the statistical average of any age, but to the view of life held by the integrated man of the milieu in question. And even in this sense of the expression we must recognize that common sense develops from age to age with the growing experience of mankind. Homer's tragic view of life, combined with the ethical intuition of *arete,* his rich sense of various human values, was the exalted common sense of an age just emerging from barbarism. His view of life would of course be an anachronism today, if adopted mechanically; yet the contact with an integrated mind is always liberating and always constitutes an aid to sanity, in whatever age this mind may have appeared.

The humanists hold that Croce is wrong in simply identifying beauty and expression. Beauty is dual. Classical art, which is the expression of an integrated mind, is a higher type of beauty than romantic or naturalistic art, which are the expressions of disintegrated minds. "Either beauty cannot be defined at all," Babbitt says, "or we must say that only is beautiful which seems so to the right kind of man, and the right kind of man is plainly he whose total attitude towards life is correct, who views life with some degree of imaginative wholeness, which is only another way of saying that the problem of beauty is inseparable from the ethical problem."[19]

19 *Rousseau and Romanticism*, p. 208.

Joseph Baldacchino

Babbitt and the Question of Ideology

I

"THE PERSON WHO confides unduly in 'reason' " Irving Babbitt writes, "is . . . prone to set up some static 'absolute'; while those who seek to get rid of the absolute in favor of flux and relativity tend at the same time to get rid of standards. Both absolutists and relativists are guilty of an intellectual sophistication of the facts, inasmuch as in life as it is actually experienced, unity and multiplicity are indissolubly blended."[1] With these two sentences, Babbitt points to a question that has long divided intellectuals. That question is directly relevant to the nature and validity of ideology.

In the English-speaking countries particularly, conservative thinkers since Edmund Burke have tended to look with suspicion on attempts to formulate a systematic or "ideological" account of human life and values, believing that such systematic efforts must inevitably incorporate dangerous abstractions and oversimplifications. Russell Kirk has stated, for example, that "conservatism is not a political system, and certainly not an ideology. In the phrase of H. Stuart Hughes, 'Conservatism is

---

1 Irving Babbitt, *Democracy and Leadership* (Indianapolis, 1979; first published in 1924), p. 194.

the negation of ideology.' "[2] However, a number of contemporary writers—including Irving Kristol, Erik von Kuehnelt-Leddihn, and, in a more philosophical context, Folke Leander and Claes G. Ryn—have argued that a failure to address life's central questions in a systematic conceptual fashion is politically costly, philosophically inadequate, or both.

Kristol asserts in a *Wall Street Journal* article that, "in an age of ideological parties, conservative parties have to develop a sharp ideological identity." Though many conservative academics will oppose his position and "lament any ideologization of American politics," he writes, such ideologization is necessary; for "ideological politics rallies its supporters around a vision for the future and sees politics itself as being, above all, a force for the shaping of the future. . . . You can't beat an ideology with no ideology."[3]

On this last point Kuehnelt-Leddihn emphatically agrees. If the "still-free world" is to survive the challenge of Marxism, he writes, it is not enough to provide a negative critique of the Left, however brilliant. Rather, the West must oppose to the Marxist vision a coherent vision of its own—and one capable of appealing to people "all over the world"—for it is only such a vision that ultimately gives men a purpose and makes their lives seem worthwhile. Unless the West offers a constructive and well-coordinated ideology, writes Kuehnelt-Leddihn, totalitarianism will win by default; for men prefer the "sense of belonging, fulfillment, and identity" that is provided by even a wicked ideology to the emptiness that results when no animating vision is present. But under American leadership, he continues, the free world is floating in a frightening ideological vacuum. "Its subconscious, unexpressed, and ill-defined ideologies have very little if any value as cohesive or combative instruments. The military weakness of the West is much talked about, but it

2 "Introduction," *The Portable Conservative Reader,* ed. Russell Kirk (Harmondsworth, England, 1982), p. xiv.

3 Quoted in Erik von Kuehnelt-Leddihn, "Is Ideology Useless?" *National Review* (June 10, 1983), 686.

derives from an ideological void." As a direct result of the failure of conservatives to put forth a coherent ideology, Kuehnelt-Leddihn states, "various forms and degrees of Marxists"—Stalinists, Trotskyists, Eurocommunists, Socialists, Social Democrats, New Leftists, pseudo liberals—enjoy "what amounts to a near-monopoly" in "the present-day ideological domain."[4]

But if Kristol and Kuehnelt-Leddihn are correct that the development of a rationally coherent world view would prove immensely valuable from a practical standpoint—and experience would seem to support this contention—then why the reluctance of many conservatives to think in such terms? The beginnings of an answer may be discerned in Kirk's writings, which are heavily influenced by Burke's thought.

According to Kirk, "conservatism may be apprehended reasonably well by attention to what leading writers and politicians, generally called conservative, have said and done." With reference to British and American conservatives, Kirk notes that "conservatives generally believe that there exists a transcendent moral order, to which we ought to try to conform the ways of society." Conservatives also uphold "the principle of social continuity." While mindful of Burke's dictum about "the social necessity for prudent change," conservatives believe that such "change ought to be gradual and discriminatory, never 'unfixing old interests at once.' " Another, related principle, according to Kirk, is the belief in "prescription": the notion that our rights and moral obligations are embodied to a great extent in the patrimony bequeathed by our ancestors. Other principles cited by Kirk include an emphasis on prudence (the belief that public measures should be judged by their "probable long-run consequences"); respect for diversity, for differences of property, class, and moral authority; and, not least, the recognition that since human nature "suffers irremediably from certain faults," "no perfect social order can ever be created." But while such principles derived from experience are broadly descriptive,

4 "Is Ideology Useless?" 687–690.

writes Kirk, they should not be taken as fixed definitions. Precisely because it is based on historical experience, which varies
with circumstances, conservatism cannot be reduced to "a body
of immutable secular dogmas." It "offers no universal pattern of
politics for adoption everywhere." Hence, Kirk suggests, it
cannot be defined systematically.[5]

But though the Burkean view, with its apparent elevation of
prudence over abstract principle, represents what has been the
dominant tendency in Anglo-Saxon conservatism over the past
two centuries, it has not held sway unchallenged. The Burkean
view has been forced throughout most of its existence to coexist
in uneasy juxtaposition with a contrary tendency to see the
transcendent moral order as inhering in precisely the kind of
abstract norms of conduct that Burke believed should be
transcended by "expedience" or "prudence." This latter viewpoint, which dates from at least Plato's time and has been
common in older European thought, has tended to downplay
individual uniqueness and historical particularity for the sake of
a universality conceived as ahistorical. Critics writing from this
perspective often assume that emphasis on man's inescapably
historical nature must necessarily be associated with mere
utilitarianism and relativism.[6]

Reflecting this older approach, Kuehnelt-Leddihn attributes
the Burkean emphasis on experience over abstract reason to
a "post-Protestant," Anglo-Saxon predilection toward "relativism," "pragmatism," and "empiricism." While "systematization
and absolutism in thought" have long been alien to British conservatism, this has not been true on the Continent, he writes.
"There, Rome and Byzantium, with their thirst for the absolute,
are pitted against 'post-Protestant' relativism and pragmatism."[7]
Exhibiting this "thirst for the absolute," Kuehnelt-Leddihn, in
words that are almost antithetical to Kirk's, defines conservatism as a "set of values which are perennial" and as a "coherent

5 *Portable Conservative Reader,* pp. xiv–xix.

6 See Claes G. Ryn, "American Intellectual Conservatism: Needs, Opportunities,
Prospects," *Modern Age,* XXVI (Summer/Fall 1982), 310.

7 "Is Ideology Useless?" 686–687.

set of ideas." What is more, he describes the kind of ideology he is seeking as a "blueprint" and a "utopia."[8]

Despite his identification of conservatism with immutable norms of behavior, Kuehnelt-Leddihn cannot finally avoid recognizing with Burke that human life is experienced historically and that changing circumstances must be given due consideration. It is "obvious," he writes, that

the conservative aim cannot be a totally static world, because that is undesirable and impossible. The "state" and "society" of the ants, the termites, or the bees are completely immutable. Man is always faced with change. . . . There must be action among men and there must be thought, and with these two elements in the Western World change is unavoidable. The problem is to achieve organic progress, which means the preservation of real values, the resuscitation of past, forgotten or abandoned values, and the addition of new values harmonizing with the patrimony we have received. . . .[9]

Similarly, though Kuehnelt-Leddihn says that the kind of ideology needed should "speak a global (and not a local) language,"[10] he is not unmindful of the significance of differing cultural and historical circumstances. Indeed, he reluctantly concludes that conservatism may be incomprehensible except in terms of historicism:

The definition of conservatism is . . . difficult because this term bears a relation to time and space. Can it perhaps be understood only in a framework of Historicism? What about a Japanese conservative? Would he have to oppose Christianity in the name of Buddhism? Or Buddhism in favor of Shintoism? If this is the case, then conservatism becomes a completely relative term, unlike democracy which always and everywhere means equality and majority rule, or liberalism which stands for a maximum of personal liberty. I am afraid that conservatism in a purely etymological sense can only be understood in the context of a given culture and civilization.[11]

We see, then, a fundamental contradiction in Kuehnelt-Led-

---

8 Erik von Kuehnelt-Leddihn, *Leftism: From de Sade and Marx to Hitler and Marcuse* (New Rochelle, N.Y., 1974), p. 384, p. 394, p. 406; "Is Ideology Useless?" 687–688.

9 *Leftism,* p. 382.

10 "Is Ideology Useless?" 690.

11 *Leftism,* pp. 393–394.

dihn's position. He identifies conservatism with immutable
principles on the one hand and with historicism on the other.
Perhaps in an attempt to overcome the contradiction, Kuehnelt-
Leddihn adds this stipulation: "If we (i.e., Western conservatives)
... speak here about conservatism, we can only do so in
referring to a set of values which are *perennial* in our Christian
civilization, values which we want to conserve, which we want to
defend not only because we like them, because they are congenial to us, but also [because] we carry the deep conviction that
they are true. And if they are true, they are true independently
of time and space."[12] But even this attempt is not very successful.
For if conservatism is to be defined as "a set of values which are
perennial," how does one allow for the element of change that,
as we have seen, Kuehnelt-Leddihn considers both unavoidable
and desirable? Also, if Kuehnelt-Leddihn's conservatism can be
understood only in relation to the doctrines of Christianity,
what of his desire for an ideology that speaks "a global (and not
just local) language"? In apparent recognition of this problem,
Kuehnelt-Leddihn suggests that the desired ideology, though
intended ultimately to appeal to "people all over the world,"
might appeal "as a starter, [to] all Christians and Jews."[13] But
does this concession to the values of a particular religious tradition, and hence to "historicism" as understood by Kuehnelt-
Leddihn, mean that he himself must be considered a relativist?
Or is there, unknown to him, a kind of historicism that is not
inconsistent with a universal moral standard: one that simultaneously recognizes "the existence of a transcendent moral order
and the historical nature of man's participation in that order"?[14]

We have dwelt at some length on the tensions in Kuehnelt-
Leddihn's thought because they illustrate a problem that has
long plagued efforts to define the moral order in terms of
abstract principles: that of mediating between the universal and
the needs of particular situations, which might be ill served by

12 *Leftism,* p. 394.
13 "Is Ideology Useless?" 690.
14 "American Intellectual Conservatism," 310.

strict adherence to a preexisting moral blueprint. Such efforts usually employ a form of rationality that begins with the good as experienced in particular circumstances and tries to make of it an abstract standard (or set of standards) to be applied in all circumstances. Ideologies based on such reasoning fail to account for the element of variety and change that is everywhere present in life, and this failure leads to serious difficulties. Insofar as they are static, such ideologies are doomed to lose credibility—sometimes quickly, sometimes over a long period—as the needs they were initially intended to serve fall victim to changing time and circumstances. When this happens, the temptation is often great for the adherents of these doctrines to attempt to maintain them at all costs; and down this road lie authoritarianism and fanaticism.[15] Those who are aware of these difficulties but nevertheless persist in conceiving of the universal in terms of abstract norms often look for a solution in some form of casuistry. It is frequently suggested that the abstract norms in question are retained and remain controlling but that they are "tempered" or "moderated" to meet the requirements of specific situations. Yet it should be obvious that, whenever a supposedly controlling principle is "tempered," this principle is in fact transcended by the very act that brings the "tempering" into being.

From this last statement it appears that the transcendent moral standard may not exist as general rules or principles but

15 Claes G. Ryn points out ("History and the Moral Order," *The Ethical Dimension of Political Life*, ed. Francis J. Canavan, [Durham, N.C., 1983], p. 102): "The belief that true justice in the individual and society requires the imitation of a preexisting intellectual model of perfection tends to treat individuality as such as unimportant. This belief breeds suspicion of the view that government and society in general should try to accommodate diverse competing interests. Must not the moral approach be simply to disregard particular interests and to implement the disinterested moral blueprint? But such an approach to ethics and politics underestimates the requirement of continuous adjustment to the varying moral needs and opportunities of individuals and groups in a forever changing society." And Kuehnelt-Leddihn himself acknowledges (*Leftism*, p. 388) that nineteenth-century European conservatism, which tended to think in such absolutist terms, "had a strongly authoritarian bent and . . . operated with affirmations which brooked no discussion. . . . The idea that one could rule *fruitfully*, effectively and efficiently through an executive of policemen, *gendarmes*, informers, and jail wardens was (let us admit it) pretty widespread."

as a certain kind of action or quality of will. It is this emerging insight, and not mere utilitarianism or relativism, that underlies the Burkean emphasis on prudence exemplified by Kirk. To their considerable credit, those in the Burkean tradition have managed—through a direct, imaginative, and experiential intuition of the transcendent in concrete history—to overcome the difficult problem of mediation between the universal and the particular.[16] They have understood in a way that older Western thought did not, that the transcendent exists for man not in the abstract (i.e., apart from particular circumstances) but in particular good actions. Their emphasis on experience and their corresponding distrust of abstract reason are not without considerable justification. But if the critique of "desiccated reason" has been a major strength of this point of view, its failure explicitly to recognize another kind of reason that is faithful to the whole of experience has been a major weakness. As Ryn has pointed out, those like Kirk who have best understood the role of the imagination in shaping man's view of reality have "typically limited themselves to criticizing" the kind of abstract, metaphysical, or pragmatic thinking that normally has been

called reason . . . as being inadequate to understanding the essence of the human condition. This criticism has been amply justified. Rationalistic and positivistic reason sets reductionistic abstractions in the place of life as directly experienced; it knows nothing about the living and infinitely complex reality of human existence. . . . To grasp what is truly universal, it is necessary to have recourse to actual experience. . . .[17]

But, Ryn stresses, "the tendency within some strains of American intellectual conservatism to assume a conflict between conceptual intellection and the needs of humane knowledge is based on a one-sided notion of reason. . . . [A]bstract and reified thought-processes . . . have no monopoly on rationality."

---

16 For an examination of this aspect of Burke's thought, see Joseph F. Baldacchino, Jr., "The Value-Centered Historicism of Edmund Burke," *Modern Age*, XXVII (Summer 1983).

17 "American Intellectual Conservatism," 313.

Widely overlooked is a kind of reason that does not violate immediate awareness of the whole but is "scrupulously faithful to this awareness." Such truly philosophical reason is important, says Ryn, because experience alone "is intellectually mute; it offers direct intuition of reality, not argument. . . . The office of philosophical thought is to raise intellectually mute intuition into conceptual, systematic self-awareness. Experience *per se* has no voice in intellectual debate, but *conceptual accounts* of experience can refute distorted views of life."[18]

The intuition of what life is really like is necessary but not sufficient for the philosopher. To be effective in intellectual discourse, the intuitive awareness of good or evil must be raised to conceptual clarity. It must, to use the word in a special way, be expressed ideologically. Thus, Kuehnelt-Leddihn is correct when, in criticizing the "Anglo-Saxon" (i.e., Burkean) approach, he writes: "A discussion based on noble feelings is impossible. Any program to which a large number of people is pledged needs a rational profile."[19] Yet the Burkeans have been equally correct in stressing that ideologies composed of abstract and reified ideas, which present only part of experience as the whole of it, are not merely incomplete but dangerous. An "ideology" is needed that is capable of accounting for human life at its fullest, leaving out neither those aspects of experience that are universal and abiding nor those that are particular and fleeting, but systematically defining both, including their interrelationship. To be capable of appealing "to people all over the world," such an "ideology" must not require the acceptance of dogmatic formulations specific to particular times and places but must be able to "make sense" on the basis of universally available experience.

18 "American Intellectual Conservatism," 313–314 (emphasis in the original).
19 *Leftism*, p. 406.

II

Although Irving Babbitt lacks the idea of a philosophical reason, the foundations for a philosophical system or "ideology" meeting all these criteria are present in his work. As noted earlier, those who conceive of the transcendent in terms of abstract principles often attribute the Burkean emphasis on experience to mere utilitarianism and empiricism. Babbitt would agree that there is a certain resemblance between Burke's position and that of an empiricist in that both profess to look to experience rather than to the pronouncements of an external authority like the Church as the ultimate test of reality. But, Babbitt stresses, the resemblance is at bottom superficial; for the empiricists, in contrast to Burke and his followers, have a reductionist conception of experience and have ignored the supraindividual ethical dimension of human experience, with the result that their view of reality, and of human nature in particular, is seriously distorted.

Babbitt explains that the kind of "experience" to which the empiricists have devoted exclusive attention is aimed at controlling external matter in the interest of power and mechanical efficiency. And he readily acknowledges that this Baconian "outer working" has contributed to material progress on a grand scale. But the empiricists have gone astray in claiming far more for the kind of experience they are willing to recognize than it can possibly deliver. Not content "merely to minister to man's power and utility," the "apostles of modernity" have "professed to have a substitute for the spiritual unity" that was once provided in the West by the Church. And this claim, when put to the test of experience, which is to say, when judged by its fruits in the world of action, fails miserably: "The results of the material success and spiritual failure of the modern movement are before us. It is becoming obvious to everyone that the power of Occidental man has run very much ahead of his wisdom."[20]

20 *Democracy and Leadership,* pp. 166–167.

To attain true wisdom, Babbitt points out, it is not sufficient to accumulate empirical "facts" or "data," which are but bits and pieces of information torn from their experiential context. Rather, one must be attentive to the evidence offered by the whole of human history: by life as it is experienced directly and concretely. This evidence consistently demonstrates, says Babbitt, that all of man's power to control nature and his fellow human beings (i.e., the power supported by mere empiricism) is ultimately dangerous or meaningless unless ordered by the higher, ethical purpose that is felt within the individual as a power of self-control. "If our society continues to listen to those who are seeking to persuade it that it is possible to find mechanical or emotional equivalents for self-control," he comments, "it is likely, as Rousseau said of himself, to show 'a great tendency to degenerate.' "[21]

At the center of man's experience, according to Babbitt, is a neverending conflict between two competing qualities of will, and it is this inner conflict or "civil war in the cave" that defines man's essential moral predicament. The "lower will," which is alternately described as man's "impulsive," "natural," or "ordinary" self, is toward self-indulgence for oneself or one's group. The "higher" or "ethical" will, which is a will to goodness, is experienced as a "check" on merely selfish impulse in favor of a unifying and more deeply satisfying goal. The higher will "is not itself an expansive emotion but a judgment and a check upon expansive emotion."[22] To the extent that man disciplines his impulsive self, including even his ruling passion, in deference to this transcendent purpose, he not only unifies his own personality and achieves lasting happiness (as distinguished from momentary pleasure), but "moves toward a common center with others who have been carrying through a similar task of self-conquest."[23] The individual thus promotes what is simultaneously good for himself and good for all and thereby

21 Irving Babbitt, *Rousseau and Romanticism* (Austin, Texas, 1977; first published in 1919), p. 130.
22 *Rousseau and Romanticism*, p. 130.
23 *Democracy and Leadership*, p. 335.

brings into being such unity (community) as can exist in this imperfect world. The lack of such deference to the higher will leads to disharmony within the personality and society.

That man is a creature torn between contrary inclinations, who achieves happiness by deferring to a higher purpose, is an insight that is shared by many of the world's great religious and philosophical traditions, including Christianity, Buddhism, Judaism, Islam, Aristotelianism, and Confucianism. But, Babbitt argues, it is not necessary to subscribe wholly to any of these doctrines to recognize the essential duality of human nature; for the existence of "an ethical will that is felt as a power of control over the natural man and his expansive desires" is "one of the 'immediate data of consciousness.' "[24]

Babbitt stresses that man never experiences the universal in the abstract but always in and through particular circumstances. Hence it is impossible to devise an abstract rational blueprint that will serve "once for all" as a moral standard.[25] Rather, the morally disciplined imagination creatively perceives life's tran- scendent purpose through the noble examples of the past and creatively envisions new ways of serving this higher purpose with the means presently at hand.[26] The noble deeds of past and present generations; the symbols emerging from the great religious and philosophical traditions; works of artistic and literary merit; habits, customs, behavioral norms; the laws and political constitutions of the world's nations—all provide mate- rial for our imaginative grasp of the universal moral order to the extent that they embody ends that were shaped by the ethical will.

One of Babbitt's salient contributions is his recognition that the imagination, rather than the critical intellect, or reason, is the faculty that fundamentally shapes man's view of reality and that the ability to intuit reality is a function of an individual's moral character. It is part of the human predicament that every

24 *Democracy and Leadership*, p. 250.
25 *Democracy and Leadership*, pp. 170–171.
26 *Democracy and Leadership*, pp. 127–128.

individual is torn to some extent between contrary dispositions of will. Babbitt points out, however, that the individual who has been striving to humble his expansive self in deference to life's transcendent purpose and who is likely, therefore, to have experienced some of the true happiness that accompanies such "inner working" will tend to envision new potentialities of action that are similarly motivated. Those, on the other hand, who have made a habit of yielding to their passions will tend to erect elaborate, albeit false, justifications for continuing their self-indulgence. The quality of their imagination will be distorted by their lower will, and this will adversely affect their perception of reality. Babbitt observes, for example, that the man who does not impose ethical "control upon his ordinary self does not usually avow that he is a mere materialist. The ethical problem would be comparatively simple if he did. The egocentric individualist is, however, prone to give fine names to his own unrestraint. As Plato says, he will call insolence breeding, anarchy liberty, and waste magnificence; and may even go to the point of deifying his own impulses." Such a man, Babbitt adds, "also frequently calls what is at bottom only an hypostasis of his ordinary self in his dominant desire either progress or justice."[27]

It is helpful to note at this point that Babbitt's understanding of the role played by reason is somewhat deficient. As both Leander and Ryn have shown, Babbitt tends to conceive of reason as a pragmatic and analytic faculty that, though useful in critically assessing the content of imagination and in achieving particular, practical purposes, is based on abstraction and therefore is incapable of describing life as known to direct experience. Babbitt notes, for example, that there is an

element of truth contained in the saying that history never repeats itself. If this were the whole truth, if history were only a whirl of unrelated happenings that did not exhibit the workings of any central human law, one would have a right to dismiss any attempt to judge the present in the light of past experience. . . . But though it is true that

27 *Democracy and Leadership*, pp. 256–257.

history never repeats itself, it is about equally true that history is always repeating itself; and this is a part of the paradox of life itself which does not give up here an element of oneness, and there an element of change, but a oneness that is always changing. This implication of unity in diversity is the scandal of reason, and philosophers have, for the most part, ever since the Greeks, been seeking with the aid of reason to abstract the unity from the diversity, or else, by similar rationalizing processes, to stress the diversity at the expense of the unity.[28]

Commenting on passages such as this, Leander and Ryn note that they illustrate Babbitt's strong sense of the shortcoming of reason, understood pragmatically, when it comes to grasping the essential facts of human life. The abstract "concepts" or "facts" produced by so-called pragmatic reason are not true to actual experience, but are rules of action procured by the will for purposes of practicality. However, Babbitt is unaware that, in criticizing the deficiencies of the "reason" that is incapable of describing life as directly experienced, he is using a kind of reason that is capable of such a task: namely, philosophical reason.[29] Partly because of his limited notion of the intellect, Leander and Ryn argue, Babbitt puts most of his emphasis on the role of the imagination, or intuition, in grasping the universal. Ryn writes:

[Babbitt] says of the element of manifoldness and change and the element of oneness that they are "intuited." And so they are. But we also articulate what we intuit by forging a term for it. We give conceptual form to experience. The "what" may be a structural trait of experience, a category. According to Babbitt, the erroneous road leading towards a "metaphysic of the One" is attending exclusively to life's recurrent elements: Man allows himself to construct a prematurely closed system, blinding himself to or explaining away life's variety and change. "The metaphysicians of the many," Bergson, for example, do not attend to what is permanent. How does Babbitt *know* all this? By what faculty is he able to explain the shortcomings of the two opposed types of metaphysics? He gives a rational account of the

28 *Democracy and Leadership*, p. 170.

29 Claes G. Ryn, *Will, Imagination and Reason* (Chicago, 1986), esp. Ch. IV, and Folke Leander, *The Inner Check* (London, 1974), whose analysis of More applies equally to Babbitt.

structure of experience and of the two ways of misinterpreting it. He expresses *conceptually* what he has also intuited. He does not argue his case by means of intuitions but by means of concepts. He is relying on philosophical reason.[30]

Babbitt is not alone in recognizing the crucial role of the morally disciplined imagination in shaping man's view of reality while simultaneously overlooking or discounting the contribution of philosophical reason. Rather, as we have seen, this tendency has been typical of Burkean conservatism. The hostility of those in this tradition to ideology in any form can be attributed in large part to their not distinguishing between abstract pseudo reason in various forms which divorces itself from concrete human experience, and the reason of philosophy. Identifying ideology with rational systems and the latter exclusively with a kind of reductionistic, abstract rationality that is deficient from the standpoint of direct experience, some have claimed to eschew systematic conceptual argument, preferring instead to express their vision of life's higher possibilities in artistic and literary works, in historical and literary criticism, or in practical example. An instance of the latter would be the way of life and development of moral character that Burke has in mind when he refers to the "spirit of a gentleman."[31]

Yet there is a sense in which the visions of life that take shape in the imagination can be described as "ideologies," whether they are conceptually developed. It is possible for the imagination to grasp the deepest meaning of human life and reality in an intuitive glance. By its nature the imagination makes use of the totality of one's past experience, including all that one has learned through reading about faraway times and places, in interpreting present circumstances. Hence the resulting visions—though they may remain conceptually undifferentiated or "compact," to use a Voegelinian term[32]—can be highly complex and, depending on the quality of the experience on

---

30 *Will, Imagination and Reason,* Ch. IV (emphasis in the original).

31 Edmund Burke, *Reflections on the Revolution in France* (Harmondsworth, England, 1969), p. 173.

32 See Eric Voegelin, *The New Science of Politics* (Chicago, 1952), especially p. 27.

which they are based, potentially comprehensive. Even in those who have raised their vision of reality to a highly systematic, conceptual level, moreover, it is their imaginative "world view" or "ideology" (*Weltanschauung*) that most directly affects their actions and, through the example they set, the actions of others. If by "ideology" is meant a vision of the whole that serves as an animating and unifying force, those conservatives who emphasize the role of the moral imagination are not necessarily unideological or antiideological.

It would be a mistake, however, to conclude on the basis of what has just been said that philosophical reason is unimportant. According to Benedetto Croce, the reason of philosophy raises to the conceptual level what man already knows about himself intuitively and experientially. Its object is human self-knowledge, and because what is known is what has become embodied in actions that have shaped new reality, this knowledge is, in a broad sense, historical. The facts with which philosophical reason is concerned are not, like those of pragmatic "reason," rules or principles of action (which, given the element of novelty and change that is a permanent aspect of the human condition, must necessarily be provisional and somewhat arbitrary) but are what Croce termed the universal categories of human action. These are ends or aims to be achieved—goodness, efficiency, beauty, and truth—which are present at least to some small degree in every individual and every society at all times. These categories in their various aspects and interrelationships make up the permanent structure of human experience. Ryn comments that, as aims, the categories of experience both "are, and . . . are not, realized: they *are being* realized." Hence formalistic logic—with its static alternative of "is" or "is not"—is inadequate to philosophical reason. The latter utilizes a "dialectical" logic that ignores neither life's permanent nor its fleeting aspects but is faithful to life as concretely experienced: as a "oneness that is always changing."[33]

---

33 *Will, Imagination and Reason* (emphasis in the original). Also see Benedetto Croce, *Philosophy of the Practical: Economic and Ethic* (New York, 1969).

Philosophical reason, resting on the disciplined and yet open imagination, diagnoses and refutes intuitions of life that leave out essential aspects of experience. Though not reflectively aware of the logic of his own thought, Babbitt uses philosophical reason quite effectively in the task he calls criticism, which entails uncovering the distorted products of the imagination. Understanding that morally corrupt vision often hides reality by using linguistic symbols in a misleading way, Babbitt insists that the role of criticism is to submit vague terms to a "searching Socratic dialectic." "Words, especially abstract words," he explains, "have such an important relation to reality because they control the imagination which in turn determines action and so 'governs mankind.' " Hence, he says, it is necessary to "dichotomize" words Socratically in order to become aware of the deceptive uses to which they can be put.[34] Toward this end, Babbitt introduces a vast array of dichotomies in his works. These include:

1. The "outer working" of Baconianism, whose goal is power, versus the "inner working" of morality, which is felt on the humanistic level as a "will to justice" and on the religious level as a "will to peace";[35]

2. True justice as the proper reward for one's work, with particular emphasis on ethical working, versus "social justice," which, based on mere "sentimentalizing over the lot of the underdog," tends toward confiscation and undermines moral standards;[36]

3. True liberty as the freedom to work ethically versus the utilitarian notion that man should be "free to cultivate his own idiosyncrasy" providing only that he does not "injure his fellow men" in a superficial, external sense;[37]

4. True peace, which in the secular realm is synonymous with justice and results from inner working, versus the illusory peace

34 *Democracy and Leadership*, p. 218. Also see *Rousseau and Romanticism*, p. 201.
35 *Democracy and Leadership*, pp. 222–223.
36 *Democracy and Leadership*, pp. 231–232.
37 *Democracy and Leadership*, pp. 226–227.

sought by the pacifists, who want the reward of ethico-religious striving without doing the necessary work;[38]

5. The market economy and private property as means to ethical ends, versus the same institutions in the service of un-bridled materialism;[39] and

6. Direct democracy, which seeks to put into effect the unre-strained will of the majority, versus constitutional democracy, which seeks to reflect the popular will "but only after it has been purified of what is merely impulsive and ephemeral."[40]

Referring to such dichotomies, Ryn notes that Babbitt "in-troduces them one by one almost as if they were unrelated items. On closer inspection they turn out to be so interrelated that each one implies all the others. Together they form a conceptual network. . . . The network of Babbittian dichotomies turns out to be a comprehensive philosophy." While Babbitt does not claim to be presenting a systematic world view, such a system is nevertheless strongly implicit in his writings. To quote Kuehnelt-Leddihn, his work presents a "rational profile." Sig-nificantly, Babbitt's outlook does not consist of rigid principles, whose validity is contingent on particular circumstances. Rather, the concepts developed by Babbitt—the higher and lower will, happiness as distinguished from mere pleasure, etc.—describe aspects of experience that are present at all times and in all cultures, regardless of the needs and opportunities present at any given moment.[41]

Despite ambiguities that hint at another solution, the thrust of Kuehnelt-Leddihn's thought is toward an ideology consisting of immutable moral precepts or rules of action. Because intuitively aware of the need for flexibility and adjustment to changing conditions, he is not fully comfortable with such a system. But

38 *Democracy and Leadership*, pp. 221–222.
39 *Democracy and Leadership*, pp. 231–235, 298.
40 *Democracy and Leadership*, p. 273.
41 *Will, Imagination and Reason*, Ch. IV. What is here said of Babbitt's concepts is equally true of the "principles" outlined by Kirk. This is hardly surprising, considering that Kirk has described Babbitt's writings as providing, with Burke's, the most significant influence on his own thought.

under the influence of traditional Western thought and its
tendency to identify the transcendent with abstract principles,
Kuehnelt-Leddihn apparently sees no middle ground between
doctrinal rigidity on the one hand and a view of reality that sees
only flux and relativity on the other. And with the choice
narrowed to these two extremes, Kuehnelt-Leddihn opts for the
former, albeit somewhat hesitantly.[42] Of course, the predominant tendency over the past few centuries has been in the opposite direction. If traditionalists like Kuehnelt-Leddihn have
suppressed whatever doubts they may have entertained about
the continued relevance of old dogmatic formulations, those of
a more liberal bent have shown no such reluctance to abandon
the old forms. And since, in the West at least, the notion of a
transcendent good had become widely identified with the acceptance of such static, sometimes theological, formulations,
the ascendancy of moral relativism followed almost inevitably.[43]

The overriding lesson of Irving Babbitt is that man does not
have to choose between the extremes represented at one pole
by adherence to some form of ahistorical dogmatism and at the
other by the pursuit of novelty. Indeed, far from being a requirement, the acceptance of either position is, says Babbitt, a
fundamental mistake. We have already quoted his observation
that both absolutism and relativism involve "an intellectual
sophistication of the facts, inasmuch as in life as it is actually
experienced, unity and multiplicity are indissolubly blended."
He adds: "It is the wont of man to oscillate violently between
extremes, and each extreme is not only bad in itself but even
worse by the opposite extreme that it engenders."[44] Babbitt
points out, for example, that the romanticist's antipathy to any
form of social restraint on individual impulse and temperament
is in large part a reaction against the tendency of an earlier age
to divinize lifeless rules and conventions. Babbitt himself takes

42 A similar tension is evident in the writings of the twentieth-century philosopher
Leo Strauss. For an analysis and a solution along lines suggested by Babbitt's insights,
see Ryn, "History and the Moral Order," pp. 92–95.
43 See *Rousseau and Romanticism*, p. 104.
44 *Rousseau and Romanticism*, p. 106.

an intermediate position. Every society needs to work out rules or norms of behavior, he writes, if only to serve "on practical grounds . . . as a barrier to the unchained appetites of the individual." Yet the "elements that enter into any particular attempt to circumscribe the individual in the interests of the community are very mixed and in no small measure relative." They are at best "a very imperfect image, a mere shadow" of a "higher law"—one that transcends particular times and places and yet is immediately perceptible to the disciplined imagina-tion. To the extent that they "approximate" the transcendent moral order, the conventions of a particular country—its cus-toms, laws, and traditions—should not be "sacrificed lightly." Yet because only an approximation, they should not be given "an undue reverence" either.[45]

How is it that Babbitt succeeds, where so many have failed, in avoiding both the straitjacket of doctrinal inflexibility and the meaninglessness that follows from relativism? How, in other words, does he reconcile the idea of a universal moral order, which implies a "constant element in human experience," with life's undeniable historicity? The key is provided by his identify-ing the transcendent as a form of volition rather than intellect. For Babbitt the transcendent is a supraindividual element of will that is felt as a check on arbitrary desires. This special will

---

45 *Rousseau and Romanticism*, p. 51, p. 79. Discussing this aspect of Babbitt's thought, Ryn writes ("History and the Moral Order," p. 100) that an "activity which is rational in a sense but not really philosophical because not concerned with what is universal, is the effort to formulate particular rules or principles of conduct. These rules range from the temporary and trivial to the long-lasting and highly significant. . . . Respect for the law is a fundamental political need of civilization. To the extent that norms of various kinds are formulated with genuine sensitivity to the demands of ethics, they tend to induce in those who attempt to respect them a sense of that universal right which lies beyond all specific rules. Together with ethical philosophy proper they help to orient the individual to the kind of life which is intrinsically good and happy. Yet no specific rules, however general they be or however elaborate is the casuistry used to apply them, can anticipate all possible circumstances. They offer at best pragmatic guidelines for action. . . . The uniqueness of circumstances calls for a creative synthesis of the moral universal—the higher will—and the particular: The specific content of the moral act is the incarnation of the transcendent good through ethical ordering and development of the potentialities immanent in the situation. Awareness of possibly relevant rules or principles, and of philosophical truths, is a part of the complex challenge of circumstance out of which the ethical will finally creates the new action."

always obligates men to seek the just solution (an effort requir-
ing both imagination and reason), and in this sense it is immutable. But what the just solution will be in a given instance
depends upon circumstances, which in no two cases are ever
quite the same. Pragmatic principles can provide necessary
support to man's higher disposition in its continual struggle
against opposing impulses, but the morality of a particular
action is ultimately a function of whether it was informed by the
higher will. As Ryn has observed:

The higher will draws each individual towards its own transcendent
purpose by ordering his impulses. It is experienced as a negative, an
"inner check," on inclinations destructive of the moral enhancement
of life. In relation to impulses which are being shaped by the higher
will into actions of the opposite quality, it becomes their inspiring
sense of meaning and worth. In moral action, individuality and
universality, immanent and transcendent, merge. The good is "incarnated."[46]

In developing the various implications of his notion of the
moral universal as a living force (i.e., will) rather than a set of
static principles, Babbitt offers an entire world view, one that is
capable of full systematic elaboration.[47] If by "ideology" is
meant a "systematic . . . or coordinated body of ideas or concepts especially about human life or culture"—a definition from
Webster's Third that seems to express one of the major uses of the
term—then it is fair to say that Babbitt provides an "ideology."
Because this "ideology" is centered in an experience (the
struggle within the individual between good and evil inclinations) that is known to some extent to everyone, rather than
based on specific theological or dogmatic formulations, it can
appeal more effectively to people of different cultural and

46 "History and the Moral Order," p. 98.
47 Babbitt's account explains the existence of good and evil, for example, in a way
that relativism cannot; at the same time it reconciles "the constant and the variable
factors in human experience" in a way that traditional Western rationalism has
perennially failed to do. Babbitt's description of the effect of character and imagination
on man's perception of reality also explains why it is, for example, that apparently
intelligent people can still defend Marxism as moral in the face of vast historical evidence
to the contrary.

religious backgrounds than one based on a specific tradition, which is what Kuehnelt-Leddihn seems to advocate.[48]

Now when Kirk expresses his hostility to ideology, he has in mind not the broad sense of the word used here but the more narrow connotation that John Adams had in mind when he described ideology as the "science of Idiocy": namely, the insistence on applying abstract and impractical ideas to politics without regard to the harm or injustice that results. It should be obvious from what has been said that Babbitt's thought is in no wise ideological in this latter sense. On the contrary, his "ideology," by defining both the need for and limits of pragmatic principles, enables us to see precisely what it is that distinguishes a good ideology or world view from a bad one. To the extent that a world view formulates universally valid aspects of experience and does so systematically, it merges with philosophy, and its practical effects will be salutary. Equally legitimate, though not philosophical, is the formulation of pragmatic principles, provided that

    1. They are demanded by the higher will in the circumstances in which they are initially created, and

    2. They are continuously evaluated as to their applicability in changing circumstances.

Danger arises when rules that are at best provisional and temporary are confused with eternal verities. "Life does not give here an element of oneness and there an element of change," writes Babbitt. "It gives a *oneness that is always changing.* The oneness and the change are inseparable."[49] "Wisdom is found in mediation between the constant and the variable factors

---

48 As an example of how the conception of the moral universal as a quality of will transcends historical and creedal differences, Leander notes (*Humanism and Naturalism* [Gothenburg, 1937], p. 139) that a Moslem and a Christian may both share the same hierarchy of values—both can believe in sexual restraint, for instance, though one is polygamous and the other monogamous; both share a certain spiritual attitude— although "their concrete ways of life can be shaped very differently on account of the dissimilarities between the social conventions under which they live."

49 *Rousseau and Romanticism,* p. 7 (emphasis in the original).

in human experience." However, rationalism, with its tendency "to abstract the unity from the diversity, or else . . . to stress the diversity at the expense of the unity" has been singularly ill equipped to support such mediation.[50] This is what has given ideology a bad name.

50 *Democracy and Leadership*, pp. 170–171.

Peter J. Stanlis

Babbitt, Burke, and Rousseau: The Moral Nature of Man

AMONG THE MANY philosophical convictions that Irving Babbitt held in common with Edmund Burke (1729–97) was their conception of the moral nature of man. Both Babbitt's classical humanism and Burke's Anglican Christianity rejected the naturalistic theory, which had evolved during the seventeenth and eighteenth centuries and culminated in the moral "sensibility" of Jean-Jacques Rousseau (1712–78). The theory of man's moral nature that was based upon sensibility held that man's nature is innately or inherently good, and therefore does not need the aids to grace or normative reason provided by the personal discipline and social controls of religious and civil institutions. Babbitt agreed wholly with Burke's description, in the *Reflections on the Revolution in France* (1790), of the necessary function of social institutions. Burke had written that the institutions of society provide humanity with "the wardrobe of a moral imagination, which the heart owns and the understanding ratifies, as necessary to cover the defects of our naked, shivering nature." Both Babbitt and Burke believed that the moral clothing provided by man's institutions protected him from his vulnerability to yield to his destructive instincts and passions, thus redeeming mankind into civility. Therefore, they believed that any "return to nature," as advocated by Rousseau, whether primitivistic or merely more "simple" than the polished European society inherited from the past, would result in a regression into the savagery of a Darwinian jungle, and not a return to the idyllic nature of a Garden of Eden. Burke's strong attacks on Rousseau's moral conception of man during the French Revolution, and Babbitt's lifelong criticism of Rousseau, cannot be understood apart from their common conception of the moral nature of man, such as had been preached by Christianity for many centuries.

There were some philosophical differences between Burke and Babbitt, but their common Aristotelian belief that organized civil society was the normal or "natural" condition for man, in all its varieties of historical development, provided them with a common ground from which to criticize theories of a supposed idyllic "state of nature" prior to organized society, or apart from it. History and experience, including the experience of living according to inherited or revealed ethical norms, rather than a fictional theory of a social contract, gave both Burke and Babbitt a basis for criticizing Rousseau's naturalistic sensibility.

I

A detailed comparison between Burke and Babbitt as critics of Rousseau would be highly illuminating. This essay will be limited to Burke's and Babbitt's criticism of Rousseau as the archetypal embodiment of eighteenth-century naturalistic "sensibility," an important movement that challenged the long-established Christian conception of the moral nature of man.[1] To understand fully their criticism of Rousseau as a moralist it is essential to comprehend the genesis and development of romantic "sensibility" as an ethics of feeling, from the seventeenth century and throughout the whole eighteenth century,

---

1 On Burke's attacks on Rousseau between 1756 and 1791, see Peter J. Stanlis, "Burke and the Sensibility of Rousseau," *Thought*, 36 (1961), 246–276.

and, as Babbitt shows, to the twentieth century. That in turn would require a thorough knowledge of the intellectual history of Europe in all that affected man's conception of himself in relation to the universe and to European society, from the Renaissance and Enlightenment to the dominance of romantic literature and philosophy.

For many centuries before Rousseau and Burke, Christianity had taught that, although man was created in the spiritual image of God, and therefore had seeds of divinity in him, by virtue of the Fall he is alienated from God. In his innate or "natural" state, because of original sin, man's reason is clouded, his will is weak, and he is subject in times of temptation to fall into one or more of the seven deadly sins: pride, covetousness, lust, anger, gluttony, envy, and sloth. Some Christian theologians even advanced the theory of "the decay of nature" in man, that mankind was growing progressively worse since the Fall.[2] But in general, Christianity taught that through faith, hope, and charity man could acquire prudence, justice, temperance, and fortitude and through these cardinal virtues could overcome his innate natural depravity and be redeemed into spiritual and temporal salvation. To redeem himself from his innate moral weaknesses, the "natural man" needed to acquire knowledge of the principles of good and evil, and to strengthen his will through the spiritual discipline of the sacraments and God's gift of sanctifying grace. As Burke noted, the basic institutions of society, the family, church, and state, and even all lesser institutions, were the necessary means by which the "natural man" overcame his innate deficiencies in the intellectual, social, aesthetic, and moral virtues, and fulfilled his highest potential as an individual and in society:

Every sort of moral, every sort of civil, every sort of politic institution, aiding the rational and natural ties that connect the human understanding and affections to the divine, are not more than necessary, in

---

2 Victor Harris, *All Coherence Gone* (Chicago, 1949). See especially the chapters "The Decay of Nature" and "The Fall of Man and Nature."

order to build up that wonderful structure, Man—whose prerogative it is, to be in a great degree a creature of his own making, and who, when made as he ought to be made, is destined to hold no trivial place in the creation.[3]

In brief, as Burke noted, Christianity taught that man is by nature innately weak and prone to sin, but that by accepting all the necessary aids to grace and reason provided by his social institutions he can be redeemed in both his spiritual and temporal life into a magnificent destiny.

Burke noted that religion had both a private and a public function, that it existed both "in the sanctuary of the heart" in its "personal capacity," and in a "corporate character," as in public religious ceremonies that recognize God as "the Institutor and Author and Protector of civil society, without which civil society man could not by any possibility arrive at the perfection of which his nature is capable, nor even make a remote and faint approach to it." The public function of religion justified a Christian conception of the state as one of the most vital instruments given by God to man for his temporal redemption: "They [Christians] conceive that He who gave our nature to be perfected by our virtue willed also the necessary means of its perfection: He willed, therefore, the state: He willed its connection with the source and original archetype of all perfection."[4] Burke believed with Aristotle that politics was a branch of ethics, that constitutional government, corporately organized within civil society, exercised its sovereign legal power subject to the norms of moral law. The governments of the world, in their relationship with their subjects and citizens, therefore, were not free to exercise power by the arbitrary will of rulers, but were bound by moral necessity to rule in accordance with the moral natural law. Burke's social contract is not merely between rulers and subjects, as with Hobbes and Locke, but includes the sovereign-

---

3 Edmund Burke, *Reflections on the Revolution in France* in *Edmund Burke: Selected Writings and Speeches,* ed. Peter J. Stanlis (New York, 1963), p. 462.
4 *Reflections*, p. 472.

ty of God-given moral law. The "partnership" includes man's relation to God and is therefore "a partnership in every virtue and in all perfection." It includes all the generations of men, "those who are living, those who are dead, and those who are to be born." To Burke the validity of the social contract of each state was sanctioned by its connection with the archetypal fixed moral compact of God with man: "Each contract of each particular state is but a clause in the great primeval contract of eternal society, linking the lower with the higher natures, connecting the visible and invisible world, according to a fixed compact sanctioned by the inviolable oath which holds all physical and all moral natures each in their appointed place."[5] Clearly, in Burke's theory of the social contract the constitution of each state is valid only as it conforms to the higher moral law.

Burke argued that as the moral law cannot be altered by the arbitrary will of rulers or subjects, the whole relationship of man to civil society is not a matter of choice, but a matter of moral necessity. In advancing this vital point Burke described the effects that would result if mankind were to assume a voluntaristic relationship to society:

This law is not subject to the will of those who, by an obligation above them, and infinitely superior, are bound to submit their will to that law. The municipal corporations of that universal kingdom are not morally at liberty, at their pleasure, and on their speculations of a contingent improvement, wholly to separate and tear asunder the bands of their subordinate community, and to dissolve it into an unsocial, uncivil, unconnected chaos of elementary principles. It is the first and supreme necessity only, a necessity that is not chosen, but chooses, a necessity paramount to deliberation, that admits no discussion and demands no evidence, which alone can justify a resort to anarchy. This necessity is no exception to the rule; because this necessity itself is a part, too, of that moral and physical disposition of things to which man must be obedient by consent or force: but if that which is only submission to necessity should be made the object of choice, the law is broken, Nature is disobeyed, and the rebellious are

5 *Reflections,* p. 471.

outlawed, cast forth, and exiled, from this world of reason, and order, and peace, and virtue, and fruitful penitence, into the antagonist world of madness, discord, vice, confusion, and unavailing sorrow. . . .[6]

As the culmination of Burke's conception of the social contract, this passage contains the essential basis for much of his most perceptive criticism of the political theory of man and society assumed or advanced by the French revolutionists. It also underscores his strong criticism of Rousseau as a moralist.

Burke's attack on Rousseau's revolutionary view that man is by his innate nature morally good, and without need of help acquired from his institutions, was in essence a defence of the orthodox Christian conception of the moral nature of man. Burke was well aware that Rousseau did not originate the theory that man is naturally good. But he came to believe around 1790 that Rousseau had become the most powerful propagandist and advocate of the theory. He would have agreed with Madame de Stael's famous remark that Rousseau originated nothing but set everything afire. It is not necessary here to describe in detail the genesis and historical development of the theory of man's natural moral goodness. But a brief summary of its main features will be useful in clarifying the criticism of Rousseau by both Burke and Babbitt.

Probably the modern theory that man is by his innate nature morally good derives largely from the development of science and speculative rational philosophy during the sixteenth and seventeenth centuries. For more than fifteen centuries the Christian world view of most Europeans was rooted in the Ptolemaic system that the earth was the center of the physical universe, that man was the center of the moral universe, and that a transcendent and personal God was the source, means, and end of all reality and meaning in human life. This meta-physical and humanistic conception of reality, with its attendant principles and values, was called into doubt by the revolutionary astronomy of Copernicus and Galileo. The "new philosophy" of

6 *Reflections,* p. 471.

modern science, and especially the empirical and rational scientific methods of Bacon and Descartes, gradually displaced the religious and humanistic view of reality and man's place in the universe with an essentially naturalistic philosophy that nullified and denied the Christian conception of the moral nature of man.[7]

Even before the so-called Enlightenment, the "ethical calculus" of Descartes and Hobbes, centered in the systematic application of geometric reasoning to every branch of knowledge—including religion, ethics, history, law, politics, society, and aesthetics—provided the methods and objectives that came to dominate the entire eighteenth century.[8] What had been considered intellectual pride in Dr. Faustus late in the sixteenth century became the norm during the Enlightenment. Men had come to believe that through science and speculative reason they could so master external nature, and even the historical processes that controlled human affairs, that in time man could become God. Such an optimistic belief left no room for much concern with man's finiteness and fallibility, or inherent limitations and weaknesses, such as had been stressed in the traditional Christian conception of the moral nature of man.

Ironically, the most swift and complete changes toward an optimistic conception of man's moral nature occurred within Calvinism, the branch of Christianity that had held the darkest view of the "natural man." Between 1662 and 1800, British Calvinist students of medicine in the Netherlands carried over

7 For the destructive impact of the new science upon the traditional conception of the moral nature of man see Victor Harris, *All Coherence Gone* (1949); Michael Macklem, *The Anatomy of the World* (1958); and Marjorie H. Nicholson, *The Breaking of the Circle* (1960). These and other writers have shown that the dark view of human nature inherited from medieval times was reversed by the new science during the seventeenth century. Locke's *tabula rasa* neutralized the Christian doctrine of man's innate depravity, and the revolutionary optimistic conception of man began to evolve. In the words of a contemporary, Newton's *Principia* (1687), showed that "the wisdom of God manifests itself in the skies," and by the time of Pope's *Essay on Man* (1733-34), both moral and physical evil in man were explained as illusory.

8 See Louis I. Bredvold, "The Invention of the Moral Calculus," *The Seventeenth Century* (Palo Alto, Calif., 1951). Also see Ernst Cassirer, *The Philosophy of the Enlightenment* (Boston, 1955); Sir Isaiah Berlin, "Introduction," *The Age of Enlightenment* (New York, 1956).

into their theology the scientific methods and discursive reasoning they had learned in their medical studies. They discarded
everything in Calvinist dogma that did not square with scientific
reason, such as belief in miracles and such mysteries as the
Incarnation and doctrine of the Trinity. In time the orthodox
trinitarian theology of Calvinist dissenters, which had limited
salvation to a small minority, God's "elect," and had taught the
dogma of universal depravity for the nonelect, was largely
abandoned in favor of the opposite doctrines of Unitarianism,
which preached the natural goodness and rationality of mankind, and held out universal salvation.[9]

Another important development of eighteenth-century naturalism was romantic "sensibility," which further extended faith
in man's natural goodness. As a movement of moral thought
and feeling, sensibility conceived of ethics in terms of human
emotion rather than as a code of normative principles by which
to judge man's behavior. Christianity and sensibility provided
opposite answers to the question: Do men feel deeply about an
action because it is morally good or bad, or is an action morally
good or bad because men feel deeply about it? In Christianity
emotion is not the basis of ethics, but ethics (including "moral
sentiment") may be the basis of emotion, so that emotion is
either irrelevant in judging actions, or it is derived from adherence to principles of morality, or to violations of the principles.
In Christianity the norms of good and evil are revealed by God
to man through Scripture: they are considered valid and binding
regardless of how men feel about them. The Christian feels
deeply about an action because it is intrinsically good or evil,
and no action is regarded as good or evil because of how he
feels about it.

But to the man of romantic sensibility human emotion is the
source, test, and end of morality, so that how deeply men feel
about an action or law determines its moral truth and value.

9 For a full account of the way British Calvinism was turned inside out during the
eighteenth century, see Olive M. Griffiths, *Religion and Learning* (Cambridge, England,
1935).

Indeed, the theory of sensibility holds that all human values, not just ethical values, are based upon emotion or feeling.[10] The essence of sensibility is the doctrine that man is by his innate nature good, that therefore his impulses, instincts, emotions, and passions are also wholly good and trustworthy, and that all evil behavior can be explained by the restraints placed upon him by external conditions in his physical or social environ- ment. As a theory of ethics based upon feeling or emotion, sensibility taught that man is born pure and free, but becomes corrupted and enslaved by organized society.[11]

Like scientific rationalism, the ethics of feeling, or sensibility, which culminated in Rousseau, Wordsworth, and other "roman- tic" writers, originated at least as early as the seventeenth century. Such scholars as Ronald S. Crane, C. A. Moore, and Louis I. Bredvold have traced out the origins and development of the "man of feeling," whose doctrine of ethics permeated British and French "romantic" thought and literature during the later Enlightenment.[12] In this period the Christian doctrine of

10 Thus William Wordsworth, the first major English poet in the tradition of Romantic sensibility, stated his aesthetic theory in terms of values based solely upon emotion. In his famous preface to the second edition of his *Lyrical Ballads* Wordsworth wrote: "Another circumstance must be mentioned which distinguishes these poems from the popular Poetry of the day; it is this, that the feeling therein developed gives importance to the action and situation, and not the action and situation to the feeling." In short, the value of a poem does not depend upon its artistic skill, but upon how men feel about it, or the feelings it contains or generates.

11 In his "Ode on Intimations to Immortality" Wordsworth conceived of man as born not in original sin, but "trailing clouds of glory" from his divine origins, until society imprisons and corrupts him:

> Heaven lies about us in our infancy:
> Shades of the prison-house begin to close
> Upon the growing boy. . . .

12 See Crane's important article, "Suggestions toward a Genealogy of the 'Man of Feeling,' " *Studies in the Literature of the Augustan Age,* ed. Richard C. Boys (Ann Arbor, Mich., 1952). Crane's article appeared originally in *A Journal of English Literary History,* I (1934). Crane's article extended the pioneer scholarship on sensibility of C. A. Moore, "Shaftesbury and the Ethical Poets in England," *PMLA* (June 1916), and "The Return to Nature in the Enlgish Poetry of the Eighteenth Century," *Studies in Philology* (July 1917). For Bredvold's excellent scholarship on sensibility see "Some Basic Issues of The Eighteenth Century," *Michigan Alumnus Quarterly Review,* LXIV, No. 10 (December 7, 1957); "The Sentimental View of Human Nature," and "Following Nature," in *The Brave New*

divine grace was replaced by the human concept of natural virtue. During the decade of the 1740's in Britain, sensibility became a self-conscious and aggressive force; afterwards it supplied the underlying emotional and sentimental spirit in the reform and revolutionary movements of the last half of the eighteenth century. The doctrine that man is by his innate nature morally good, and becomes corrupted by laws, customs, institutions, and organized society, functioned as a silent revolution in religion and ethical theory and provided the emotional thrust in those revolutionary social and political theories that reached fulfillment in the French Revolution.

In the light of modern scholarship on eighteenth-century romantic sensibility, the criticism of Rousseau by Burke and Babbitt takes on enormous significance. Burke believed that Rousseau, as a man, writer, and moral and political thinker, personified in an archetypal form the revolutionary conception of the moral nature of man that was at the core of romantic sensibility. Like many men of feeling, Rousseau was born a Calvinist but abandoned its doctrine of universal depravity for the "natural man" in favor of a much more optimistic conception of man. Rousseau believed that man is at his best when living in a simple state of nature away from the complex and highly polished organized society of Europe. It may indeed be true, as Professor A. O. Lovejoy maintained, that Rousseau was not a primitivist but simply made the case for a return to a more "simple" society. But his eighteenth-century critics made no such distinction: To Johnson, Burke, and many of their contemporaries, Rousseau was clearly opposed to organized society as inherited from history and proposed a "return to nature" that freed mankind from its traditional social controls.

At age twenty-seven Burke published *A Vindication of Natural Society* (1756), a satire on the supposed blessings of living in an idyllic, precivil, unorganized "state of nature," or "natural society." Thus, at the beginning of his public career Burke

---

World of the Enlightenment (Ann Arbor, Mich., 1961); and *The Natural History of Sensibility* (Detroit, 1962).

perceived and rejected the theory of morality based upon sensibility and implicitly defended traditional organized society and
its institutions as "natural" to man. The fact that Burke's
sustained irony went unperceived by some readers, that he was
forced to write a preface to his second edition in 1757, assuring
his readers that his defense of "natural society" and attack on
"artificial society" was a satire, indicates that theories of primitive or "natural" society could be made plausible even to intelligent people. As an Aristotelian political thinker, Burke
believed that "artificial" society was normal or "natural" for
man, that "art is man's nature." His satire was clearly directed
against Lord Bolingbroke's rationalistic deism, but it applied
equally well to anyone who made an antithesis between the moral nature of man and organized civil society, such as Rousseau.

The year before Burke's satire appeared, Rousseau had published his *Discours sur l'origine de l'inégalité parmi les hommes* (1755),
which immediately had established his reputation as a brilliant
writer of paradoxes and an advocate of the virtues of the simple
life close to nature. There is good reason to believe that Burke's
satire was directed as much against Rousseau's sentimental
naturalism as against Bolingbroke's deism.[13] Burke's book
review of Rousseau's *Lettre à d'Alembert,* in the *Annual Register*
(1759), concluded with a mild but serious admonition against
what he supposed might be satirical in Rousseau: "A satire upon
civilized society, a satire upon learning may be a sport, but if
carried further could only unsettle notions of right and wrong
and lead to scepticism." Three years later, in 1762, Burke
reviewed Rousseau's *Émile,* and again noted his "paradoxical
genius:" "To know what the received notions are upon any
subject is to know with certainty what those of Rousseau are
not." Burke's second book review has in it a growing tone of
impatience with Rousseau for sporting with paradoxes and

13 Richard B. Sewall, "Rousseau's Second Discourse in England from 1755 to 1762,"
Philological Quarterly 17 (1938), shows through many parallel passages in Rousseau's
discourse and Burke's satire that Burke certainly was refuting Rousseau as well as
Bolingbroke.

treating them as though they were normative principles: "A tendency to paradox, which is always the bane of solid learning, and threatens now to destroy it, a splenetic disposition carried to misanthropy, and an austere virtue pursued to an unsociable fierceness, have prevented a great deal of the good effects which might be expected from such a genius."[14] The central paradox in Rousseau's thought—that man is by his innate nature morally good, but becomes corrupted in a highly polished and competitive society by the demands of social customs and institutions— was the reverse of Burke's conviction that man needs his institutions to cover the defects of his naked and shivering nature and to bring him to some degree of perfection. From his central paradox Rousseau derived the paradox with which he opened his *Contrat social* (1762): "Man is born free, but everywhere he is in bondage." But in 1759–62, when Burke first reviewed Rousseau, the belief in man's natural goodness when living close to nature was not yet fully formulated in Rousseau's mind. Indeed, paradoxes, ambiguities, and flat contradictions were to characterize Rousseau's writings throughout his life.

After 1762, for the twenty-seven years preceding the French Revolution, Burke had almost nothing further to say about Rousseau, although when David Hume had his Swiss friend visit England in 1766 Burke received a very unfavorable impression of his character. This confirmed his negative judgments in his book reviews. In his *Reflections* (1790), Burke noted that the paradoxes he had criticized in Rousseau in 1759 and 1762 were being applied seriously by Rousseau's disciples, along with "the declamations and buffooneries of satirists" such as Voltaire. He observed that these writers would "be astonished if they were held to the letter of their own descriptions." Burke concluded: "I believe that were Rousseau alive, and in one of his lucid intervals, he would be shocked at the practical frenzy of his scholars, who in their paradoxes are servile imitators; and even in their incredulity discover an implicit faith." But the real madness, Burke

14 *Annual Register* (1759), p. 479.

believed, lay in Rousseau himself; his writings "carried marks of a deranged understanding. . . ." That aberration was not merely mental or emotional but moral. Burke believed that Rousseau's sensibility was a private physiological instinct, conforming to the changing moods of his temperament, rather than a moral intuition, conforming to the universal ethical norms of moral natural law and religious revelation. This made Rousseau's sensibility identical with the ruling passion that moved him in any given instance; it served him in place of conscience and was its equivalent to him.

Burke's extended attack on Rousseau in *A Letter to a Member of the National Assembly (1791)* was the most devastating criticism inflicted upon him as a man, writer, philosopher, and influence by any British writer of the eighteenth century and provided many of the essential points found in Irving Babbitt's lifelong philippic against Rousseau. Burke's attack cannot be dismissed as an argument *ad hominem.* Even before Rousseau's *Confessions* had revealed in revolting detail the depths of personal degradation into which he had fallen in following the impulses of his sensibility, Burke had regarded him as a half-mad writer whose great rhetorical powers made plausible a moral theory based upon whimsical feelings, a theory totally impractical and highly dangerous to any sound social order.

Burke believed that even Rousseau's prose style reflected his lush and sensual sensibility: he found it diffuse and discursive, uneven and at times uncontrollable, alternately flaccid and distended or hysterical and intensely lyrical, as the impulse of his ideas and feelings moved him in his expression. Burke believed that Rousseau's prose style was an important clue to his character, temperament, and philosophy, because by his appeal to the passions it was able to disguise "depravity of sentiment" as austere eloquence and sound morality:

We certainly perceive, and to a degree we feel, in this writer, a style glowing, animated, enthusiastic; at the same time that we find it lax, diffuse, and not in the best taste of composition; all the members of the piece being pretty equally labored and expanded, without any due

selection or subordination of parts. He is generally too much on the
stretch, and his manner has little variety. . . . It is not that I consider
this writer as wholly destitute of just notions. Among his irregularities,
it must be reckoned that he is sometimes moral, and moral is a very
sublime strain. But the general tendency of his works is mischievous;
and the more mischievous for this mixture: for, perfect depravity of
sentiment is not reconcilable with eloquence; and the mind (though
corruptible, not complexionally vicious) would reject and throw off
with disgust, a lesson of pure and unmixed evil.

Burke's analysis of Rousseau's prose style gives added significance to his statement that "Rousseau is a moralist, or he
is nothing." To Burke, the morality he represented, both in his
private life and in his writings, was centered in romantic sensibility.

Burke believed that the doctrine that man is by nature innately good was very flattering to the human ego. This conviction underlies Burke's reference to Rousseau as "the philosopher of vanity," a vanity that consumed the whole man and
wished to remove all restraints upon the will as unnecessary
impediments to total freedom. This was how the ethics of
feeling functioned in practical human affairs. Burke observed
that one of the worst characteristics of sensibility in practical
affairs was that it made personal virtue as feeling purely
theoretical. To Burke theoretical virtue was practical vice. He
noted that Rousseau exhausted "the stores of his powerful
rhetoric in the expression of universal benevolence," but had
not "one spark of common parental affection" for his children.
"Benevolence to the whole species, and want of feeling for every
individual . . . form the character of the new philosophy." Burke
noted that Rousseau, as a man of feeling, was filled with mere
theoretical virtue:

He melts with tenderness for those only who touch him by the
remotest relation, and then, without one natural pang, casts away, as
a sort of offal and excrement, the spawn of his disgustful amours, and
sends his children to the hospital of foundlings. The bear loves, licks,
and forms her young; but bears are not philosophers. Vanity, however, finds its account in reversing the train of our natural feelings.

Thousands admire the sentimental writer; the affectionate father is hardly known in his parish.[15]

Burke characterized Rousseau as "a lover of his kind, but a hater of his kindred." This disparity between exalted moral theory and practical behavior was not merely an instance of a sound moral teacher whose personal actions out of weakness fell far short of his professed principles. Burke believed that the "painted theatric sentiments" of the ethics of feeling necessarily inverted "all natural sense of wrong and right."

To Burke the proper order of progression in expressing a general love for people was from love of kin to love of kind: "To be attached to the subdivision, to love the little platoon we belong to in society, is the first principle (the germ as it were) of public affections. It is the first link in the series by which we proceed towards a love of our country, and to mankind." Although Burke maintained that "we begin our public affections in our families," and that "we pass on to our neighborhoods, and our habitual provincial connections," yet "the love to the whole is not extinguished by this subordinate partiality."[16] Burke believed that Rousseau's sensibility not only inverted moral principles in relation to feelings, but also inverted the normal order of progression for public affections, from the concrete local to the abstract remote relationships between people.

15 Even in the novels of his era Burke's distrust of morality based upon sentiment is illustrated in his preference of Fielding to Richardson. He disliked the sentimentality of Richardson's *Pamela*, which had served as a model for Rousseau in *La Nouvelle Héloïse*. Burke believed that the sentiments of a theoretical exalted morality expressed in fiction could not be carried over into practical life. Burke's conviction that appeals to sensibility reversed the principles of normative ethics has been confirmed by two recent scholars on sensibility. See Jean H. Hagstrum, *Sex and Sensibility* (Chicago, 1980), for how sensibility is an important element in ideal and erotic love in poetry since Milton and in Music up to Mozart's time. R. F. Brissenden, in *Virtue in Distress: Studies in the Novel of Sentiment from Richardson to Sade* (London, 1974), presents the villain in *Clarissa*, the aristocrat Lovelace, as exposing the myth of man's natural goodness that was used by the sentimental middle class to conceal its avarice in practice.

16 *Reflections, Works*, V, 352. See John MacCunn for a good account of the importance of "civil vicinity" in Burke's political philosophy, in *The Political Philosophy of Burke* (London, 1913), pp. 16–37.

In a letter to Claude-Francois de Rivarol (June 1, 1791), Burke
elaborated several important points in his criticism of Rousseau:

I think of late that the Parisian Philosophers have done upon meditated System, what the Poets are naturally led to by a desire of flattering
the passions. To you, as a Poet, this is allowed. To Philosophers one
cannot be so indulgent. For perhaps ladies ought not "to love too well"
like the Phaedras and Myrrhas of old, or the ancient or modern
Eloyses. They had better not pursue their lovers into convents of
Carthusians nor follow them in disguise to camps and slaughter
houses. But I have observed that the Philosophers in order to insinuate
their polluted Atheism into young minds, systematically flatter all their
passions natural and unnatural. They explode or render odious or
contemptible that class of virtues which restrain the appetite. These
are at least nine out of ten of the virtues. In the place of all these they
substitute a virtue which they call humanity or benevolence. By these
means, their morality has no idea in it of restraint, or indeed of a
distinct settled principle of any kind. When their disciples are thus left
free and guided only by present feeling, they are no longer to be
depended on for good or evil. The men who today snatch the worst
criminals from justice, will murder the most innocent persons
tomorrow.[17]

From this important passage it is clear that Burke's criticism of
the sensibility of Rousseau and his disciples is perhaps the most
important single element in all his attacks on the French
Revolution. Sensibility, with its self-conscious cultivation of an
indiscriminate outgoing sympathy, supplied the emotional
foundation of the Revolution, and permeated the important
aspects of revolutionary theory and practice concerning man
and society. Sensibility encouraged a moral impressionism in
place of an adherence to the common ethical norms of moral
natural law and Christianity. Through an appeal to private
feelings, the sensibility of Rousseau made vanity into a social
virtue and instituted an attitude and spirit destructive of any
personal restraint and social authority. Burke believed that
through an anarchical conception of civil liberty the belief in the

17 Edmund Burke, *Correspondence* (Chicago, 1967), VI, pp. 269–270.

natural goodness of man fostered the complete freedom of private impulses and produced a state of civil anarchy in which men were "disconnected into the dust and powder of individuality." Rousseau's sensibility converted vanity and affectation into virtues and encouraged men to dramatize themselves against their social environment, as individuals unique in feeling, and above the established code of social manners and morals. In brief, Rousseau's theory of morality based upon sentiment radically contradicted Burke's Christian and moral natural law conception of man's moral nature and his Aristotelian view that man is by his innate nature a social animal, in need of all the aids to grace and reason that organized society can provide.

<h2 style="text-align:center">II</h2>

Although Irving Babbitt's criticism of Rousseau was a recurrent theme in many of his writings, his essential arguments on Rousseau's philosophy are centered in four works: "Two Types of Humanitarians: Bacon and Rousseau," in *Literature and the American College* (1908); *Rousseau and Romanticism* (1919); "Rousseau and the Idyllic Imagination," in *Democracy and Leadership* (1924); and "What I Believe: Rousseau and Religion," in *Spanish Character and Other Essays* (1940). The essential thesis about Rousseau in Babbitt's later work was also anticipated in *The New Laokoon* (1910).

Before examining in detail Babbitt's analysis of Rousseau it will be useful to note in general how his views compare with those of Burke. Babbitt was able to identify with Burke's conception of individual liberty under moral and constitutional law, because the principles and values of his humanism coincided in many vital points of common morality with Burke's Aristotelian and Anglican Christian philosophy. Like Aristotle and Burke, Babbitt believed in the social nature of man as a norm and therefore rejected the Rousseauistic theory of an idyllic "state of nature" as a norm. Burke's satiric attacks on "natural society" find their counterpart in Babbitt's attacks

upon primitivism. Like Burke, Babbitt rejected the concept of
the social contract based upon popular collective will, and the
derivative French revolutionary abstract doctrine of the "rights
of man" and the political theory of unlimited popular sovereignty in one unchecked legislative assembly. Indeed, what Burke
wrote against the French Revolution in general, and against
Rousseau in particular, found many parallels in Babbitt's
humanistic criticism of naturalism, Rousseau's sensibility and
idyllic imagination, and the whole "romantic" movement in
European thought and literature.[18]

In Babbitt's essay, "Two Types of Political Thinking" (1924),
he reveals a thorough knowledge of the historical genesis of
romantic sensibility in England, as it applied to the conception
of the moral nature of man and his place in the universe and
society:

The rise of emotional ethics may be studied, especially in the England of the early eighteenth century, in connection with the deistic
movement. The trend of deistic moralists like Shaftesbury and Hutche-
son is all towards what we should call, nowadays, altruism and social
service. With the decline of the doctrine of total depravity, the age of
theology is beginning to give way to the age of sociology. The word
beneficence gains currency about this time. The sympathetic man, the
good-natured man, the man of feeling are emerging and are being held
in ever-increasing estimation. Those who believed in the intrinsic evil
of human nature on either theological or naturalistic grounds were still
numerous and aggressive. The divergent views concerning the goodness or badness of human nature were combined in almost every
conceivable proportion in different individuals.[19]

In "Rousseau and the Idyllic Imagination" Babbitt had
actually placed the genesis of the sentimental view of man's

---

18 Professor Arthur O. Lovejoy, one of Babbitt's chief critics, considered his severe
strictures on "Romanticism" nothing more than a personal bias. Without mentioning
Babbitt by name, Lovejoy condemned his "determining what . . . Romantic essence is"
by being one of "those for whom 'Romantic' is an adjective of disparagement, guided
only by a determination to apply that damning epithet to all the ideas or tastes which
they most dislike." *The Reason, the Understanding, and Time* (Baltimore, 1961), Preface, pp.
xi–xii.
19 Irving Babbitt, *Democracy and Leadership*, p. 48.

moral nature earlier than such scholars as Louis Bredvold, C. A. Moore, and Ronald Crane: "In the period between Hooker and Locke, the conviction of man's depravity undergoes a notable diminution."[20] But the real triumph of the theory of sensibility, as Babbitt noted, occurred after Shaftesbury, later in the eighteenth century: "The decisive victories of both rationalistic and emotional ethics over the traditional dualism were won in the eighteenth century."[21] Babbitt was aware that by the middle of the eighteenth century the fusion of scientific and sentimental naturalism had occurred: "Diderot . . . was both a scientific and sentimental naturalist. . . ."[22] According to Babbitt, this fusion of science and sentiment has continued down to the twentieth century, with Rousseau providing the driving force for the sentimental element in naturalism, centered in the idea that a man's feelings and passions are essentially good in determining behavior.[23]

Like Burke, Babbitt was aware that Rousseau did not originate sensibility, but that he was the most eloquent voice in its propagation: "We inevitably think of Rousseau as the most important figure in this emotional reaction, as the great apostle of the original and the spontaneous. That such a reaction would have taken place without Rousseau is certain; but it is equally

20 *Democracy and Leadership*, p. 71.

21 *Democracy and Leadership*, p. 52.

22 Irving Babbitt, *The New Laokoon*, p. 215. Babbitt considered Diderot an embodiment of a harmonized science and sensibility in mid-eighteenth-century France. In England, later in the century, William Godwin was also to combine science and sentiment. It is significant that Louis I. Bredvold, after describing in two chapters "The New Promise of Science" and "The Sentimental View of Human Nature," noted that "the scientific study of man and the sentimental belief in the natural goodness of man . . . converged and reinforced one another." *The Brave New World of the Enlightenment*, p. 77.

23 Babbitt made the case that the fusion of science and sentiment in naturalistic philosophy has been a disaster for art and aesthetics in modern times. The "general malady" of modern art, he wrote, reflects "that excess of sentimental and scientific naturalism from which . . . the occidental world is now suffering." *The New Laokoon*, p. 185. See also, pp. 118–122 and 205–207. Babbitt believed the problem extended to other fields as well: ". . . We are now seeing in nearly all fields of human endeavor, in art and philosophy and education . . . a violent extreme—the extreme of scientific and sentimental naturalism." *The New Laokoon*, p. 238.

certain that he first gave powerful expression to it and profoundly influenced the forms it assumed."[24]

In Britain the writer who most clearly anticipated Rousseau
was Anthony Ashley Cooper, Third Earl of Shaftesbury (1671–
1713). In the celebrated battle between Shaftesbury and Bernard
Mandeville (1670–1733), over the innate moral nature of man,
Babbitt clearly preferred Mandeville's cynical realism over
Shaftesbury's idyllic moral sensibility. Babbitt's critical power in
dissecting these writers went far beyond that of any of his
predecessors. Many scholars had noted how Shaftesbury had
anticipated Rousseau and had viewed Mandeville as Rousseau's
antithesis. But Babbitt perceived that despite Mandeville's
strong opposition to Shaftesbury's optimistic conception of man
in his innate moral nature, he too had foreshadowed Rousseau.
He quoted a passage from Rousseau's *Émile*, Book IV, "as a
sample of the fully developed emotional ethics of which the
beginnings are found in Shaftesbury," and he also noted that
the English writer had anticipated the "type of 'enthusiasm' "
found in *Nouvelle Héloise*, Part II, Letter XI.

Babbitt then quoted with approval Mandeville's central point
against Shaftesbury, which he used himself in much of his
criticism of Rousseau: "He imagines that men without any
trouble or violence upon themselves may be naturally virtuous." Mandeville's statement was applied by Babbitt in his
remark that Rousseau abandoned what Diderot had termed the
"civil war in the cave," the idea that since man was conceived to
be innately good he did not need to struggle to become good.
Mandeville, like Rousseau, was a former Calvinist turned
secular. Babbitt did not mention this important point they had
in common, but he did note that Mandeville, while attacking
Shaftesbury's "sympathy of the humanitarian type . . . was
himself an emotional moralist" and had conceded that "natural
pity" was an instinctive emotion in man. This point, combined
with Mandeville's belief that men are motivated primarily by
self-interest, put him squarely in Rousseau's camp, for Rousseau

24 *The New Laokoon*, p. 65.

had asserted that self-love and instinctive pity together were the whole basis of man's "natural rights."

Babbitt then very skillfully nailed down the vital points in common between Mandeville and Rousseau:

One has only to exalt this passion of pity and, at the same time, to take seriously Mandeville's occasional praises of ignorance and the simple life, to be in sight of the primitivistic solution of the problem of luxury and of civilization itself that Rousseau was to set forth in his two Discourses. Mandeville is on the side of decorum, and yet he admits that decorum is not only "artificial," but is, as Rousseau was to say later, only the "varnish of vice" and the "mask of hypocrisy." He affirms that vice in general is nowhere more prominent than where arts and sciences flourish, and that we shall find innocence and honesty nowhere more widely diffused than among the most illiterate, the "poor silly country people."[25]

Babbitt does not identify the anti-aesthetic elements in the original Calvinist theology of both Mandeville and Rousseau as a source of what they had in common regarding man's moral nature. But he does note that they both conceived of society as "artificial" and this resulted in their making an antithesis between "art" as evil and "nature" as good. When applied to the moral nature of man in society, their logic led them to their belief that the "artificial" in society, such as institutions, corrupts man's nature. They appeared different because Mandeville accepted that corruption as the necessary condition of economic prosperity in organized society ("Private vices" create "public benefits"), whereas Rousseau advocated escaping the complex corruptions by a "return to nature."

Babbitt was keenly aware that the very vocabulary used to discuss man's moral behavior in society was revolutionized by the sentimental conception of man's moral nature. The traditional religious concept of "grace" as a gift of God to men faithful to His revelation was replaced by "virtue" or "benevolence" originating in man's feelings. Babbitt observed that in Rousseau's *First Discourse* (1750), he never referred to "grace," but used "virtue" forty-three times, and that by "virtue" he meant "a glorification of the instinctive and the subrational" in man living the simple life close to nature, without the luxuries of polished society to corrupt him.

In his *Second Discourse,* Babbitt noted, Rousseau added the idea that fraternal pity is "natural" to man in the state of simple nature. Thus Rousseau rejected both Hobbes' concept that war dominates man in the precivil state of nature and also Locke's claim that "reason" ruled man in the state of nature: "By his refutation of Hobbes, and his substitution of fraternity for reason, Rousseau gave to naturalism the driving power it still lacked."[26] To the claims of Hobbes and Locke that liberty and equality characterized the state of nature Rousseau added the vital claim of fraternity: "It thus became possible to develop it [Naturalism] into a new evangel that seemed to culminate, like the old evangel, in love. This conception of love in terms of expansive emotion is . . . a sort of parody of Christian charity."[27] Humanitarianism, based upon an ethics of feeling, is indeed a parody of Christian charity, based upon the commandments of Scripture. There is no doubt, as Babbitt's criticism inferred, that many modern people who regard themselves as Christians are in fact Rousseauists and don't even know it. This applies to both the laity and the clergy of practically all Christian denominations. A sentimental conception of the moral nature of man, which makes emotion or feeling identical with conscience, and bases its whole value system in things spiritual upon subjective feelings, is not Christian but Rousseauistic and humanitarian. In place of the traditional religious doctrines of salvation by faith and good works [Catholicism], or salvation by faith alone [Lutheranism], Rousseau taught the doctrine of salvation by feeling alone. Babbitt believed that this type of confusion was

---

26 *Democracy and Leadership,* p. 74.

27 *Democracy and Leadership,* p. 74–75. In this connection Babbitt has said: ". . . Religion, even after it has lost all effective hold on the reason and character, still lingers in the sensibility." "Introduction," *Souvenirs D'Enfance et de Jeunesse* (Boston, 1902), p. xvi.

inspired by Rousseau's moral inpressionism, when "Nature" displaced the Judaeo-Christian God of revelation, and feeling became the basis of ethics.[28]

Babbitt noted that by identifying virtue with poverty and vice with wealth the logical extension of Rousseau's ethics of feeling into economics and politics led inevitably to theories of class warfare and revolution. The social mythology of revolution, based on the idea that private property is the greatest evil in society, also derives from Rousseau's sentimental conception of the moral nature of man. The "equality" and "liberty" that supposedly existed between men in a precivil "state of nature" was destroyed when private property became legally established in civil society. Private property led to class divisions between rich and poor and to the miseries of peasant labor and slavery. Thus Rousseau created what Babbitt called "a new dualism" in his social and economic theory, aimed at securing justice for the dispossessed and oppressed. This dualism of economic classes, of rich and poor individuals in a class-structured society, replaced the old classical and Christian moral dualism: "The old dualism put the conflict between good and evil in the breast of the individual, with evil so predominant since the Fall that it behooves man to be humble; with Rousseau this conflict is transferred from the individual to society."[29] Thus, as Babbitt interpreted Rousseau, moral vice and intellectual error exist not in man's innate constitution, as something to be eradicated by religion and education, but are "introduced from without" through his social institutions.

Babbitt argued further that from this theory it follows that those who administer the institutions of society, parents in the family, teachers in schools, priests in the church, kings in the state, and employers in business and capitalists in industry, are the evil powers preventing the ordinary man's natural moral

---

28 Babbitt died in 1933, so that he did not live long enough to see the culmination of this kind of incredible confusion among Christians who identified Christian charity with not only humanitarianism but with Marxist revolutionary theory and practice.

29 *Democracy and Leadership*, p. 76.

goodness and talents from blossoming. Remove these tyrants and mankind will be on the road to utopia. This is the logical revolutionary consequence that follows from the myth of man's natural goodness. The revolutionary myth is popular, because it flatters human vanity and offers an escape hatch for failure, since those who fail in the competition of life can always see themselves as victims of a corrupt society.

As Babbitt noted, Rousseau perceived himself as a victim of society, particularly in his *Second Discourse:* "What one hears through this discourse, as elsewhere in Rousseau, is the voice of the angry and envious plebeian, who in the name of love is actually fomenting hatred and class warfare."[30] Babbitt reinforced his point through a revealing sentence from *Émile:* "What was hardest to destroy in me was a proud misanthropy, a certain acrimony against the rich and happy of the world as though they were so at my expense, as though their alleged happiness had been usurped from mine."[31] The idea that the wealth of the rich is the cause of the poverty of the poor was screened through Rousseau's emotions and imagination and was a vital element in his political ideology.

Babbitt interpreted Rousseau's conception of the "state of nature," combined with his theory of the "social contract," as original elements in his revolutionary philosophy: "Starting from the premise of a fictitious state of nature, [Rousseau's logic] leads to conclusions that justify emotional revolt against everything established. ..." To reinforce his point, Babbitt quoted Gustave Lanson, a well-known authority on Rousseau. Lanson described Rousseau's conception of the individual's relationship to society and noted that as a man of feeling Rousseau "exasperates and inspires revolt, ..." that his philosophy "is the mother of violence, the source of all that is uncompromising. It launches the simple souls who give themselves up to its strange virtue upon the desperate quest of the absolute, an absolute to be realized today by anarchy and

30 *Democracy and Leadership*, p. 77.
31 *Democracy and Leadership*, pp. 77–78.

tomorrow by social despotism."[32] In Rousseau the revolutionary impulses of the heart are only partly nullified by contradictory convictions in his mind. Babbitt was well aware that these splits between emotion and reason in Rousseau created ambiguities and contradictions that made possible a great range of interpre-tations of his moral and social thought, by such different scholars as Albert Schinz, Arthur O. Lovejoy, and Ernest H. Wright.[33] Indeed, the multiple interpretations of Rousseau's philosophy continued to grow after Babbitt's death.

Babbitt defined Rousseau's political contradictions in terms of isolated individuals and collectivist social tyranny: "From the unflinching individualism of the 'Second Discourse,' where man is conceived as a sort of isolated and unrelated particle, he passes to the no less unflinching collectivism of the 'Social Contract.' He fluctuates between extremes even in his collec-tivistic ideal."[34] According to Babbitt, the contradictions in Rousseau may be explained in part by his belief that it was impossible to be both a good man and a good citizen. This is most evident in such famous paradoxes of Rousseau as that "Man is born free, and everywhere he is in bondage." Babbitt interpreted this paradox to mean that Rousseau believed "the only free and legitimate government is that formed upon a true social compact." But since all men are born without their consent into a historically developed society, no man is "born free," and no such social contract based upon individual volun-tary will is possible.

Yet the idea of man's equality in society is central in Rous-seau's political theory. Since the social contract sanctifies the "general will" of society, and there can be no check upon the general will, each individual is reduced to an equal status under the collective power of the whole community. Like several other interpreters of Rousseau's Contrat social, Babbitt believed that Rousseau made a political absolute of his doctrine of popular

---

32 *Democracy and Leadership,* pp. 82 and 86.

33 See Babbitt, "What I Believe: Rousseau and Religion," in *Spanish Character and Other Essays* (Boston and New York, 1940), pp. 4–5.

34 *Democracy and Leadership,* p. 86.

and individual sovereignty and thus prepared the way for modern collectivist totalitarianism: ". . . Rousseau transfers to the people the doctrine that the king can do no wrong. But he does more than that. The king, if not responsible to what is below him, is at least responsible to what is above him—to God. But the sovereign people is responsible to no one. It *is* god."[35] Thus, in Rousseau the idea of constitutional government is replaced by a permanently shifting revolutionary government based upon the claimed sanction of popular sovereignty. As Babbitt put it: "On all ordinary occasions the general will means a numerical majority at any particular moment."[36] Rousseau held that the majority will would force men to be free in their collectivist society.

Babbitt perceived some close affinities in Rousseau's political theory with the political philosophy of Hobbes: "Perhaps he is more closely related to Hobbes than to any previous political thinker. . . . His state of nature and his sovereignty are merely the state of nature and the sovereignty of Hobbes reversed. In Rousseau the people can do anything it pleases with its ruler, in Hobbes the ruler can do anything he pleases with the people."[37] Babbitt noted that Hobbes' state is fixed permanently; Rousseau's state is permanently unfixed. But under neither Hobbes' nor Rousseau's state would there be any right of free individual conscience against the tyranny of the omnipotent state: ". . . Rousseau does not propose to leave the individual any such refuge."[38] Hobbes' monarchical tyranny is replaced by Rousseau with a democratic or popular tyranny, which contradicts Rousseau's exalted appeals to absolute individual liberty.

Babbitt makes an important distinction between Rousseau and Burke in their respective conceptions of liberty:

Rousseau, as he never tires of telling us, has a horror of every constraint upon his emotional impulses. He does not spurn certain special barriers and limitations but all barriers and limitations whatso-

35 *Democracy and Leadership,* p. 89.
36 *Democracy and Leadership,* p. 91.
37 *Democracy and Leadership,* p. 90.
38 *Democracy and Leadership,* p. 92.

ever. When he speaks of liberty, he does not mean, as a typical Englishman (let us say Burke) would mean, liberty defined and limited by law, but an indefined liberty that is tempered only by sympathy, which in turn is tempered by nothing at all. An undefined liberty and an unselective sympathy are the two main aspects of the movement initiated by Rousseau—the poles between which he oscillates.[39]

Babbitt's analysis of the final chapter of Rousseau's *Contrat social* brings him closest to Burke's criticism of Rousseau and the French Revolution.

Babbitt noted that Rousseau attacked not only traditional organized orthodox Christianity but also the nominal Christianity of the sentimental deist who retained his church membership, because every kind of allegiance to the church separated the citizen from his civic earthly concerns. Rousseau attacked the basic Christian virtue of humility, because like Nietzsche he claimed it made men slaves. Also, like Machiavelli and to some extent Hobbes, he substituted for humility the pride of nationalism. Rousseau's conception of religion is strictly social and utilitarian. The practical manifestation of Rousseau's "civil religion," Babbitt observed, was in Rousseau's disciple, Robespierre, in his "Festival of the Supreme Being" during the French Revolution: ". . . It also looks forward to the Civil Constitution of the Clergy and to the guillotining as 'fanatics' many priests who refused to forswear their allegiance to Rome."[40] Rousseau's theories on man and society were not treated seriously by Burke until they were put into practice, which, according to Babbitt, was what compelled Burke to attack Rousseau so violently in the course of his early criticism of the French Revolution.

The chief element in Rousseau's theory that troubled Burke most was Rousseau's doctrine of the natural innate goodness of man. On this vital point Babbitt and Burke join company in their criticism of Rousseau. From the hindsight of the twentieth century Babbitt noted: "The consequences that have flowed from this new 'myth' of man's natural goodness have been incalculable."[41] The pseudo religion of "brotherhood" that

39 *The New Laokoon*, p. 195. See also pp. 196–197.
40 *Democracy and Leadership*, p. 95. See also pp. 93–94.
41 "What I Believe: Rousseau and Religion," p. 5.

permeates so much modern social and political thought, and especially the revolutionary movements, is perhaps the most evident manifestation of persistent faith in man's natural good-ness. Babbitt and Burke, in their criticism of Rousseau, provide powerful weapons with which to combat all that is false and delusory in modern man's sentimental conception of his innate nature.

T. John Jamieson

Babbitt and Maurras
as Competing Influences
on T. S. Eliot

The reasons why the various ideologies were wrong were sufficiently well known in the 1920's, but no ideologist could be persuaded to change his position under the pressure of argument. Obviously, rational discourse, or the resistance to it, had existential roots far deeper than the debate conducted on the surface. In the interwar years, truth was definitely what did not prevail.

—Eric Voegelin[1]

IRVING BABBITT'S reputation has never recovered from the qualified repudiation made by his most accomplished pupil, T. S. Eliot, in the 1927 essay, "The Humanism of Irving Babbitt." Yet Eliot's ostensible argument—that humanism cannot take religion's place in conserving civilization—needs to be sifted for a certain confusion concerning the ends of civilization and the ends of religion, a confusion detected in Eliot's later works by fellow Christian conservatives C. S. Lewis and Christopher Dawson.[2] One may trace this confusion to the influence of

---

1 *Anamnesis,* ed. and transl. Gerhart Niemeyer (South Bend, Ind., 1978), p. 6.
2 See C. S. Lewis, "Christianity and Culture," *Christian Reflections,* ed. Walter Hooper (London, 1967); although Lewis does not name Eliot, the essay was written in the wake

Action Française leader Charles Maurras, an influence that goes
nearly as far back in Eliot's life as the influence of Babbitt.
The Action Française, an ostensibly monarchist and pro-
Catholic organization that published a newspaper of the same
name, called for a *coup d'état* that would abolish the parliamentary democracy and replace it with an authoritarian (though
decentralized) regime. Its ideology, developed chiefly by Maurras at the time of the Dreyfus affair, was anticapitalist and
anti-Semitic. During World War II, Maurras supported the
Vichy regime; convicted of collaboration after the war, he
barely escaped the death penalty.

In 1927, Eliot was Maurras' only significant promoter in the
English-speaking world, so much so that he could be described
as "a softened and domesticated Maurras, the Maurras of
Anglo-Saxon liberal society."[3] Because Eliot would have described both Babbitt and Maurras as "classicists" (in some sense
of the word), the critics, who have usually read neither, assume
that their respective influences upon Eliot were continuous and
complementary and even seem to endorse Eliot's preference for
Maurras.[4] But if one examines the sources seriously, one finds
that, no matter how Eliot himself felt those influences (and his
was a personality susceptible to influences), the intellectual
positions of these two powerful personalities contradicted each
other radically.

Babbitt's humanism was indeed philosophy in the original

---

of *The Idea of a Christian Society*. In a letter to Paul Elmer More (May 23, 1935), Lewis calls
Eliot "the very spear head of [the] attack on *peras*"—the Parmenidean "limit" or One.
See also Christopher Dawson, "T. S. Eliot on the Meaning of Culture" (a response to
Notes towards the Definition of Culture), in *Dynamics of World History* (New York, 1957): "The
paradoxes that are inherent in [Eliot's] view are gratuitous difficulties that are due to his
ignoring the transcendence of the religious factor," pp. 107–108.

3 J. H. Cameron, "T. S. Eliot as a Political Writer," *T. S. Eliot: A Symposium for His
Seventieth Birthday*, ed. Neville Braybrooke (London, 1958), p. 145.

4 This is only to accept Eliot's version of things. In the article on "Classicism" in the
Dictionary of the History of Ideas I (1968), p. 455., René Wellek incorrectly alleges that Babbitt
approved of Maurras—and used Brunetière as a source. Hugh Kenner admits that Eliot's
attack on humanism discouraged him from studying Babbitt, and agrees that the
influence of Maurras prevailed over the influence of Babbitt, although "surely Eliot was
not the product of that influence." (In conversation, March 13, 1984.) The reader may
decide.

sense, the "love of wisdom" that engages man in a skeptical search for a reconciliation of his divided experience of the noetic and the immanent. Maurras' Integral Nationalism was ideology—a reductionist system promoted by demagogy and supported by taboos upon questions concerning its premises. Eric Voegelin has written on the phenomenon of the alienated megalomaniac who invents an ideological "second reality" and conceals the essentially mythical character of his work beneath a grand system. While the most notorious "intellectual swindlers" identified by him have generally escaped detection, it is still troubling to imagine a Harvard doctoral candidate in philosophy, and especially one who had briefly studied under Babbitt, being unable to expose a man who, in comparison with Voegelin's *grandes hommes,* is a rather clumsy, petty crook. To the extent that any explanation of this paradox can be satisfactory, one will not find it, as Voegelin indicates, within the terms of the debate conducted on the surface.

The importance of the two figures, Babbitt and Eliot, compels us to explain thoroughly the process by which the great thinker's most well known pupil came to leave him behind. The task requires us, however, to open the question of Eliot's influences in all its complexity and even to scrutinize Eliot's personality as expressed by his intellectual "style." But the investigation will establish that Babbitt and Maurras are not of the same party and that the single attack upon Babbitt that one may have been inclined to take seriously was launched from a Maurrassian position.[5]

---

5 *Note:* in the later sections of the essay, I discuss Eliot's psyche to explain what has been practically ignored, in all likelihood, because it seemed inexplicable: the attraction of a trained philosopher towards a mediocre ideologist. Eliot's neurotic condition does not justify any attempt to dismiss him; indeed, the poet Randall Jarrell believed that the chief interest of Eliot's poetry lay in its power as a study of neurosis. The effect upon ideas of a personality in existential crisis, however, is a legitimate area of critical concern.

I

The plausible assumption that Babbitt, as one of the undergraduate Eliot's first intellectual contacts, propelled him towards
his later career as a defender of Western values (serving as a
model for the Arnoldian role of "critic of ideas" superior to
Arnold[6]) receives support both from what we know about
Babbitt's teaching style and from the poet's own words. Because
Babbitt's humanism was a system with consequences far beyond
literary criticism, it challenged the student in the classroom in
such a way as to leave no alternative but acceptance or rejection:
It was at once a religious philosophy (though it treated the claims
of religious revelation with scepticism) and a psychological theory. (Though his "inner check" has been maligned as a merely
negative force, Babbitt defined it as a faculty that by the
cumulative effect of its choices creates the positive content of the
personality—making it, in his words, "the supreme factor in
that which we know as our individual character"[7]). His lectures
and seminars brought one into direct confrontation with Babbitt's very forceful personality. "What held the lectures or talks
together was his intellectual passion, one might say intellectual
fury; what made them cohere was the constant recurrence of his
dominant ideas." There were "perambulatory conversations,"
and the likes and dislikes of the master grew to be those of his
pupils also. "If one has once had that relationship with Babbitt,
he remains permanently an active influence; his ideas are
permanently with one, as a measurement and test of one's
own."[8]

Eliot says also that Babbitt's influence directed him toward
Paris for graduate study at the Sorbonne. But when he got there,
the Action Française cast its spell. The system of Maurras provided answers to questions Babbitt had never even asked and
offered a comprehensive political program to be acted upon; the

6 See Austin Warren, *New England Saints* (Westport, Conn., 1976), pp. 190–191.

7 Quoted in Paul Elmer More, *On Being Human* (Princeton, N.J., 1936), p. 41.

8 T. S. Eliot in *Irving Babbitt, Man and Teacher*, eds. Frederick Manchester and Odell
Shepard (New York, 1941), pp. 102–104.

organization that advocated the system provided the experience of camaraderie and the thrill of action, even violence. Whereas humanism was critical and sceptical, Maurrassianism was assertive and absolutist. The principle of unbounded pride in one's convictions was written into the ideology: Maurras had said, "It is exceedingly pleasant to be right, to know it, and to know why." Jean Verdenal introduced Eliot to Maurras. Almost forty years later he wrote that he believed it was Babbitt who directed his attention to the movement.

That may be so, but it is highly unlikely that Babbitt mentioned the Action Française to Eliot without a warning. In 1909 Babbitt wrote of the "brilliant and virulent attack on French Romanticism" made by Pierre Lasserre, but objected that his book, *Le romantisme français,* tended to be "extreme, and in the French sense reactionary," and described his shock at seeing Lasserre's work in a Parisian shop devoted to books recommending the restoration of the monarchy. "Now I for one regret that a legitimate protest against literature should be thus mixed up with what we may very well deem an impossible political and religious reaction."[9]

The Action Française ideology that Babbitt found unpleasantly "reactionary" was well summed up in an article on Maurras' "aesthetic of the three traditions" in 1913 by one of Maurras' partisans, an article probably read by Eliot; the traditions were styled "classique, catholique, monarchique."[10] Needless to say, Babbitt was a classicist, drawing inspiration for his system from both Plato and Aristotle; he held the Roman Catholic Church in high regard as a religious institution, though not a confessional Christian himself.[11] Having no quarrel with monarchy per se, he

---

9 Irving Babbitt, *The New Laokoon, An Essay on the Confusion of the Arts* (Boston, 1910), pp. xii–xiii.

10 Albert Thibaudet, "L'Esthetique des trois traditions," *La Nouvelle Revue Française* (January 1913). See Herbert Howarth, *Notes on Some Figures Behind T. S. Eliot* (Boston, 1964), pp. 175–177.

11 One must distinguish Babbitt's ambivalent attitude toward Christianity from Maurras'. Babbitt regarded Christ much as he did Buddha—as a religious sage whose wisdom was unfathomable to the modern liberal Protestant churchmen he despised.

held an ideal of democracy that was aristocratic in character and rejected the supremacy of mere numerical majorities. Now to Babbitt these three terms would have indicated ethical, not aesthetic, traditions; he would have perceived immediately a mistake in the Action Française critic's priorities. But what he would have rejected as "reactionary" was an obvious indulgence in historical fantasy, the building of an imaginary utopia in the *grand siècle,* the so-called *moment privilegié.*

A short time later Babbitt elaborated his charges against the Action Française writers in *The Masters of Modern French Criticism;* presumably he had come to most of these conclusions by the time Eliot was taking a course from him in French criticism as a Harvard undergraduate. Babbitt warned that though an anti-romantic reaction draws nourishment from tradition, "it must not dream of an impossible return to the past." The subservience of the movement's enterprise to nationalism did not escape his notice: "This problem of discipline and standards is not to be solved in terms of French life alone, as a whole school of contemporary French thinkers incline to believe, but is international." The ideological (rather than philosophical) nature of the movement, its devotion to the philodoxical manipulation of concepts, is reflected in his observation that "If France is to maintain her high place in civilization she will have to expel both the Jesuitical and the Jacobinical virus from her blood."[12]

It is evident that Babbitt has sensed the disordered priorities of the Maurrassian when he says that "the Frenchman has a way . . . of connecting the literary problem with the religious problem and then running the religious problem in turn into the political problem"—a statement superficially resembling his assertion in *Democracy and Leadership* that the economic problem runs into the political problem, the political problem into the philosophical problem, and the philosophical problem at last

---

Maurras held Christ to be a "grubby Jew" preaching socially subversive doctrines that the Church neutralized with its pagan genius.

12 *The Masters of Modern French Criticism* (Boston, 1912) p. 368, p. 381.

into the religious problem.[13] The fault of the Frenchman, in Babbitt's eyes, lay not in connecting unrelated spheres of life but in connecting spheres that are ultimately related in the wrong way: for religion is concerned with the "last things," being at the same time the basis of "first principles." *The Masters of Modern French Criticism* ignores Maurras except as a name in a move-ment to which Babbitt objects: A brief mention in his "List of Critics" complains of Maurras' tendency to "mix up the whole question of classic and romantic art with politics."[14] The "poli-tical problem" is a problem in the Maurrassian system precisely because it is analyzed in terms of utopian nostalgia and not in terms of political philosophy.

Babbitt detects the influence of Brunetière upon the Maurras-sians, and suggests that his objections to that critic's work should be applied to theirs also. Anyone familiar with the Action Fran-çaise's ideology would be able to tell immediately which objec-tions he meant. The chapter on Brunetière notes the absurdity of that critic's attempts to justify Roman Catholic dogma with the theories of Comte and Darwin and disapproves of his self-avowed "social" conversion to Christianity, regarding it as a mere "escape" from egoism and subjectivity, that is, an evasion of deeper issues. A position that insists on the total subjection of the individual to traditions and institutions, Babbitt says, has ignored the fact that the answer to Rousseauistic individualism is not to reject individualism altogether but rather to embrace a correct individualism based on the aristocratic ideal of the cultivation of character.[15]

Babbitt scarcely referred to the Action Française critics again until 1929 when discussing the attack made on Maurras in Julien Benda's *Belphégor*. Eliot had recently come out as a "classicist in literature, royalist in politics, and anglo-catholic in religion," a formula inspired by Maurras' "aesthetic of the three traditions." Eliot had already made his attack on humanism, and in the

13 Irving Babbitt, *Democracy and Leadership* (Indianapolis, 1979), p. 23.
14 *Masters*, p. 408.
15 *Masters*, pp. 330–337.

pages of the *Criterion* was promoting Charles Maurras. Babbitt felt it was time to take another look at a movement that had previously seemed to be of no intellectual consequence—to take a stand lest there be any confusion. He observed that Maurrassian critique of Rousseauism was an odd nationalist theory that perceived the romantic movement as "an alien intrusion into the French tradition" and that the three traditions, "classical, Catholic, and monarchical," were to be restored such as they existed "in the age of Louis XIV. The members of this group, it is important to note, are less interested in classicism and religion for their own sake than as necessary supports for what they term an 'integral nationalism.' " Then comes Babbitt's final condemnation, in terms of his antiromanticism:

[Benda] detects again romantic elements in the cult that M. Maurras renders to reason, and is unable to see that "integral nationalism" of the type promoted by *l'Action française* is genuinely Catholic or classical. Rousseau would, as a matter of fact, have the right to say (in the words of Emerson's Brahma) of many of those who profess to be reacting from him: "When me they fly, I am the wings."[16]

II

Because Maurras appeared to be of little importance outside France, Babbitt did not launch a systematic attack upon him. Then, as now, it would have been very easy for anyone from the Western liberal tradition to find Maurras instantly and utterly repulsive. But Eliot had rejected that tradition. Moreover, in rejecting Babbitt as too closely related to that tradition, Eliot found himself with no other authority for an attack on democracy but Maurras.

By the time that Eliot was calling for Babbitt and Maurras to merge their doctrines and influence, he was entirely familiar with Action Française ideology. Doctrines of the Action Française that were not fully exposed in its own extensive propaganda were aired in the controversial literature that sprang up in

16 *On Being Creative and Other Essays* (London, 1932), pp. 187-189.

1926 when the Vatican officially condemned the movement; Eliot's exchange with Leo Ward over the significance of the Vatican's position reveals his complete familiarity with both sides of this literataure.[17] But it was easy enough to see what Maurras was about well before then. Within the personality cult surrounding Maurras there was no mystery about his actual beliefs and their import, only hypocrisy. If Maurrassianism was "classical, catholic, and monarchist," then the terms must be redefined.

For the classicism lacked Plato—a philosopher infected by "Asiaticism" (a mystical current contrary to Western rationalism). For Maurras, the Epicurean Lucretius incarnated the Western genius. A recent scholar has observed that Maurras' "great admiration for the legacy of Hellas" was "very much the wistful classicism of nineteenth-century romanticism, a wistfulness that can be found in the writings of a Nietzsche or a Pater."[18]

The Catholicism lacked God. In adolescence, Maurras felt "an implacable need to experience the absence of God"; the positivism of Auguste Comte (the modern Lucretius) was his alternative.[19]

The monarchism lacked legitimacy—let alone divine right. Maurras supported the regicide House of Orleans; even so, its candidate, the Count of Paris, had repudiated the Action Française. A Maurrassian king would be only a royal dictator; thus Maurrassian monarchism was merely a version of the Bonapartist/Boulangist faith in a "man on a horse" and would lead eventually to Vichy. The amoral principle of national interest, *raison d'état* was the principle of Maurrassian political justice; the late nineteenth-century French vogue of Nietzsche

17 *Criterion,* VII (1928), 195-203, 364-378.
18 Michael Sutton, *Nationalism, Positivism, and Catholicism: The Politics of Charles Maurras and French Catholics 1890-1914* (London, 1983), p. 124.
19 Quoted in William C. Buthman, *The Rise of Integral Nationalism in France* (New York, 1939), p. 124. Although Babbitt and Comte have both been considered agnostics, and Babbitt chose to apply the term "positivist" to himself in an unusual sense, his strongly held dualistic beliefs point toward theism, while Comte's positivism was only a dogmatic atheism.

prepared the way for such a teaching, though Maurras would deny any debt to Nietzsche as a source.[20] The most important of the three terms was classicism, an aesthetic principle of order and symmetry that could be applied to an "organic" society as well as to a work of art. This "organicism," however, did not attempt to explain the interrelations of a social fabric that one embraced realistically (and conservatively) as the status quo; rather it was the rationale for stigmatizing social elements perceived as "alien." As a symbol of national destiny and purpose, classicism served to distinguish Integral Nationalism superficially from other radical and obviously romantic nationalisms such as Nazism and Fascism: A mythical genius of the West born among the columns of the Acropolis and later inherited by France placed the point of ideological breakdown into "mystique" at one remove from movement's own soil.

In the end, the Maurrassian position was a utopian fantasy calculated to attract alienated literary men, a simplistic explanation of how the forces of economic change (presided over by Jewish, Protestant, Masonic, and "cosmopolitan" business interests and supported by the Semitic ideology of individualism) destroyed the *ancien régime*'s paradise of literary patronage. Maurras makes his demagogic appeal to the degraded elite of writers in *L'Avenir de l'intelligence,* which Eliot purchased while at the Sorbonne.

Of course, Eliot's own straitened circumstances do not sufficiently explain Maurras' hold on him. Unfortunately, historians of the movement do not analyze its attractive power other than in terms of social forces and the mob passions to which they gave rise. What demands explanation is how so many brilliant young men came to believe what we cannot—that Maurras was a true "philosopher" with a coherent and substantial "system." In criticizing the French weakness for the "Jesuitical and Jacobinical virus," Babbitt intended an attack on the illusion of the French that intellectual systems are not only desirable but that they are easily constructed and defended. One gets a sense of how Maurras both suffered from the virus and consciously played on the French weakness from the analysis of his "system" offered by Georges Bernanos, an ex-Maurrassian who sought to defend Catholicism and monarchy without Maurras, and who, foreseeing the scandal of Vichy, tried to exorcise the Action Française's influence on the eve of World War II. As a critic of Maurras, Bernanos is unique, indispensable, and persistently overlooked.[21] What he shows us is the ideologist at work—circumventing the taboo questions concerning his premises. The analysis then proceeds from methods to motives, and is, on either score, a study in pathology.

Bernanos says, "One understands nothing about M. Maurras if one judges the man by his work," for the work is an exercise in concealment, a "vast defensive system, of which he is at once the master and the prisoner." "His doctrines define him as the theologians have defined God, not by what he is, but by what he is not." His "delicate articulation of the true and the false, of the just and the unjust" affords him a position of minimal risk, from which he cannot be dislodged "without compromising the whole edifice." The precarious balance—of obvious truths with errors couched in the language of the Catholic philosophy—is itself a defense: The author may call any attempt to isolate these errors "a substantial distortion of his thought." Obviously, one cannot argue on Maurras' own terms: "more than one enemy, incapable of forcing the guard of this rude jouster, has not hesitated to seize his foil with the left hand." Which is to say, one cannot get at Maurras if one fences by the rules; one's willingness to suspend them proves one's suspicion of the opponent's bad faith. Manipulated by an intellectual thimblerigger, the game will go on until someone knocks the thimbles off the table. Our civility—or credulity—is being used against us. Bernanos's *ad hominem* attack on Maurras explains itself: Behind the attempt

<hr />

21 Thomas Molnar's *Bernanos* (New York, 1960) brought this new source to my attention, though Molnar's use of it is entirely unsatisfactory.

to manipulate reality lies a man with a poor grasp of reality; but one cannot expose his falsification of reality so long as one accepts his endless evasions, out of politeness, as a legitimate defense. Nor is consistency, which Maurras has aplenty, the final criterion of truth: "One does not judge an error by the place it seems to hold in a system; one measures the seriousness of the evils which it fosters, of the good which it hinders." ("By their fruits shall ye know them," Babbitt would have said.)

The only good that Maurras' system offered the world was the beneficent principle of order—an order adjudicated by no authority (since there is no authority in a godless cosmos) and opposed only to disorder (the "organized chaos" of parliamentary democracy). Why did Maurras' brilliant young men feel (as he said) the need of "order in their thought, of order in their life, of order in society"? Bernanos answers that order is "not at all a mistress of illusion who seduces and consoles, but a mistress of certitude. . . . Whoever has been a Maurrassian, and is no more, runs the risk of being nothing."[22] Very likely Bernanos means that *rien* quite literally and, if so, casts a new light on Babbitt's phrase, "the affinity of the jellyfish for the rock."

Fear of losing possession of oneself and thereby lapsing into nonexistence is the pervasive characteristic of the pneumopathological condition defined by R. D. Laing, the "divided self." May we not suppose that the ideologist seeks to palliate this fear by constructing the "second reality" of ideology as a version of reality under his complete control? Bernanos portrays Maurras as an existentially divided self, "fired with passion for the truth of the disciplines within which he persists in pursuing his thought, while his being denies them, thus denying their eternal substance, their profound reality"—a state that is "one of the most cruel forms of damnation in the world"; at the same time, this contradiction is his animating principle.[23]

Bernanos had unmasked an insecure man with no real claim

22 *Nous autres, francais* (Paris, 1939), 61-62, 72-73.
23 *Scandale de la Verité* (Paris, 1939), 28.

to intellectual significance. Something in the personality of Eliot blinded him to the nature of Maurras' "system": an insecurity analogous to Maurras' insecurity, but not identical with it.[24]

III

While in Paris in 1923, Babbitt met a young American journalist who found the Action Française attractive and attempted to dissuade him from his interest. The young man was surprised and confused to learn that the conservative Babbitt saw danger in the ideas of Maurras; but Babbitt then "made clear to [him] how deep-rooted was his objection to the combination of political, religious, and literary aims in a single program like that of *l'Action Française*." How unlikely it seems that Babbitt would fail to confront his own pupil on the same subject—particularly during their meeting in London in 1926, when he convinced Eliot of his duty to "come out into the open" and account for his new religious position. Eliot's tripartite declaration in *For Lancelot Andrewes* for classicism, royalism, and Anglo-Catholicism was the result.[25]

As Eliot entered this new position, he was just getting to know Paul Elmer More, who was now an established Anglican theologian; in a letter to Austin Warren, More referred to Eliot's change as "*a kind of* conversion, due largely I believe to the influence of Maurras. . . . He is avowedly and, no doubt, sincerely religious; but just what his religion means to him, I do not know."[26] The man who could write *Ash Wednesday* obviously understood the issues and emotions of faith and doubt; yet the poem's "sincerity" (or usefulness as biographical evidence) is

24 Maurras' insecurity was that of all conspiracy theorists. Eliot's desperations were many and various: See George Whiteside, "T. S. Eliot: The Psychobiographical Approach," *Southern Review*, VI (1973), 3–26, and my essay, "Eliot on the Couch," *Hillsdale Review*, IV (Winter 1982–83), 10–18.

25 Marcus Selden Goldman in *Irving Babbitt, Man and Teacher*, p. 235; Eliot, p. 103.

26 Quoted in Arthur Hazard Dakin, *Paul Elmer More* (Princeton, 1960), p. 269. (My emphasis.) Eliot indicated the importance of Maurras to his conversion in the exchange with Ward [*Criterion*, VII (1928), 202]. Later he said that 'for some of us, Maurras was a kind of Virgil who led us to the doors of the temple' ["Hommage a Charles Maurras," *Aspects de la France et du Monde* (April 25, 1948)].

undercut by the knowledge that Eliot sought this understanding, and desired his civilization to seek it, so that poetry might
flourish.

The declaration was a scandal, both to the Right and the Left,
and as the initial "disclaimers" accompanying it proved insuf-
ficient, Eliot provided others in *After Strange Gods,* denying in
particular that the three terms were of equal importance, that
they were to be accepted on the same grounds, or "that they all
hang together or fall together, which would be the most serious
misunderstanding of all." "I now see the danger of suggesting
to outsiders that the Faith is a political principle or a literary
fashion, and the sum of all a dramatic posture."[27] But the history of the Maurrassian movement shows exactly how the three
terms share a common basis, for some minds, in political faith,
religious fashion, and aesthetic religion; how each was invoked
to support the others; and how the sum of all often was a
dramatic posture—an anticlimax to the nineteenth-century
tradition of the ultraroyalists, the "intransigents," and the
dandies.

Experienced readers of Eliot's prose will have to admit that he
tended to retreat from argument into his "disclaimers," as though
he really believed that conceding an objection nullifies it: Following Bernanos' analysis of Maurras, we might say that Eliot's
disclaimers define him by what he is not rather than by what he
is. It is no coincidence that this "Maurrassian" strategy appears
chiefly in Eliot's attitude towards Maurras and towards his own
version of Maurrassianism. We know that Maurras was a fixture
in Eliot's mind; he persisted in defending Maurras as late as
1955.[28] More significantly, his great critical undertaking, the
Criterion, may be seen as a Maurrassian project.

A principal concern of the *Criterion* was establishing an organ-
icist concept of Western culture, the "mind of Europe," an idea

27 *After Strange Gods* (New York, 1934), pp. 29-30.
28 Lecture, "The Literature of Politics." For an albeit inconclusive summary of Eliot's
pronouncements on Maurras, see Roger Kojeck, *T. S. Eliot's Social Criticism* (New York,
1972), Ch. 3. Eliot seems to approach a realization of Maurras' intrinsic flaws but finally
cannot attain it.

that traditionalists may find themselves accepting uncritically.[29] On the public level, the "mind of Europe" was a cultural identity for artists that would overcome the barrier of Anglo-Saxon temperament (the principal source of provincialism in Anglo-Saxon letters) and would reunite modern Europe with its classical roots. On the personal level, it served as an artificial nationality for a man who felt that he "was never anything anywhere,"[30] and who supposed that he might be a European if he could not be an American, Englishman, or Frenchman; it served also as a haven from the shame of his "provincial" origins (America and humanism). On the ideological level, the "mind of Europe" enabled the non-French to participate in the salvific enterprise that Maurras' nationalist doctrine reserved to the French. It failed on all levels. The public mission was too large for Eliot to undertake by himself. The private mission was impossible because individuals must live on the plane of the particular (a "cosmopolitan" identity is no identity at all) and, accordingly, cannot deny the particularity of their origins. The ideological mission ran directly against Maurrassianism's primarily political motives, which did not allow it, and in practice it conceded too much to the Maurrassians—particularly their claim that France was the cultural "center."

As Denis Donoghue observes, the "mind of Europe" enterprise implies a claim by Eliot of having taken that "mind" unto himself. If the claim is not simply "outrageous," it nonetheless carries "an air of failure" because of its virtual impossibility. "The whole effort was somehow artificial, a function of [Eliot's]

---

29 Whatever the symbol "the West" actually signified to Eliot, one should find troublesome his passive consent to the Maurrassian Henri Massis' use of it in *The Defence of the West* (New York, 1928, with preface by G. K. Chesterton; entire text published also in the *Criterion* during 1926). In that book, "the West" is a vague abstraction opposed to an equally vague abstraction, "the East," and finally serves as a blind for nationalist-racist theories whose true nature Massis denies. Thus the Maurrassian conceals premises that would discredit him, but extracts a mystical affirmation from the reader of conclusions drawn from them. (Irritated by Massis' wholesale attack on the Orient, Babbitt charges him with "sectarian narrowness" and "sheer ignorance of the facts" in *Spanish Character* (Boston, 1940, p. 205.)

30 From a letter to Herbert Read, quoted in *T. S. Eliot: The Man and His Work,* ed. Allen Tate, (New York, 1966), p. 15.

will at odds with his talent." "What shows, for the most part, is
the strain." "We are continually aware of severances and dis-
junctions between one tone and another, insecurities of feeling
and the desperate labour of transcending them."[31] In short, Eliot
was struggling, valiantly though wrongheadedly, against personal insecurity as well as the inherent weakness of his chosen
position.

Eliot rounded out his Anglo-Maurrassian position by endors-
ing the anticapitalist agrarian economics of Distributism; by por-
traying the early seventeenth century in England as a utopian *moment privilégié* (complete with an organic "undissociated
sensibility" and a demonologically vilified Hobbes— to corre-
spond to Maurras' Rousseau); by stigmatizing "free-thinking
Jews" as subversive to tradition; and by calling for absolute
definitions from Anglican bishops that the skeptical argument of
the *via media* does not authorize them to provide.[32] The Maurrassian flavor of Eliot's Anglicanism appears also in his emphasis
on the mundane and the aesthetic elements in the church, as
when he says: "A Church is to be judged by its intellectual fruits,
by its influence on the sensibility of the most sensitive and on
the intellect of the most intelligent, and it must be made real to
the eye by monuments of artistic merit."[33] Such was the paradoxically Maurrassian position from which Eliot assailed
Babbitt and his attitude to the church.[34]

31 "Eliot and the *Criterion,*" *The Literary Criticism of T. S. Eliot,* ed. David Newton-de
Molina (London, 1977), pp. 40–41.

32 See "Catholicism and International Order," "Lancelot Andrewes," and "John
Bramhall"; Part I of *After Strange Gods;* "Thoughts After Lambeth."

33 "Lancelot Andrewes," *Essays Ancient and Modern* (London, 1936), p. 13.

34 Space does not allow consideration of Eliot's problematic attempt to define his
position by listing the names of men who may have had no use for each other: Sorel,
Maurras, Benda, Hulme, Maritain, Babbitt [*Criterion* IV (1926), 5]. The names of Maurras
and Benda are curiously yoked in Eliot's letter to *La Nouvelle Revue Francaise,* XXI (1923),
620. I believe that Eliot intended Hulme to serve as a transatlantic and acceptably
"modernist" substitute for Babbitt. Eliot began studying another "authority" of his, the
idealist philosopher Bradley, upon returning from the Sorbonne; I would therefore
suggest that Maurras' positivist-absolutist amalgam provoked this. The humanists, as
sceptics and Platonic dualists, rejected the possibility of any absolutes in the realm of
immanence; Bradley's philosophy suggested to Eliot that an approach to an absolute
point of view could be made through a dialectical process that attempted the unification

IV

What psychological forces prevented Eliot from becoming disil-
lusioned with Maurras? Perhaps Maurras' existence proved
something that Eliot could not prove for himself. Perhaps Eliot
believed in a personal destiny—the leadership of a rightist
movement made possible by the almost astrological coincidence
around 1930 of the apogees of humanism, Distributism, Anglo-
Catholicism, and the political reaction on the continent. Belief in
this destiny and in the benign intentions of Maurras would then
have been mutually supportive ideas. At the very least, the
persistence of Maurras and his movement vindicated a belief in
the power and influence of intellectual elites. But the validative
function Maurras performed in Eliot's thinking may have been
much more radical. One catches a glimpse of this function in
Eliot's recoil from Babbitt, particularly from Babbitt's philo-
sophic acceptance of the unanswered question—"the quest
concerning the mysterious ground of all being."[35]

One turns, of course, to "The Humanism of Irving Babbitt,"
where Eliot blurs the distinction between two different attacks:
one on the failure of humanism to provide civilization with a
sense of the transcendent, and one on its failure to contribute
the immanent structure of "culture." If transcendence is confined to a rigidly defined category of "revelation," then Eliot
was right; otherwise, Babbitt's distillation of the meaning of
transcendence from the world's philosophies and faiths stands
unimpaired. But one senses the Maurrassian influence upon
Eliot in the charges of "individualism" and "Protestantism":
Eliot seems to fear that there is a void in man—that human
nature is so inchoate that the unaided will never can impose
structure on the personality, that degeneration is almost inevi-

---

of disparate points of view: Partial truths could add up nearly to a whole through an
intellectual method of correction through contradiction—a "symbiotic form" for the
unification of experience. See Adrian Cunningham, "Continuity and Coherence in
Eliot's Religious Thought," *Eliot in Perspective*, ed. Graham Martin (New York, 1970), p.
215.

35 Voegelin, *The Ecumenic Age* (Baton Rouge, La., 1974), p. 320.

table because of the sheer arbitrariness of individual choice. To Eliot, "culture" provides relief from this arbitrariness, and it possesses authority by virtue of its continuity. Humanism, he charges, is discontinuous, being the exclusive possession of a few individuals of genius and a few highly organized societies at their best period. What Eliot fears in the alleged discontinuity of humanism, one suspects, is something like the discontinuity of human nature, or the discontinuity of truth.[36]

"For us," Eliot says, "religion is Christianity." In the course of the argument, religion becomes "the religious habits of the race" —"our heredity"—in the Maurrassian sense, an organic component of Western culture.[37] The argument for religion and against humanism has dwindled to the superiority of one over the other as an ideology for conserving the city of man. The issue was not humanism's lack of transcendence after all; there was no talk of saving souls. One senses that Babbitt has paid more attention to transcendence and to the priority of truth than Eliot.[38]

Eliot's fear that "the sum of a population of individuals, all ideally and efficiently checking and controlling themselves, will never make a *whole*," and his assertion that civilization is "merely a frame to be filled with definite objects, not a definite object itself," seem to deny that civilization has ethical meaning in itself.[39] Eliot's next step, logically, should have been to declare that civilization's purpose is the saving of souls (which it cannot do without Christianity); his failure to do this suggests the cynical belief that "purpose" is the necessary myth, true or false, which preserves a culture. One suspects the worst when Eliot asks Babbitt to incorporate the church into his program so that

36 This is not to deny the essential validity of Eliot's perception of the psychic need for "roots"—cultural specificity that satisfies one's sense of moral and aesthetic fitness. Alienation enabled Eliot to perceive this truth in a way that Babbitt—whose psychic condition was the complete opposite of "alienation"—would not have.

37 "The Humanism of Irving Babbitt," *Selected Essays* (New York, 1950), p. 421.

38 The fact that Paul Elmer More's continuous development toward conversion to Christianity began with humanism, and the study of Plato, lends credence to the element of transcendence in Babbitt's philosophy.

39 "The Humanism of Irving Babbitt," p. 424, p. 426. (Emphasis mine.)

"his influence might thus join with that of another philosopher—Charles Maurras—and might, indeed, correct some of the extravagances of that writer."[40] (Is Maurras' failure to believe in the existence of a transcendent order an "extravagance"?)

With characteristic ease in self-contradiction or self-misrepresentation, Eliot felt that he had "rejected nothing that seems to me positive in [Babbitt's] teaching." But there is little left of Babbitt's teaching that is recognizable in Eliot, if one traces his ideas to their apparent primary assumptions. One must indeed ask whether Eliot ever comprehended the full depth of that teaching. Babbitt was disappointed in Eliot's betrayal of his "movement"; but more than this, Babbitt must have known the personality of his sometime pupil quite well and may have reserved to himself the right to judge the nature of Eliot's conversion in the light of his allegiance to Maurras; Babbitt's disappointment may finally have been over Eliot's shirking the burden of intellectual, and hence spiritual, integrity—regret over the loss of a soul through complacency in its own weakness. In the end, one may have to face some unpleasant conclusions about the personality of a widely respected poet. Fortunately, a few critics have anticipated these conclusions.

Richard Wollheim believes that Eliot went into steady intellectual decline after his dissertation on Bradley. He notes two "dispositions of the psyche": on the one hand, "a certain fear of the intellect: rather as though it were envisaged as something having the power to damage or dement those who used it in a literal manner." This well describes the odium in which the humanists held an instrumentalized faculty of "reason"; as More said, "rationalism is unreasonable."[41] Yet Wollheim seems to suggest something deeper than this common-sense suspicion. Alongside this "fear of the intellect," he states,

And at certain crucial points linked with it, there would appear to be in Eliot's make-up another disposition, which we may characterize by

40 "The Humanism of Irving Babbitt," p. 427.
41 More, *Pages from an Oxford Diary* (Princeton, 1937), Ch. XIV.

saying that it was only after he made some kind of initial submission to a force, felt in itself to be uncongenial or external, that he possessed the liberty to do something for himself or on his own account.[42]

(Adrian Cunningham refers to "the palimpsest nature of Eliot's mind"—suggesting Eliot's susceptibility to influences.[43]) Wollheim continues:

> If we tend in Eliot's case to overlook or discount [the operation of these two dispositions,] this (I suggest) is only because we are so seduced or beguiled by the highly evolved ironical manner, by means of which they are characteristically represented in his work, that we fail to appreciate the very real emotional tasks that this discharged for him. . . .
>
> The effect of the two dispositions that I have tried to characterise might be put by saying that Eliot, in the pursuit of a certain kind of security or reassurance that we are in no position to define, was progressively led to substitute, in his mind, on the one hand, ideas of less content for ideas of more content, and, on the other hand, poorer or softer ideas for better and stronger ideas. . . .

Wollheim remarks that the "consistent self-depreciation" in Eliot's writing "masks but also reveals a sustained attack that Eliot made upon himself"; Eliot was "compelled to deny an idea of his own once he had asserted it."[44] Cunningham, however, discerning as "a pervasive characteristic of Eliot's processes of thought" his "fairly consistent and deliberate evasion of precise definition," considers the self-contradictory tendency to result from perceiving, through Bradley, the dialectical nature of experience and intellectual discourse, leading to a perhaps endless "project of unification by antithesis." The quest of Eliot's life, Cunningham believes, is the "ultimate validation of experience"—the "security" that Wollheim would not define, perhaps deliverance from solipsism, which was not only a philosophical problem but a psychological reality for Eliot.[45]

To the extent that Eliot undertook this quest not by choice or,

---

42 "Eliot and F. H. Bradley: An account," *Eliot in Perspective,* p. 190.
43 Cunningham, p. 215.
44 Wollheim, "Eliot and F. H. Bradley."
45 Cunningham, p. 227.

Platonically speaking, out of an erotic desire for the truth, but rather under the compulsion of a fear of indeterminacy (a reluctance to accept the degree of indeterminacy with which we must all live), Eliot was doomed to exhaust himself, intellectually and spiritually, and was also doomed to leave himself helpless to resist an uncritical solution; an early fascination with Maurras led eventually, in a time of desperate insecurity, to surrender.

It is tragic to contemplate that, if Eliot, as the "jellyfish" of Babbitt's metaphor, chose Maurras as his rock, then he had only attached himself to another jellyfish. One hopes that he gradually transferred his adherence to the genuine rock; in any event, his predicament seriously limits his authority to criticize other people's solutions.

J. David Hoeveler, Jr.

Babbitt and Contemporary Conservative Thought in America

I

SUCH WATERSHED events in our history as the American Revolution, the election of Andrew Jackson, the Progressive reform movement, and Franklin D. Roosevelt's New Deal have rightly prompted historians to examine the intellectual and cultural backgrounds that generated these changes. The election of Ronald Reagan to the presidency may someday rank as another of these phenomena that redirect the course of American history. Should that be the case, historians should have no difficulty identifying a marked gain in currency for conservative opinion within the American intellectual community in the decade or so before the 1980 election.[1] Already the term *neoconservatism* has given at least a journalistic label to this revival,

---

[1] Conservative journalism, as one measure, has attained both wider readership and new respectability. Such journals of opinion as *The Public Interest,* appearing in 1965, and *The American Spectator,* 1967, have usefully supplemented older periodicals like *The National Review* and the more scholarly *Modern Age* and *University Bookman.* They have brought attention to a new generation of conservative writers. Also, it seems inconceivable that such an organization as the Conservative Historians' Forum, founded in the late 1970's, could have flourished unharassed in the previous decade.

though most thinkers included in that reference have abjured it. It will be a more challenging assignment to illuminate the several strands of ideas that mark the conservative renaissance and to identify their roots, influences, and interrelationships. The effort has so far yielded one outstanding study, George H. Nash's *The Conservative Intellectual Movement in America: Since 1945*,[2] and one less worthy survey, Peter Steinfels' *The Neoconservatives: The Men Who Are Changing America's Politics*.[3]

The question of influences is important in helping us understand the character of contemporary conservative thought in the United States. In this century, conservatism received its first and perhaps most powerful formulation in the writings of Irving Babbitt. From his earliest works in the 1890's to his two most powerful statements, *Rousseau and Romanticism* in 1919 and *Democracy and Leadership* in 1924, Babbitt's scholarship prepared the way for the *annus mirabilis* of the New Humanism in 1930. In that year Babbitt and his colleague Paul Elmer More, joined by a coterie of younger but zealous writers, enjoyed a rare public limelight. Separate "manifestos" from the humanist camp and from their rivals[4] highlighted the controversy. But the deepening economic depression made the debate about morals, the wisdom of antiquity, and the need for "inner checks" somehow less urgent, and the New Humanism faded from attention. Like most great intellectual issues, this one was never settled; it was more or less forgotten.

But not entirely so. What remained was the "remnant," a core of intellectuals of decidedly traditionalist temperament, who adhered to a system of absolute or permanent moral ideals and who, whether from a theistic or humanistic perspective, waged a kind of rear-guard defense against the continuing triumph of relativism and materialism in American life. These individuals kept Babbitt's influence alive. But they won little

---

2 (New York, 1976).
3 (New York, 1979).
4 *Humanism and America: Essays on the Outlook of Modern Civilization*, ed. Norman Foerster (New York, 1930); *The Critique of Humanism: A Symposium*, ed. C. Hartley Grattan (New York, 1930).

public attention, and even in academic spheres their influence, at least for the time being, was probably marginal. The impact of World War II, however, certainly changed the intellectual climate in the United States to the point that a traditionalist viewpoint seemed relevant and needed. In colleges and universities, where the New Humanist movement always had its greatest strength, curricular revisions reflected the urgency with which educators stressed cultural continuity and the permanent values of Western civilization. The legacy of Charles William Eliot's elective system, against which Babbitt had railed for years, now met its first sustained attack, symbolized by the reforms at his own Harvard College. The sense that Western civilization had suffered a "cultural hemorrhage," of which the war was but a manifestation, motivated the "new conservatism" of Peter Viereck. Viereck's conservatism, of course, was new only within the limited context of the American experience. Viereck stood squarely in the old European conservative tradition of Burke and Disraeli and acknowledged Irving Babbitt as a major intellectual influence. So also did Russell Kirk, whose 1953 volume, *The Conservative Mind,* made that subject again topical. Kirk identified Babbitt as perhaps the strongest conservative author in the whole range of modern American letters; his book appropriately marked the second decade of Babbitt's death.[5]

Besides influencing those like Viereck and Kirk who cited a direct influence of Babbitt on their thinking, the conservative intellectual movement developed in directions that paralleled Babbitt's. Here again another postwar constellation of intellectuals led what Nash has labeled "the rediscovery of tradition and values." These intellectuals experienced painfully the moral vacuum of twentieth-century culture, and their common perspective was an anti-naturalist ideology with clear overtones of Platonism. Richard Weaver, John Hallowell, Walter Lippmann, Leo Strauss, Eric Voegelin, Thomas Molnar, and others all

5 Claes Ryn, "Peter Viereck: Unadjusted Man of Ideas," *Political Science Reviewer,* 7 (1977), 325–366; *A Program for Conservatives* (Chicago, 1954), p. 20.

opposed liberalism on the grounds of its naturalistic character and its moral agnosticism. Clearly Babbitt would have been a spiritual friend of this group. His own humanism posited naturalism as an offshoot of romanticism, and he attacked both for their erosion of permanent ethical norms. On the other hand, however, most of these postwar thinkers incorporated a religious and metaphysical content into their conservatism, one that contrasted with Babbitt's "empirical" humanism. Babbitt constantly insisted that he was prepared to meet the moderns on their own ground by defending human dualism on the im-mediate data of consciousness, without appeal to revelation. There are among the recent antimodernists explicit Roman Catholic and Anglo-Catholic affiliations.[6]

Probably at no other time since his death was Babbitt's stock lower than in the 1960's. Amid the clamor and hysteria that surrounded antiwar protests and the calls for a new order in America, the "remnant" felt its isolation. For the generation of the 1960's was nothing if not a romantic generation. "Do your own thing" became a battle cry for a culture that celebrated whim. On the campuses, the demand for "relevance" not only personalized courses in Shakespeare, in which a student's dance interpretation of *Hamlet* might substitute for a research paper, but enhanced the solipsistic mentality that became pervasive. How might any conservative individual imbued with the spirit of a Burke or a Babbitt address a culture whose advertising media mindlessly worshipped youth and invited young and old alike to join the "Pepsi Generation"? Conservatism became "a still small voice" indeed.

Throughout the decade of upheaval, however, a new conser-vative spirit was fermenting. It had many roots and many locations. It could not be identified by any geographical, ethnic, or religious denominators. It flourished in journalism and at Harvard. But this diversity has been a troubling factor to some. Paul Gottfried, for example, has criticized "neoconservatism" as too much an ad hoc phenomenon, merely an issues-oriented

6 Nash, pp. 36–41, pp. 44–46, pp. 49–54, pp. 57–83.

response to 1960's causes such as feminism, environmentalism, and racial quotas. Gottfried believes these characteristics will assure this movement only a "provisional" status in American conservatism. "The neoconservatives are political commentators," he writes, "not the authors of timeless truths."[7] Such a castigation raises the question whether some cohesive philosophy underscores contemporary conservative thought, something akin to those first principles that animate all Irving Babbitt's writings.

For this reason it may be useful to examine the recent conservative literature from the perspective of Babbitt's own scholarship. There may be in fact no better way to ascertain whether some kind of continuity underlies modern American conservatism, some commonality of belief concerning human nature, history, politics, and social change. Here it is not just a matter of demonstrating that Babbitt directly influenced the contemporary writers. As Claes Ryn has suggested, Babbitt's "influence" may be implicit.[8] The comparison would then be useful in helping us indicate a core of opinion that has given conservative thinkers a consensus, however independently each may have arrived at it. Such an effort, of course, must be selective. This chapter will discuss Babbitt and contemporary intellectual conservatism with reference to three individuals: a New York Jew of a Trotskyite background, a Roman Catholic of Eastern European background, and a Protestant of midwestern background.

Wise readers have always recognized in Irving Babbitt a concrete guide for the conduct of life. The less perceptive, however, have charged that Babbitt and his followers pursued only vague abstractions and did not sufficiently outline a program for social amelioration. Now Babbitt and More partly validated this criticism themselves. For both, even an immersion in a contemporary novel induced malaise. Babbitt's political and

7 "On Neoconservatism," *Modern Age: A Quarterly Review*, 27 (1983), 40–41.

8 Claes Ryn, "American Intellectual Conservatism: Needs, Opportunities, Prospects," *Modern Age: A Quarterly Review*, 26 (Summer/Fall 1983), 307.

social commentary was unspecific at least in the sense that he did not propose corrective legislation for the ills of the day. His criticism was trenchant in its Burkean perspective, but even his theory of justice, he admitted, applied primarily to the inner lives of individuals.[9]

The contemporary conservatives we shall examine have been eager, on the contrary, to give their ideas concreteness. They are journalist intellectuals who study the daily news to make it the substance of their larger ideologies. At the very least they give us a fairly good intimation of how a Burkean mentality might assume flesh and blood in the United States of the 1980's.

Babbitt stood clearly in the tradition of Burke, and his differentiation of the "moral imagination" of Burke and the "idyllic imagination" of Rousseau stood at the heart of his political philosophy. And that philosophy, like all Babbitt's intellectual efforts, was essentially an exploration of human nature and an application of his dualistic philosophy of man. Specifically, Babbitt was interested in how the modern intellect, since the Renaissance, had lost the sense of sin. The dissolution of the higher will under the forces of romanticism and natu-ralism had conspired, in Babbitt's extended analysis, to de-prive human beings of any restraints on their natural instincts. Modern culture had thus become both sentimentally emo-tional—self-indulgent with respect to individual feelings and humanitarian with respect to feelings towards others—and materialistic, hedonistic in individual living and imperialistic in the relations between nations. These trends, Babbitt believed, could be understood only as the result of our relocating the source of sin, in Rousseauistic fashion, away from the individual and on to society. Human beings were essentially inculpable regarding their situations in life. Naturally good in their given nature, they probed society for the roots of their discontent.

9 Thus the oft-quoted remark by Malcolm Cowley: "And what . . . has Humanism to do with the scene outside my window: with the jobless men who saunter in the dusk, or the dying village, or the paper-mill abandoned across the river—this mill whose owners have gone South where labor is cheap?" in *Critique of Humanism*, ed. Grattan, p. 84.

The political consequences of this new mentality horrified Babbitt.[10]

Most troubling to him was the zealous reformer, the utopian reshaper of the world. For anyone who legitimates his own inherited innocence is free to redesign the world, the source of all evil, as his imagination dictates. The reformer is motivated by a quest to recover a lost innocence, an idyllic state that will reclaim humanity's original birthright. To Babbitt, such a reformer could be only a menace. For all along the way to the new world, reality interferes. Imagination and fact war against each other. But for the reformer it is reality that must submit; therefore, coercion and eventually tyranny become the vehicles of revolutionary change. Those most eager to serve us become those most eager to control us. Those who begin with an inordinate love for humanity end in oppressing it.[11] And the reformer who has escaped the "war in the cave" is not unlike the modern nation, equally ruled by its own sense of innocence. Babbitt warned against the dangers of the most recent of our many "sham" religions, the religion of nation, another product of the romantic age. Both the utopian reformer and the chauvinistic nationalist registered the dangers to civilization of the expansive temperament at work. The undisciplined will stood at the service of the undisciplined imagination.[12]

In 1924, Babbitt outlined these views, which received mostly scorn or indifference. But it is instructive to discover that among the contemporary conservative thinkers we are considering here, some form of Babbitt's humanistic dualism applied to politics constitutes a common perspective. Mostly it emerges as a critique of utopianism and its totalitarian consequences. And it is not difficult to understand why this particular concern of Babbitt has gained currency. Babbitt's *Democracy and Leadership*

10 For a summary of Babbitt's political views, see J. David Hoeveler, Jr., *The New Humanism: A Critique of Modern America, 1900-1940* (Charlottesville, Va., 1977), Chapter 6.

11 Babbitt, *Rousseau and Romanticism*, p. 377; *Democracy and Leadership*, pp. 69, 197-198, 287-288.

12 Babbitt, *Rousseau and Romanticism*, pp. 344-347.

coincided with the socialist movements that rose in Germany and Italy in the middle 1920's and soon brought their tragic consequences when their fascist characteristics emerged in the ensuing years. Babbitt died in 1933, just before the great communistic experiment in the Soviet Union was demonstrating that this worker's paradise was no Brook Farm. Slowly and painfully over the ensuing decades intellectuals, save those lost in a stubborn refusal to observe facts, have witnessed the outcome in tyranny of the "progressive" forces of the twentieth century. Many conscientious liberals in the 1940's did begin to warn that totalitarian forces were not the accidents of history and that intellectuals and others must recover the sense of evil in the human personality to guard against these dangers.[13] But since that time what probably has most changed many minds have been the political directions of the Third World and the failures of socialism. Among intellectual conservatives in America today there are many who saw the socialist dream die hard amid the repressive political course of the world's former colonial nations.

The link between Babbitt and the contemporary conservatives must also take note of some indigenous developments in the United States. Intellectual conservatism enjoyed a lively revival in the 1950's, but the character of "neoconservatism" seems to owe as much to the direction of liberalism and the New Left in the 1960's, into which many conservatives had brought radical and liberal pasts. Two factors seem influential. First, the utopian character of the New Left, with its "new order" rhetoric, its Freudian emphasis on the transformed personality, its call for a "new consciousness," and its sense that all these were in ready reach of a militant revolutionary push—this character of the New Left certainly caused many to take exception and view skeptically, in Babbitt's fashion, all such easy promises that a different human nature lies just below the surface of our evil capitalistic and bureaucratic society. Second, a new conserva-

13 For example, Arthur Schlesinger, Jr., *The Vital Center* (Boston, 1949), and Reinhold Niebuhr, *The Children of the Light and the Children of the Darkness* (New York, 1944).

tism emerged because a new liberalism emerged. Partly as a defense against the New Left, liberalism shifted from an emphasis on equality of opportunity and the large role that government would play in achieving it, to equality of results and the role that government would play in bringing that about. Liberalism became obsessed with numbers. Busing, racial quotas, the working incomes of the sexes, and other measurements gave a new and disturbing meaning to democracy, an ideal of statistical uniformity. To many who had been liberals, there was in these prospects something rash and utopian, and something frightening too.

II

The utopian mentality has been the subject of some analysis by Irving Kristol. Kristol, who willingly applies the term "neoconservative" to describe his political position, is coeditor of *The Public Interest,* an issues-oriented conservative publication, and frequent contributor to other journals. His collection of essays, *Reflections of a Neoconservative: Looking Back, Looking Ahead,*[14] contains some biographical remembrances of his college years at the City College of New York and the student rivalries between the Stalinists and his own Trotskyites. In previous works, *On the Democratic Idea in America* and *Two Cheers for Capitalism,* Kristol covers a considerable number of issues, from economics to pornography. But one may legitimately ask if these writings generate a unifying view of history and life that helps provide an intellectual framework for Kristol's neoconservatism. Without in the least maintaining that Kristol's reflections on politics and economics reflect, as do Babbitt's writings, a sustained and consistent ideology, we can nonetheless discern in Kristol a perspective on human nature that makes neoconservatism something more than a merely ad hoc response to contemporary events. And that perspective resembles Babbitt's in a very clear way.

14 (New York, 1983). This anthology includes many early Kristol essays, and most of the items in the book have been previously published.

Kristol believes that the American experience is exceptional and owes its special character to the influence of certain cultural traditions. These traditions have their beginnings in the Western religious experience. In a suggestive essay Kristol argues that Judaism and Christianity have always reflected certain dialectical tensions, which he describes as rabbinic (orthodox) and prophetic. Borrowing from Eric Voegelin, Kristol describes the prophetic tradition as gnostic in character. It finds the world sinful, imperfect, and unyielding. It confronts the world not within these limitations but by opposing to it some new kind of metaphysical order by which it hopes to reshape the world. Its temper is millenarian. "These gnostic movements," Kristol writes, "tend to be antinomian—that is, they tend to be hostile to all existing laws and to all existing institutions."[15] The political form of gnosticism is utopianism. The prophetic mind envisions an ideal order that it strains against all in its path to make a reality. It differs to that extent from the "orthodox" character of religion. Orthodoxy seeks improvement in human life through practice in daily living. Its spirit, in the face of the world's evils, is stoical. Its faith teaches that somehow these evils can be made the vehicle of good, but it warns that in this life things may not ultimately be "fair."[16] What really divides the prophetic from the orthodox, Kristol believes, are fundamentally different views of human nature, or what Babbitt would call differences of "first principles." The prophetic vision turned much of Judaism and Christianity increasingly away from the doctrine of original sin. The doctrine of original innocence, which replaced it, "meant that the potential for human transformation here on this earth was infinite, which is, of course, the basic gnostic hope." The hope was illusory. Writes Kristol: "Human nature and human reality are never transformed. . . ."[17]

Western culture has ever since felt these tensions. Kristol observes that Christianity was born at a time when Jewish gnosticism was very active and that Christianity inherited a

15 Kristol, *Reflections*, p. 320, p. 317.
16 Kristol, p. 317.
17 Kristol, p. 318.

large measure of its spirit. The different mentalities continued to be influential even in the more secularized world of the eighteenth century, and Kristol believes that the opposing courses within the Enlightenment were especially important for American history. Kristol compares the Anglo-Scottish Enlightenment with the French-Continental Enlightenment. The latter, culminating in the French Revolution, saw a new order emerging from the progress of history. Its temper was gnostic and antitraditionalist. From its prophetic roots in religion, the French-Continental Enlightenment imposed on the world a secular eschatology.[18] But the Anglo-Scottish Enlightenment envisioned no immanent new order. Its spirit, Kristol says, was melioristic rather than eschatological. Whereas one Enlightenment yielded a Robespierre and a Saint-Simon, the other yielded a James Madison and an Adam Smith. The Anglo-Scottish Enlightenment accepted an imperfect human nature and tried to channel self-interest safely into a competitive marketplace economy. It used existing social institutions as safeguards in this process and trusted to traditional moral values to civilize it.[19]

Its disdain for existing institutions also made the French-Continental Enlightenment hostile to capitalism. French Physiocrats emphasized "real" wealth drawn from the soil.[20] But the later socialists, both utopian socialists and "scientific" socialists like Marx, were the genuine heirs of the radical Enlightenment and of the prophetic religious tradition. Marx was the more realistic only in the sense that he knew that the new human consciousness needed to transcend the limitations of the human condition heretofore thought to be natural would not be spontaneous. That task must then fall to a socialist elite that would lead the masses into their own self-transformation. The Marxian origins of communism are no different in outcome from those of any other grand scheme of reform. Socialists, communists, and fascists all have roots in the temperament of the French-Continental Enlightenment. Kristol states: "The

18 Kristol, pp. xi, 143.
19 Kristol, pp. 143–155.
20 Kristol, pp. 146–147.

germs of twentieth-century totalitarianism, whether self-declared Left or Right, were activated by that grandiose, indeed utopian, commitment."[21] But Kristol does believe that the socialist ideal flourished as a genuine albeit misguided offshoot of the Western religious tradition. It has been the quasi religion of the prophetic Jews and Christians who have found their orthodox traditions to be stale and unrewarding. The zeal with which these partisans embraced a gnostic socialism was not merely a threat to world peace; it was a corruption of religion. Kristol concludes: "All of modern socialism is a movement that says it will create a good society, which will then create good people. I can think of no political doctrine more contemptuous of both the Jewish and Christian traditions, which says that there cannot be a good society unless there are good people."[22]

Kristol believes it is a matter of great significance and good fortune that the American Revolution was born of the more sober influences of the Anglo-Scottish Enlightenment. While the French philosophers thrived in the fashionable salons of Paris, remote from the rest of society and "alienated" as an intellectual class, the Anglo-Scottish thinkers were respected community participants and active members of improvement societies in and outside the universities. "At home" in the world, they were content to find practical means of improving it.[23] The leadership of the American Revolution, Kristol finds, reflected these characteristics. Not distracted by imaginative projections of a new world to be made, the prolific pamphlet writers and publicists of the revolutionary cause did not so easily lose sight of human nature and its deficiencies. The Founding Fathers in fact were even more "realistic" in this consideration. So the Americans looked inward on human nature, not outward to a new society. According to Kristol, "They understood that republican self-government could not exist if humanity did not possess . . . the

---

21 Kristol, pp. x–xi, 33–34.
22 Kristol, pp. 324–325.
23 Kristol, pp. 150–151.

traditional 'republican virtues' of self-control, self-reliance, and a disinterested concern for the public good." James Madison's sensitivity to the "degree of depravity in mankind" fortified democracy against the unrealistic hopes that may ultimately bring the harshest judgments against it. That realistic temperament also explains why the American Revolution was, as Kristol calls it, a "successful" revolution.[24]

Thus clearly the neoconservative views of Irving Kristol resemble Babbitt's distinctions between the individual who places primary attention on the external world and its reconstruction and the individual who considers the self the only proper vehicle of reform. And for Babbitt and Kristol alike the differences were not inconsequential. What Babbitt described in general terms Kristol elucidates with history. Babbitt may have founded his ideas on a fuller outline of human nature, but Kristol is no less useful for being the more concrete.

III

Irving Babbitt's social conservatism embraced capitalism. But it never waxed eloquent in that embrace. Babbitt greatly feared the dangers in all leveling programs of reform and decried the pretensions of socialism. Private property he accepted as a needed safeguard against the rule of numbers, and he acknowledged as valid the rewards won by successful competition. But Babbitt knew too much history to rest content in the assurance that the leadership class would not betray its trust. Social decay always sets in at the top first. Since Babbitt accepted the trickle-down theory of degeneration, he issued his famous warning: "Our real hope of safety lies in our being able to induce our future Harrimans and Rockefellers to liberalize their own souls, in other words to get themselves rightly educated."[25]

Recently, another effort to give contemporary conservatism a large intellectual framework has been undertaken by Michael

24 Kristol, pp. 81–82.
25 *Literature and the American College* (Boston, 1908), p. 71.

Novak, and as its specific subject is "democratic capitalism," it bears comparison with Babbitt on that subject.

Novak's family roots were in the hills and farms of eastern Slovakia. His religious influences were Roman Catholic, and his social influences were small industrial communities in Connecticut and Pennsylvania. Like the Eastern European Jewish background that inspired the religion of socialism in the younger Kristol and his ethnic contemporaries, these factors in Novak's life shaped his early leftist views. "I identified with the sense of community of the European villages and the familiar neighborhoods of my youth," he writes, "and with 'labor' rather than 'capital.' " For these identities had religious and ethnic associations. "Capitalists seemed always to be Protestants, either Calvinist or Episcopalian."[26] Novak's education seemed to rationalize and intensify these prejudices. He read heavily in European Catholic literature—de Maistre, Lamennais, Chesterton, Belloc, Marcel, and especially Charles Péguy. Now the socialist ideal became especially compelling to Novak. It seemed to express the best of the Judaeo-Christian moral system. However more effective capitalism was in providing material goods, socialism had moral superiority over it.[27] But for Novak too the dream faded. He came to ask, "If an ideal doesn't work, isn't that evidence that it is out of touch with human reality? Isn't that a sign that it is a *false* ideal?"[28]

So Novak eventually resolved to examine capitalism for its theological meanings and significance. *The Spirit of Democratic Capitalism*[29] became an effort at justification and at the same time a critique of the rival socialist alternative. Such an effort led to some considerations of human nature.

Novak's comments on this question raise a familiar theme. The socialist ideal, he says, carries a large promise, a promise

---

26 Michael Novak, *The Spirit of Democratic Capitalism* (New York, 1982), p. 23.

27 Novak, p. 23, pp. 197–198.

28 Novak, p. 198.

29 Novak's subject does not embrace all countries that are formally capitalistic in their economic structures; it excludes such "authoritarian" capitalist nations as Brazil.

that a "new socialist man" will emerge from the ruins of destructive capitalism, a virtuous individual unexemplified in human history heretofore. But democratic capitalism "promises no such thing." "Its political economy ... is designed for sinners. That is, for humans as they are."[30] And again a fundamental difference in perspective maintains. Novak describes two types of revolutionary traditions, the utopian and the realist. "Utopian revolutionaries," he writes, "imagine that the source of human evil lies in social structures and systems and that in removing these they will remove evil and virtue will flourish." Realists, on the other hand, insist that evil lies in the self and in the inherent deficiencies of all collective organizations. Morality cannot be generated by a new social order, neither spontaneously by a new human nature thus realized nor by an elite entrusted to its imposition on the larger group. "For the realists," Novak says "morality flows from individual will and act."[31]

The democratic capitalist spirit, according to Novak, is suspicious of any rule of the saints; it knows that it will eventuate in a rule of tyrants. And this concern necessarily focuses the attention of the realist inward. Those European thinkers and American statesmen who effected the American Revolution illustrate the best tradition of realist revolution. "The seminal thinkers who set democratic capitalism upon its historical course," Novak writes, "were exceedingly practical men, thoroughly sobered by the human capacity for sin and illusion."[32] And by this kind of emphasis Novak places himself in the tradition of Burke and Babbitt. For if human nature is disposed to evil, how is freedom justifiable? Burke's formulation is classic: "Society cannot exist," he writes, "unless a controlling power upon will and appetite be placed somewhere, and the less of it there is within, the more there must be without. It is ordained in the external constitution of things, that men of intemperate

minds cannot be free. Their passions forge their fetters."[33] So
the thinkers who shaped the spirit of democratic capitalism,
Novak says, were obsessed with inner controls. Even the maxim
"time is money" was a reflection of this obsession, a new
command for inner self-discipline. Furthermore, democratic
capitalism cannot survive without a traditionalist moral culture
that will furnish these controls. Democratic capitalism is liberal
in its respect for freedom and in its demands for a competitive
economic system. But it is conservative in its reliance on existing
social institutions and ethical social norms. These, Novak argues,
must furnish the means for an inner discipline that will make
outer freedom effective.[34]

Novak goes even further in his book than Kristol does in
trying to relate contemporary conservatism, that is, his defense
of democratic capitalism, to the religious traditions of the West.
He does so in a manner that again reveals continuity in the line
of conservative thinking from Babbitt to the contemporaries. To
be sure, in considering capitalism as a theological issue, Novak
disavows any claim that capitalism is supported by Christianity
or that the verity of one depends in any way on that of the other.
Only liberationist theologians today take the truly transcendent
character of the Gospels and try to make them a blueprint for
social policies. But Novak does believe that democratic capitalism has absorbed certain ideals that derive from a Christian
outlook and understanding of life.[35] He discusses six points of
Christian theology that he judges appropriate to the spirit of
democratic capitalism, of which one, the Incarnation, is especially germane to this discussion.

Christians who know and accept the true meaning of the
Incarnation, Novak says, must disavow the whole tradition of
utopian socialism. For the Incarnation informs us first that God
entered the world as flesh and walked among human beings as

---

33 Quoted in *The Portable Conservative Reader*, ed. Russell Kirk (New York, 1982),
p. 48.
34 Novak, p. 91, pp. 120–121.
35 Novak, pp. 353–356.

man. "He accepted for Himself the human condition, including
the worst it might offer. . . ." God did not send legions of angels
with Christ to save the world. Christ brought a message of hope,
not of utopia. However persistently some Christians have tried
to derive a larger promise from the Incarnation and to make it
the means of deliverance from all constraints of human evil,
they have really misread its meaning.[36] "The point of the Incarnation," Novak declares, "is to respect the world as it is, to
acknowledge its limits, to recognize its weaknesses, irrationali-
ties, and evil forces, and to disbelieve any promises that the
world is now or ever will be transformed into the City of God."[37]
For the single greatest temptation for Christians is to persuade
themselves that the salvation brought by Christ has also altered
the human condition. Moreover, the realistic Christian will
fortify himself by the Incarnation against all promises of "an
eschatological break" with the past and a new beginning for the
human race. "The pure fury of reformers can kill," Novak
warns. "Those who claim enlightened virtue often carry unex-
amined viciousness in their hearts."[38] What Babbitt descried in
extending his view of an empirical human nature to an understanding of social and political behavior, Novak similarly comes
to describe from within the categories of a Christian view of
life.

IV

Babbitt's application of his human dualism to affairs of state
raised for him another important matter. Like the individual, a
society, insofar as it listened only to its "lower self," was free to
follow its impulses, to yield to the pressures of the hour, to
accept any bold scheme for its metamorphosis. It could do so to
the extent that it had freed itself from restraints, from a
countervailing will that served as a check on its appetites and
emotions. These restraints were critical for Babbitt. For like the

36 Novak, pp. 340–341.
37 Novak, p. 341.
38 Novak, pp. 342–343.

individual, society too had a lower and a higher self. And, like Burke, Babbitt located the sources of society's higher will in its imaginative grasp of the controlling power of tradition. For Babbitt this power, felt to be a living reality of the present, alone guarantees that any community of individuals will not succumb to the facile appeal of sensationalists and demagogues. The imaginative power of the symbols of the past, Babbitt believed, draws the individual back into an ethical center that exercises a restraining control against the "lawless expansion of his natural self." To the extent that such individuals typify any given community, so will that community be stable and orderly, and so too will the process of change avoid violence and upheaval.[39] And yet at the same time that Babbitt urged these considerations, he knew how uncertain they were for his own country. Despite Babbitt's admiration for the achievements of the Founding Fathers, he still knew the United States to be a traditionless society that celebrated its origins in rebellion from all Old World ways, a capitalist society that seemed to worship progress and technological change as the essence of its life, and not a society likely to yoke itself to an imaginative conservatism in the Burkean tradition. And is that fact not the intrinsic problem of conservatism in the United States?

George F. Will knows that it is, and that concern governs his brand of conservative thinking. Grandson of a Lutheran minister and product of central Illinois, Will traces his intellectual pedigree to the philosophical "Tory" conservatives—Burke, Newman, Disraeli, Henry Adams, Babbitt, More, Viereck, and others. And for this reason Will feels slightly uncomfortable with those writers embraced by the "neoconservative" label. They are solid citizens, Will says, but they do not have "stained-glass minds."[40] "Neoconservatives do not really mourn the passing of the thirteenth century; feudal codes, heraldic banners, serried ranks of bishops, the lower orders tugging at their forelocks—that sort of good stuff." One has the emphatic sense

39 Babbitt, *Democracy and Leadership*, pp. 142–143.
40 George F. Will, *The Pursuit of Virtue and Other Tory Notions* (New York, 1982), p. 40.

in reading Will that he, like Babbitt, was born conservative. He is exorcizing no radical ghosts from a leftist past. And, writing in the *New Republic,* he has urged that American conservatism needs "a Burke, a Disraeli," a more thoughtful, principled leadership.[41] In many ways Will's syndicated newspaper col-umns give us a fair sense of Babbitt's mentality applied to the contemporary facts of American life.

Will's glance at present-day America uncovers as many Rousseauistic influences as Babbitt's in his time. Our popular culture and conventional wisdom celebrate an unreflective in-dividualism; we wallow in subjectivity; we judge one opinion as inherently good as another, no matter how ill formed; we honor the street wisdom of the inarticulate. Our nation has become a democracy of the sentiments, and nowhere is this more danger-ously the case than in higher education. Will is at one with Babbitt on this score. He laments the tragic decline of the humanities in our universities, for these, properly pursued, create and sustain a sense of a higher wisdom beyond the whim of undergraduate genius. But this notion of humanistic educa-tion moves against the prevailing tide, against our cult of intuition and our education in self-expression. *Sentio ergo sum* summarizes our prevailing educational credo. Our modern conceit preaches that education serves to help us choose between alternative lifestyles, and such intellectual agnosticism has turned our colleges into "academic cafeterias offering junk food for the mind." The forgotten lesson in this emphasis, Will states, is that democracy is essentially irrelevant to a university's purpose.[42]

Will is saying, in short, that our educational system has betrayed its essential function. It has failed to sustain a common trust of learning, moral wisdom, and collective historical expe-rience. It has ceased to be the vehicle of America's higher self in Babbitt's meaning of that word. And if education has failed in

41 Will, "In Defense of the Welfare State," *The New Republic* (May 9, 1983), p. 21.
42 Will, *The Pursuit of Virtue,* pp. 24–26. One example of our sentimentalist culture that Will mentions was the public bathos, the vigils and weeping, surrounding the death of John Lennon, rock star.

this responsibility, what more can we expect of our public life in general? For decades, Will believes, the liberal mind has been at work in America to strip our public life of meaningful symbols of our shared experiences and values. It has flayed these ideals in the name of individual rights and private conscience. And today school children who wish to perform a Nativity play have fewer rights in the courts than the pornographer. Nazis are free to preach their venom of hatred in Skokie, Illinois, because the liberal says that truth should be decided in the marketplace.[43] This matter is not a frivolous one for Will. We suffer from an excess of individual freedom, and it takes its toll on our community. Our "public space" is being neutered, and "symbolic nakedness" erodes the common essence and spirit that give life and vitality to any society. The community's right to celebrate the various beliefs that leaven its culture, Will avers, yields dangerously today to a court system that recognizes only individuals.[44]

A great society will have an ennobling sense of its traditions; our society functions increasingly under a sentimentality of the commonplace. The culture of democracy contributes dangerously to these effects. It is a long-standing trend in America, dating probably from the time of Andrew Jackson. But Will questions what public good, what higher purpose is served when the television enters the White House and shows President Ford buttering his breakfast toast in the kitchen. Why enshroud our high public offices with the details of the commonplace? And what of the "denim presidency" of Jimmy Carter and his bluejeans Kitchen Cabinet? How can a society exercise a set of high standards and promote its higher self when its most important officers drape themselves in the garb of Georgia hillbillies?[45] For the kind of conservative that Will is, the state is important, functionally and symbolically. It must serve, somehow, as the centerpiece of a high and worthy public life.

43 Will, *The Pursuit of Virtue,* pp. 24–25, p. 93.
44 Will, *The Pursuit of Virtue,* p. 93.
45 Will, *The Pursuit of Virtue,* p. 181, pp. 242–243.

However much we may unfortunately lack the symbols of crown and scepter that give meaning in traditionalist societies, we still have no excuse to trivialize government and public life in the name of egalitarianism. But government does trivialize itself, Will says, when, for example, the Department of Transportation makes a study of car pooling and finds to its horror that mostly men are doing the driving. It ponders how it might rectify this crisis. Says one official: "The issue is equality."[46]

Will most directly confronts the problem of conservatism in America in the way Babbitt did. Babbitt had deep reservations about industrial capitalism and its dehumanizing effects, and he certainly knew that a free economic system did not coexist easily with a traditionalist view of life. Nevertheless, Babbitt did not write at length on this problem. Will is acutely aware of it and addresses it. "Capitalism," he writes, "undermines traditional social structures and values: it is a relentless engine of change, a revolutionary inflamer of appetites, enlarger of expectations, diminisher of patience." Capitalism, to use Babbitt's language, spurs the lower self of individuals and society and feeds its expansive nature. And the "neoconservatives," Will believes, are too cozy with capitalism, too indifferent to the lust of appetite that it promotes.[47] For capitalism, furthermore, has promoted a social structure that tends to minimalize the state and deprive the state of its right and necessary role as moral and symbolic bond among citizens. This situation is the legacy of Adam Smith: The weak state is left to be the prey of powerful interests; the notion of public-spiritedness declines, and the rhetoric of entitlements succeeds. Contemporary conservatism is dangerously indifferent to these effects, Will believes. "Such conservatism neglects the craving for ennobling passions and enlarging public enterprises," a craving well understood by great conservatives like Disraeli and Churchill.[48] Will once tried to convey this spirit in an eloquent and moving essay entitled

46 Will, *The Pursuit of Virtue*, p. 243.
47 Will, *The Pursuit of Virtue*, p. 36.
48 Will, *The Pursuit of Virtue*, p. 285, p. 297.

"The National Cathedral: Symphony in Stone," a tribute to Washington, D.C.'s great Gothic edifice. He made this point:

In the great cities of the civilization from which this Republic is descended, the noblest works were built to serve religion—the Parthenon in Athens, Saint Peter's in Rome, Notre Dame in Paris, Westminster Abbey in London. They are stone memories of a premodern age when cities were supposed to be something other than mere arenas for acquisition, when civil society was supposed to serve ends other than the pursuit of self-interest, when civil law was supposed to be patterned after a higher law.[49]

Very likely this concern expresses the link in intellectual conservatism between Babbitt and the contemporaries. Will is not correct in saying that writers like Kristol or Novak, in their defense of capitalism, are indifferent to the higher self of American society. In fact, each is greatly troubled by what we have come to call the "contradictions of capitalism." For capitalism, as Kristol says, generates its own discontents even as it succeeds. The demand for gratification of desires becomes ascendent, fueled by advertising media in a free press. Kristol believes that it is well to remember that the intellectual traditions from which American capitalist ideals sprang were much concerned with inner morality and control. The public and the state, moreover, have a stake in preserving these moral norms.[50] Likewise, Novak points out, the successes of democratic capitalism undermine its cultural order. Affluence corrupts; advertising appeals to base material interests. Parents brought up in poverty have trouble raising their children in affluence, in passing on those habits of self-discipline and deferred pleasures necessary for their own successes. It is all the more imperative, Novak says, that our capitalist system be tamed and corrected by "a moral-cultural system independent of commerce."[51] In fact, no conservative would deny that America will probably

49 Will, *The Pursuit of Virtue*, p. 329.
50 Kristol, *Reflections*, p. 175. See also the essay "Pornography, Obscenity, and the Case for Censorship," in this volume, pp. 43–54.
51 Novak, *Democratic Capitalism*, p. 31–32.

always confront these inner tensions in its culture. Conservative opinion will surely continue to fluctuate between the ideals of a state that is externally free in its economic life and a society that is disciplined and restrained by moral controls in its inner life. And these concerns will also mean that conservative opinion in the United States will thrive within the spirit of Irving Babbitt's earlier formulation.

Richard B. Hovey

Literature and the
American College: Irving Babbitt
Yesterday and Today

A reverence for intellect, a feeling of unity with the history of mankind.

—John Jay Chapman

ON THE SAME day I scribble this opening sentence, Irving Babbitt is in the news. Well—not explicitly named, nor his books alluded to. Granted, some qualifying is in order. I refer to an editorial in one of our great metropolitan dailies, "A Closer Look at the Colleges."[1] Almost every problem Babbitt wrestled with, nearly eighty years ago in his first book, is touched on in this bit of journalism.

To itemize the "news": About a quarter of America's youth are graduates of four-year colleges. By September 1984, more than six million more will be enrolled, plus five million in our two-year colleges. "A child's chances for education beyond high school are greater in this country than anywhere else in the

---

1 *The Washington Post* (August 10, 1984).

world, and by a wide margin." So writes the editorialist. The consequences?

He informs us that the Carnegie Foundation for the Advancement of Teaching intends soon to make a study of undergraduate education. He then lists familiar academic woes: the decline in scores made by high school seniors in the Scholastic Aptitude Test; a similar decline in the scores of college seniors on the verbal section of the Graduate Record Examination. Whatever is wrong in the lower schools, the colleges are not correcting it. Our editorial writer adds: "The confusion over curriculum and its purposes is as great at the college level as in the high schools." We learn further that a signal change in the colleges since the 1960's is a huge expansion in business administration programs, a growing "pressure for vocational specialization"; consequently more "fragmentation than ever." While increasingly the United States becomes involved in geopolitics, students become "more parochial": their competence in foreign languages diminishes as does "interest in every other subject lying outside the three-mile limit."

As to college teachers, Ernest L. Boyer, president of the foundation, thinks "that younger faculty are driven by the race for tenure and older faculty slide into isolation in their specialties." Faculty morale? It is apparently "deteriorating." At this point the editorialist interjects: "Here the Carnegie study approaches subjects that don't lend themselves to neat statistical summaries . . . the administrators' usual preoccupation with sheer numbers."

Were his ghost among us, maybe Babbitt would wear an I-told-you-so smile. None of this news—unless its quantitative immensity—would surprise him. He saw, diagnosed, and prescribed for such ills when, back in 1908, he published *Literature and the American College.*[2] At present, the main thing we can expect is that educators will redouble their status quo efforts. Only a small minority will have the insight, concern, and intellectual courage to reexamine the bases on which their

2 (Boston, 1908; Clifton, N.J., 1972 reprint.)

whole enterprise rests. Babbitt went straight to those fundamen-
tals. We may or not accept all his first principles. The questions
they entail, however, are wrenching.

For several reasons, this chapter concentrates on Babbitt's
initial volume. As one who for almost four decades and at a wide
variety of our colleges and universities has taught English, I am
curious about this exceptional classroom teacher,[3] about his
premises and how applicable they might be now. Certainly
Literature and the American College was a trail-breaking study. As
of 1908 the baker's dozen of his reputable American contemporaries in criticism had done nothing like it. Babbitt was the
first to contribute a book-length work that comprises a way of
criticism, a scrutiny of how literary studies were being conducted in our institutions of higher learning, and an analysis of the
relations among these to our culture. Like us, Babbitt lived in an
era of revolutionary expansion in education. A sizable part of his
career, both as a student and a faculty member at Harvard
(1885–1933), coincided with the presidency of Charles William
Eliot. Eliot, serene in his faith in progress and attuned to the
nation's advances in democracy and technology and industry,
strengthened the graduate and professional schools, drew to
Cambridge eminent scholars, reformed the undergraduate
curriculum with his "elective system," and converted Harvard
College into a university—on more or less the Germanic model
and at about the same time The Johns Hopkins University was
being built. Babbitt saw the necessity for the development of
universities and the accompanying specialization, recognized the
gains, and counted up the debits.

At any rate, his first book is a compendium, at least the seed
bed, of his subsequent thinking. Crucial here is a glance at the
bêtes noires on whom Babbitt settled as the source of many of our
troubles: Francis Bacon and Jean Jacques Rousseau. His interpretations of these two thinkers—*Rousseau and Romanticism* (1919)
is his most widely read work—are not entirely invulnerable. It

---

3 See *Irving Babbitt: Man and Teacher*, eds. Frederick L. Manchester and Odell Shepard
(New York, 1969).

can be charged that he is scarcely fair-minded, oversimplifies, and fails to offer a comprehensive or nuanced account of their achievements. Per contra, I submit that the polemical Babbitt uses this pair as symbols, his stalking horses, so to speak. His assault is against what might be labeled Baconianism and Rousseauism: a far-reaching complex of world views, methodologies, and values he perceives as eventuating in threats to civilization. His Bacon-Rousseau polarity provides a structure for his analysis of higher education in 1908 and underscores his persisting cogency in 1980's America.

Propagandist for science, Bacon urged us to seek, discover, and follow the laws of the natural world; thus gain dominion over nature; improve the environment; and raise hopes for "a general and systematic advance of the human race." Bacon's shibboleth is "Knowledge is power." But to the "law for man"— Babbitt translates this Emersonian phrase as "the wisdom and experience of the race"—Bacon gives little more than a perfunctory nod. He is, then, "the scientific naturalist and humanitarian." In due time he fathers utilitarianism, positivism, excessive faith in technology, and the authority of standards "purely quantitative." With the arrival of the Enlightenment, knowledge had become so extensive that Bacon's Renaissance ambitions were impossible. Perforce, Baconianism began to make for fragmentation and to require ever more specialization.

Rousseau gets a comparable tag: "sentimental naturalist." He, too, held to the law of nature, but with a difference from Bacon: i.e., to be in harmony with nature meant to follow one's impulses. These being essentially good needed few restrictions, those of wisdom or otherwise. Rousseau did not ignore the law for man; he simply equated it with his own temperament. He thus became a champion of liberty and of a vague all-embracing sympathy and the pathfinder par excellence of a new individualism, which would make its laissez-faire way to extremism. So, for the arts of the Romantics he contributed an essential. To the ego, the personal imagination, the private heart, he brought a novel preeminence: their own authenticity, the justification of untrammeled self-expression. And here these two proponents of progress, the scientist and the sentimentalist, join in a fateful union. However much they differed about society, government, schooling, with both Baconianism and Rousseauism began the disintegration of authority, whether that of religion or of the humanistic exemplars. The effect was to shunt aside any serious consideration of the past as help or guidance for the human condition.

I

Today no educator would recant his faith in the magnitude of our undertaking. For Babbitt, though, such a faith is endangered by the "fallacy of confusing growth in the human sense with mere expansion." We are now ever so busy in academe. In 1908 Babbitt explained how and why: "The task of organizing and operating a huge and complex educational machinery has left us scant leisure for calm reflection." We are fantastically bigger than when Babbitt wrote, one palpable reason being that we have so many students. He seems prophetic when he comments: "There is also a laudable desire in our colleges to give every-body a chance. Indeed the more humanitarian members of our faculties are ready to waste their energies in trying to elevate youths above the level to which they belong." Questions about his views on an élite and on humanitarianism will be taken up later in my discussion.

Meanwhile, it is worth noting how he probed the Franken-stein syndrome. Babbitt believed that the mind is more impor-tant than all the marvelous tools and techniques we might devise. Thinking of the American talent for organizing, he opposed, when it came to following the ways of the German university, "an excessive faith in intellectual machinery and intellectual appliances." He was equally alert to extramural circumstances inimical to the idea of liberal education: "the almost irresistible pressure of commercial and industrial in-fluence." To these we must now add the powers of govern-ment, local and in especial the federal. A nice question occurs:

Would Babbitt be amazed on today's campuses by the increase in number and power of those in administrative posts, layer upon layer of managerial experts, some of them with limited experience in the classroom and little proof of achievement as scholars? It is from these newly emerging types the public ordinarily hears as authoritative spokesmen on education.

What Babbitt did not quite foresee and state explicitly is that, in both our ethos and methods of operating, we academicians have created a gigantic bureaucracy. Our rhetoric is lofty. In actual fact our model is taken from the worlds of business-industry-and-big government. The bureaucrat type—whether faculty member or administrator, he is the "operator" who knows as if by second nature how to manipulate—customarily wins most of the esteem and awards, monetary and others. Babbitt had a clue when he described his own era as "an age that hopes to accomplish its main ends by the appointment of committees . . . in lieu of real communion among men." Committees, nearly countless in today's larger universities, ipso facto call for compromise. Their usual accomplishment is the lowest common denominator, arrived at by majority vote. The unuttered instruction they follow is to tinker with a cog but never to upset the machinery. The efficient running of an overcomplicated organization fosters smooth mediocrity; priority goes to the company man. An honest clash of ideas and opinions disturbs professorial decorum. Questioning, opposing, the status quo is muffled, if not easily silenced.

What is happening is a steady weakening of even the pretense to anything like the traditional faculty hierarchy, or like earned authority. No doubt, politicking occurred at the very start of the university in the Middle Ages and has continued through the centuries. I am pointing to its accelerated hypertrophy. In department meetings and committee sessions, the new arrivals, the lower ranks, the young, those as yet lacking proven credentials other than having tenure, often speak out with a self-assurance that balding grey heads might envy. Experience counts for almost zero. Evidently this change in manners is in part due to the campus disturbances of the 1960's and earlier

1970's, and the watchword "Don't trust anyone over thirty." Yet this is not exactly the perennial warfare between young turks and old guard. In the 1980's the young faculty seem certain that they are "with it," are innovative. Babbitt saw the origins as far back as 1908 in "our disregard for age and experience . . . our prejudice in favor of young men and new ideas." From what today we call built-in obsolescence he drew this analogy: "Now, just as it has been found good economy when a locomotive begins to show signs of wear to consign it to the scrap heap and substitute a new one, so there is a tendency to prefer to even a middle-aged man a young man whose vital machinery is still unimpaired."

Another reason for the gigantism and complexity of academe today is that, instead of being predominantly educational, our universities and colleges are set up to meet the multifarious ad hoc requirements of society. In this respect, they follow rather than lead: They produce leaders only in the form of specialized experts. The Baconian academic, according to Babbitt, seeks "the highest efficiency" in "certain practical or scientific results." His ideal for human advancement is to provide "training for service and training for power." How to use this power constructively? The Baconian gives no satisfactory answer—as, for instance, we recognize now in the threat of thermonuclear war. But service: How and why could Babbitt doubt the humanitarian component here, one of our noblest ideals? He questions it, not because as an anti-Rousseauist he is calloused against suffering, injustice, and all the other ills we are heir to. He attacks this ideal because humanitarianism of itself is not enough. Compassionate generosity needs, to be effective, the vision and prevision of the liberated and disciplined mind. When humanitarian values do not have their proper place in the house of intellect, both the ends and means of higher education can be seduced into chaos and self-defeat. To exalt the sympathetic at the cost of diluting the principles of self-mastery and of painstaking discrimination between alternatives, principles basic to classical humanism, encourages a facile faith in scientism and an easy self-comfort in the warmth of our good intentions. Holding to this conviction as it applies to America's professoriate, Babbitt declared: "The idea of quality, of high and objective standards of human excellence, has been equally compromised by the impressionism of the Rousseauist and by the Baconian neglect of everything that cannot be expressed in terms of quantity and power."

Remarking that we are "hypnotized by numbers," Babbitt puts this question: If the American college or university is to be in the best sense both democratic and humanitarian, should it "Level down and suit itself to the point of view of the average individual. . . . Because the claims of the average man have been slighted in times past, does it therefore follow that we must now slight the claims of the superior man?" For too many of us professors the answer seems to be yes—although who has ever heard anyone who does not verbally endorse academic "excellence"? I am thinking of grade inflation, a development that has subtly and almost unawares taken us over. How this phenomenon began is problematic. Anyhow, the "gentlemen's *C,*" a mark for generations accepted for decent and average accomplishment in most courses, is today regarded by the majority of students as edging toward "failure"; they consider a *B* as fair for a respectable average, the *A* for merely above-average achievement. Students must have *A*'s and *B*'s if they are to continue in school after college or hope favorably to impress an employer. So, in our semester reports the percentage of high marks has multiplied in the last two decades. Lumped with the other *A*'s are those students, usually few, who beyond question have done the superior work. Maybe these are the ones whose "claims" we "slight"— to their own loss and to society's. Is this one of the prices paid for big-organization schooling?

II

In a phrase I recently heard, educators are striving for "a creative tension between excellence and equality." Magic? Babbitt elucidates it: that we are trying to provide "something of everything for everybody . . . a democracy of studies to meet the needs of a student democracy." Today, responding to the swift demographic and economic developments in America, many an educator has come upon a key word that inspirits and comforts: "Pluralism." Perhaps we are approaching an equation: Plurality of values amounts to plurality of educational goals and methods. If so, then our colleges and universities had better go off in all directions as promptly as expediency dictates. Such centrifugal nonphilosophy, though, defeats not only coherence in theory, but also widens in actuality the gulf between power and ideas in this country. The pluralist will be pleased to graduate a one-sided specialist "if only this fragment is serviceable." At the antipodes, Babbitt held that the college should provide "training for wisdom and training for character." His was no naive supposition that discipline in the humanities would guarantee a bumper crop of philosopher-kings. He did, however, see that since the university offers "encyclopedic fullness" and the pursuit of many specialities, the liberal education proper to the college must "insist on the idea of quality . . . hold all the faster to its humane standards." A later historian of criticism, emphasizing what differentiates study of the humanities from the natural and social sciences, has written: "The concern of the humanities, by their very definition, is not analysis without synthesis, description without evaluation, abstraction apart from individual feeling."[4] Toward keeping this distinction clear and toward maintaining standards, Babbitt would have all college students study the past "as links in that unbroken chain of literary and intellectual tradition which extends from the ancient to the modern world." For a new nation like America in particular, it was crucial to bring home to the student this continuity, to implant "that right feeling and respect for the past . . . that feeling which, as has been rightly said, distinguishes more than any other the civilized man from the barbarian."

We have noted that Babbitt respected the need of specialization in the university. He also honored the need for the humanitarian element in the lower schools. These diverse pressures, though, one working downward from the graduate schools and

---

4 Walter Jackson Bate, *Prefaces to Criticism* (New York, 1952; 1959 reprint), p. xi.

the other upward from the kindergarten, have some dubious effects on the college, more dubious than he envisaged. He thought it only "likely between them to leave very little of humanistic standards." In fact, we now have their end products. At the one end are honors programs that too often ape graduate studies in trying to develop research and critical techniques before the student has a broad enough background, historic comprehension, and maturity of experience to read his chosen texts with insight and sound judgment. At the other end, some professors in the classroom adopt elementary school pedagogy, with "buzz sessions," field trips, even to donning costumes in playlets, the hoped-for intention seeming to be learning-by-doing history. Such premature specialization, hyperdemocracy, and misplaced humanitarianism would be, for Babbitt, virtually antieducation. One of the costs he described was a loss of "the delicate balance between sympathy and judgment."

The eroding of standards, the fragmenting of the curriculum, the heedless casting off of tradition, the passing of any vital sense of the communal—all these Babbitt assailed. Fortunately, for him, he did not live to witness how far these processes have gone. Scientists nowadays speak, honestly enough no doubt, about "the explosion of knowledge." Humanities departments fondly suppose the same thing has occurred in their disciplines. This notion has been evidenced over the past couple of decades by the staggering increase in the numbers and varieties of courses they offer—they call it "enriching" the curriculum. Often these courses are remarkably narrowed in subject matter. Some aim at linking together the study of selected works of literature with that of some current social concern: say, drugs, crime, sports, whatever. The survey courses, often requirements in the past, have generally lost favor. Granted, such courses in their attempt to introduce a period of literary or cultural history are bound to be sketchlike, to consist of selections, to be difficult for anyone to teach well. Nevertheless, the survey did at least aim to afford students an acquaintance with classic figures and works, a sense of chronology, some historic perspective, some awareness of continuities and developments and relationships, an outline of world views and their influence on the individual master artist's expression: a pattern that might make some sense to students, building blocks on which to stand before they entered advanced studies more special to their own preferences. Babbitt reminds us: "The mere fact that men once read the same book at college was no slight bond of fellowship."

Instead, we now offer a smörgåsbord. From it, undergraduates have remarkable freedom to choose. How the new varieties are set up and taught is largely catch-as-catch-can. With no concern for precedent, each teacher may pretty well choose according to his personal likes and idiosyncrasies. I myself have yet to meet a colleague who recalls that Harvard's Eliot tried a similar curricular arrangement with his "free electives." The results at Harvard were that students rushed into the easier and more popular courses; the hyperindividualism of the nonsystem did not work. Babbitt sized up this earlier reform: "Having bestowed upon the student the full liberty of Rousseau, it is evident that President Eliot would have him use this liberty in a Baconian spirit." Babbitt was not calling for a rigid hierarchy of required courses. (The "Great Books" idea and its various offspring were not of his creation.) He hoped only to check the opposite extreme: "the democratic absurdity of asserting that all studies are, and by right should be, free and equal." That was too much for him to swallow: "The wisdom of all the ages is to be as naught compared with the inclination of a sophomore."

With respect to the wrecking of standards, an odd irony enters our story. Not too long ago Yale's President Giamatti—himself a scholar-teacher of English and comparative literature—pointed out that in many places it was "those who taught in humanities departments who wrote the guidelines that displaced the requirements for a B.A., who eloquently undermined the writing and the foreign language requirements, who instituted the grading reforms."[5]

5 A. Bartlett Giamatti, *The University and the Public Interest* (New York, 1981), p. 52.

However we want to explain this self-destructiveness, our humanities departments often try to bring into their classrooms as large a number of students as we can. So, preoccupied with problems of motivation, we exert our ingenuity in offering subjects and using methods that promise to appeal to students. For Babbitt, such ploys negate "the idea of liberal culture by denying that some subjects are more humane than others in virtue of their intrinsic quality, and quite apart from individual tastes and preferences." Rank heresy today! Recently, in a sizable audience of faculty members and graduate students of English, I heard a youngish professor attacking an older colleague, a scholar-critic who for decades has earned every honor given him. The attack focused on this man's then newly published defense of the centrality of the classical ways of literary studies. He was charged with no less than "bad faith." The gravamen was that he upheld, like Babbitt, the superior value of the classics. The right position, so we learned, is that almost any readings, surely including products of "pop" culture, can, with a bright teacher having up-to-date methods and outlook, be solidly worthwhile for our students. At the finale, the lecturer drew loud, long, and hearty applause, and not a single question hinting at doubt. Anything goes? So it seems.

Babbitt, at any rate, would never abide the student-centered study of the humanities. One of his comments is à propos: "In selecting reading, the modern-language teacher often does not consult even his own impressions, but the impressions of his students, and in his endeavor to secure their interest condescends deliberately to their crudity and immaturity." Consciously or not, we today regard students as our customers; and the customer is always right. Some of us have also set up "complaint department" procedures, being more anxious about students' rights than about their responsibilities. Babbitt strikes directly: "The test of a teacher, after all, is his power so to stimulate his students as to raise their interests to a higher level. . . . the vital question is not whether a teacher inspires interest, but what kind of interest he inspires and in what quality of undergraduate." His fervor pushes Babbitt so far as to recommend that in the classroom we should strive to reach the "more capable . . . even at the risk of boring the dullards."

We are now so gingerly about introducing the older classics to our students because we attempt to relate these works to the actual here-and-now experience of the youngsters. Again, Babbitt takes the opposite direction: We should lead our students to recognize that a study of the proven classics may afford "an avenue of escape from ourselves and enable us to become participants in the universal life. It is thus truly educative in that it leads him who studies it out and away from himself." He is hardly urging escapism. Babbitt's hope was that the few truly initiated into "the Hellenic spirit" would have the power of good influence even if only through their "ability to escape from contemporary illusions." He was pointing to the bandwagon silliness and waste among intellectuals agog to take up the latest fads in education.

For instance, the most common complaint undergraduates make about a literature course is its failure to include enough class discussion. For some, the tedium of even an excellent lecture! In this protest against their being "passive receptacles" of information, they are supported by the statistics of the psychologists: that education occurs only when there is vocal give-and-take between students and professor, when students "participate" in the "learning situation," and so find the way to self-expression. The Socratic method? Yes, maybe ideal. But neither Socrates nor Plato recommended the teaching of philosophy by dialogue for those not yet prepared. I am by no means urging heedlessness to student response: To be condescending or arrogant in the classroom can be one of the deadly sins of the teacher. But for the other extreme of exalting students' opinions and impressions as our main business, of encouraging and rewarding mere self-expression, Babbitt has the rejoinder. Such a professor is like the ancient Sophist who "instructs ingenuous youth in the art of expressing itself before it has anything to express." His belief that the traditional liberal arts curriculum should be mastered, at least in its essentials, by all college students no matter what their later schooling and careers might be, Babbitt summarizes with this wisdom: "It embodied the seasoned and matured experience of a multitude of men, extending over a considerable time, as to the studies they actually found helpful and formative."

III

Studies. That word leads us to questions about the relationship between a college professor's teaching and his scholarship in the humanities. Present-day orthodoxy is that the professor whose scholarship is proved by a bulk of publication will ipso facto be best in the classroom. Yet so specialized and often esoteric are the majority of items most of us get into print that in actual practice very few of these bring consequential gains to the undergraduate courses we teach. (Directing a graduate seminar is, needless to say, a different affair.) With regard to new-made Ph.D.'s, it is rather similar. As a rule their years of graduate study are no proof of liberal culture. They foster limited views, and afford minimal preparation for what and how they will teach. Babbitt's charge is pungent: "The young Ph.D., with his one-sided interest in his own specialty, is turned loose upon it, and often allowed to inflict his naive enthusiasms on undergraduates."

At the Harvard of Babbitt's time the division of labor in literary studies was different from ours. There was, on the one hand, the "philologist," generally linguistic in his approach, trained in the Germanic fashion to be "scientific," and usually finding medieval literature the richest field for his plowing. The other sort of professor Babbitt called the "dilettante." The philologists, who predominated, were, Babbitt remarks, "ready to grant a place to literature as an occasional relaxation from the more serious and strenuous labors of philological analysis." Those whose tasks were in the relaxation area could be "nothing more than graceful purveyors of aesthetic solace, and arbiters of the rhetorical niceties." Babbitt deplored this gap: "The philologist and the dilettante are equally far from feeling and making others feel that true art and literature stand in vital relation to human nature as a whole." Neither could represent or in any way inculcate the critical spirit: e.g., meet the difficulties of discriminating, of clarifying values, or risking judgment, of facing squarely the moral issues implicit in all serious literature, of wrestling with ideas that have consequences in life as we live it.

As if cued by the scientist who quite properly might look into the tiniest details of his data, the philologist was eager to investigate the tiny details of his specialty. Babbitt warned us how such proceedings might develop distortions and sterility in the humanities: "If the minutiae rather than the larger aspects of the classics are insisted upon, the taste for small things will spread like a contagion . . . and we shall soon be threatened with an epidemic of pedantry." To be sure, pedantry has been endemic with us scholars over the millennia. The more things change, the more they remain the same, the old French saw. Today's pedantry, I am going to suggest, takes a different yet recognizable form.

To return, however, to Babbitt and a long-ago opponent of his, Dr. Hugo Munsterberg. This Doctor survives among us more than we suspect. He had been brought to the Harvard faculty from Germany, became a professor of psychology, and was the author of several works on that subject as well as on the philosophy of scholarship and education. To Munsterberg's pigeon-holing mentality there were only two sorts of scholars: the "productive" and the "receptive"—those who "discover" knowledge and those who "distribute" it. The productive were investigators, devoted to *strengwissenschaftliche Methode,* rigorously scientific methods, which nurtured "research and original work." Indisputably, all this fits nicely the training and hoped-for triumphs of the scientist. (The present-day physicist need not look very far into the past; to make a breakthrough, he would scarcely have to climb again with Galileo Pisa's Leaning Tower.) In literary studies, however, as Babbitt viewed them, our analogous fever for originality is "pedantry."

Accept or not Babbitt's position, we in the humanities today are loyal Munsterbergers when we demand, for advancement through the ranks and for merit pay increases, that our faculty be "productive" scholars. Quite simply, this means to publish, *with efficiency and on schedule and in quantity,* "original" contributions. None of us today would dare admit to a colleague that we are merely studying for a better background in, a firmer grip on, a deeper understanding of the subject of some course we are teaching or planning. Never! We are doing research. Despite hit-or-miss prizes by some intramural committee or other to an "outstanding teacher," the larger reality is that we pay only lip service to teaching. Besides the bureaucrat and/or administrative type, the "productive" scholar gets the esteem and the material rewards.

Small wonder that "older faculty slide into isolation in their specialties." Again Carnegie Foundation's Boyer hits the mark regarding "younger faculty driven by the race for tenure." With the overproduction of Ph.D.'s, competition in the academic marketplace is fierce among the young, the publish-or-perish tyranny harsh for them. To gain the foothold of tenure, they are wretchedly anxious to prove in print that they are scholars. For Babbitt, their race is a "straining after a premature 'originality.' " His own view was more kindly and much saner. He preferred that the new Ph.D. be one "who has read widely and thought maturely." Then, on this foundation those with a "turn for research" might "develop naturally" rather than "under artificial pressure." Nowadays we prefer forced feeding, so to say. The more fortunate candidates for tenure will often have a sixth sense for what is in fashion, for making a favorable show in some journal or other with a novel approach, a brand-new interpretation, regardless of its being off center or lacking solid validity. Scholar? Critic?

Babbitt could never have linked to our deluge of print the label "scholar." He held to another definition: "The final test of the scholar must be his power to penetrate his facts and dominate his impressions, and fuse them with the fire of a central purpose." He makes a further requisite for the real thing: "The maturity of judgment that can alone give value to literary scholarship comes, as Longinus has said, if it comes at all, only as the crowning fruit of long experience." He also scores the show of originality whether it comes from premature specialization or something else in this Aristotelian dictum: "The final test of art is not its originality, but its truth to the universal." He goes broad and deep when he offers this definition: "Genuine originality is so immensely difficult because it imposes the task of achieving work that is of general human truth and at the same time intensely individual." But such subtleties in questions of quality are ordinarily beyond today's busy managers. We can scarcely expect an academic boss to assess a faculty member's scholarly achievements or usefulness to the teaching staff except by a safe and demonstrable reliance on the quantitative. (*War and Peace* rates hardly more than a single line in Tolstoi's enumerative bibliography.)

One of the most curious things about our profession—maybe unique—is that often the more eminent a professor is, the less he is expected to teach. Sometimes his highest honor is to do no teaching at all. No, I am not referring to those who have been appointed as exclusively research professors. One may or may not regard this oddity as contempt for teaching; but it does devalue the teaching responsibilities of the professor. Here again, willy nilly, we are following Munsterberg. His first category of scholar, the one who discovers knowledge, is far superior to those who teach it: These latter are merely "imitative." Munsterberg thereupon passes judgment: " 'The purely imitative thinker may make a most excellent teacher. Any one who has a personality, a forcible way of presentation, and an average intellect, will be able to be a fine teacher of any subject at six weeks' notice.' " Scarcely three years ago the president of a large state university was quoted in the mass media as having made this assertion. "An outstanding research professor is not just twice as valuable as an average college teacher; he or she is often 20 to 40 times more valuable."[6] Does a geometric ratio lurk

6 *The Washington Post* (May 28, 1982) p. 1, p. 14, p. 15.

in these numbers, or did a computer disgorge them? Anyhow, this university president and Munsterberg can shake hands across the generations. At the antipodes, Babbitt—who by any rational criteria has to be defined as both a productive scholar and a teacher of unusual potency—has described the endeavor of the humanities teacher this way: "... to coordinate the scattered elements of knowledge, and relate them not only to the intellect but to the will and character; that subtle alchemy by which mere learning is transmuted into culture. The task of assimilating what is best in the past and present, and adapting it to one's own use and the use of others, so far from lacking in originality, calls for something akin to creation."

One means for a university to gain prestige is by recruiting famous scholars, titling them "distinguished professors." During the last quarter century the practice has been accelerated when some of the universities competed among themselves for Nobel Prize winners, usually scientists. Such operations are not new. In Babbitt's time, when some expected Harvard to rival Germany in "productive scholarship," there were recommendations to establish fabulously high-salaried chairs for "the most meritorious investigators and masters of scientific method . . . chosen heroes of research." Evidently the dream was to inspire everybody concerned and to bring an atmosphere of consecration to the temples of learning. Babbitt thought it an illusion that would not meet "our chief educational problem." Numerous universities now have chairs for the distinguished. We also continue to be stuck with the same troubles mentioned in the editorial with which this essay began. For our star system, Babbitt gives us this reminder: "One may shine as a productive scholar, and yet have little or nothing of that humane insight and reflection that can alone give meaning to all subjects, and is especially appropriate in a college teacher."

A figure Babbitt gaped at in his own era he called "that strangest of all anomalies, the hustling scholar." He of course knew that in its Greek root the word *scholar* is bound up with leisure. Today the hustler shines. Regularly committees charged with considering a new appointment or reviewing for a promotion make one of their chief criteria something they call being "professionally active." That means being a member of scholarly organizations, attending meetings, participating in symposia, reading papers before a group of specialists, having "connections," and so forth. The person who toils alone and in silence over the years at a task that may eventuate in a solid contribution is all but lost. Babbitt plays with a metaphor drawn from mechanics: that the scholar is considered inactive unless "the wheels are *visibly* turning."[7] Nowadays we candidly assess professorial worth according to "visibility." Visibility is skill in image making as perfected by celebrities in, say, politics and public entertainment. The professionally active may also be champions in "grantsmanship": the game of getting monetary awards for starting or carrying out some publishable project in literary studies. Connections may be helpful or not in such enterprising. So, without a trace of self-conscious apologizing, we sophisticates in academe now provide "seminars" or workshops in the art of writing up proposals that will open the purse strings. Technique, finding the exact pitch to appeal to the foundations or granting agencies, counts heavily. Perhaps we are learning from Madison Avenue?

Gone now is the old-line philologist; his linguistic descendants, increasingly technical and absorbed in theory, are generally separated from literary studies, and sometimes have departments of their own. The researcher, too, has largely given place to the academic critic—but not in Babbitt's terms.

That the capacity for writing worthwhile criticism is a rather uncommon talent seems to give no one pause. It is only a slight exaggeration to remark that, among academicians, criticism, in numerous respects, has become a game nearly anyone can play. With the revolt against tradition and the breakdown of standards, the narrowing concern with aesthetic technicalities, the inept application from other disciplines to the study of *belles lettres,* the overingenious use of innovative methodologies, the Procrustean forcing of an author or work to fit some predeter-

7 Italics are mine.

mined schema, the tenuousness of finespun analogy making, the placid ignoring of the central in preference for the peripheral, the esoteric manner of the specialist addressing fellow-specialists, the coining of high-sounding and abtruse polysyllables, the downright reveling in obfuscation: nearly anything passes— never mind how sound, comprehensive, or truly insightful it might be so long as it impresses expert manuscript readers and editorial boards as a new approach, a fresh reading. It is as if the would-be critic, uninterested in trying to get at the truth, asks himself: What novel thing can I make out of, "generate from," this piece of literature? (From too many samples I cite only one: how I lately learned that *The House of the Seven Gables* is not essentially a work of fiction; what Hawthorne concocted is "a discourse in epistemology.")

Here, then, are our current fashions. If I understand him rightly, Babbitt would say that we have run into "a veritable pedantry of originality." Both our plethora of farfetched interpretations and the professorial prose that propounds it indicate an inability to read and write. As one scholar has pointed out, this crippling comes from lack of love: i.e., those who thicken our journals this way evidently do not love literature, but read and write "only for career reasons."[8]

Maybe unconscious desperation is the urge: that we seem near to scraping the bottom of the barrel? Our hyperactivity is a symptom of failure of nerve, a loss of faith in literature itself, a lack of conviction that literature has anything valid to say to us about the human condition and that therefore it no longer has any vital or meaningful use for the education of young minds, hearts, consciences. If so, can literature professors justify their continued existence? Does an affirmative answer hide in the newborn to-do over what we call "literary theory"? No respectable English department can manage without a contingent of practitioners in this up-to-date enterprise.

In its vanguard stand, of course, the "deconstructionists."

---

8 Edward L. Comte, "Douglas Bush Remembered," *The American Scholar*, 53 (Summer 1984), 395.

Since a small library of books and articles by and about these theorists has been published, I can hardly provide anything like an adequate account of them and of their opponents. Also, I shall eschew the *ad hominem* arguments as well as the sometimes childish fracas between Yale and Harvard over the controversies the deconstructionists have raised. I can, perforce, barely touch upon the ideological ramifications, social and political, except to note that deconstructionists tend to regard the established classics and traditional ways of studying them as props for the status quo of society, a status quo sorely in need of change—by radical reform or revolution?

Insofar as I understand the deconstructionists—and they present unwonted difficulties to any common reader's mentality, for their preferred style is almost never simple or lucid and their way of thinking strikes me at least on occasion as intellectual legerdemain—they champion a dire extremism. More interested in abstract theorizing than in the concrete variousness of literary experience, they look like philosophers *manqué*. Hyperanalytic in their excessively fine logic chopping, they disclose a sorry analogy to what medieval scholasticism finally came to: a dead-end debate over how many angels could dance on the point of a pin. They have similarities to Pyrrhonism in Greek philosophy: an all-dissolving skepticism. So, the only facts we can rely on are those arbitrarily made black marks on the printed page. The attempt is to be as rigorously objective as scientism. What complicates our decision to call these black marks words is that words refer only to other words and have no reliable signification in pointing to any reality external to themselves. Literary texts are thus curiously sealed off to themselves; they cannot reflect human experience or say anything about it. So the current orthodoxy would have it. Seen thus, the critic's focus must be confined to the reader's psyche, to what goes on within that psyche in its responses to those little black marks.

We are thus landed now, not only in Pyrrhonism, but also in solipsism: no exit from the private, individual psyche. What are the consequences? Happy enough for some when such an excess

of vivisection and subjectivity can lead to free-for-all interpretations. Indeed, some deconstructionists have gone so far as to
assert that criticism is as much a creative art as are the artistic
creations to which it is addressed. Those of us who took a
humble pride in supposing our criticism only a servant of art are
hopelessly outmoded. How to discriminate between great work
and trash? Some deconstructionists answer that the justification
of the classics comes through the processes of "interpretive
communities." In other words, what makes a classic a classic is
only that it is taught in literature courses!

My readers can decide how many ironies grow like fungus
within these lucubrations. I cannot, however, resist pointing to
two of the darker sort. The deconstructionists offer a "metaphysical" demonstration of what the populace and many a
nonhumanities professor have long felt sure of: that literary
studies are not "for real," have no valid or necessary function in
education. Secondly, in their intellectual nihilism such critics,
knowingly or not, provide an excellent rationale for the suicide
of our profession. Have they done right and good service in
turning Irving Babbitt and company on their heads?

IV

From one perspective our colleges and universities have certain
reasons for self-congratulation. They function in a mass society.
And quite normally the vast majority of human beings have
always given priority to the everyday practicalities: food, clothing, housing, earning a livelihood, getting on in the world,
starting and caring for a family, hoping for a better life for their
offspring, being entertained after work is done, and so on. For
help in all such they have come to look to our schooling system.
They know, without having to be told, what is useful and
congenial for their own needs and interests. What education in
the humanities might do for their world and their young is, to
average persons, a cloudy, irrelevant notion. Given these facts of
life, we academicians are ungracious to complain about our lot
or the scholastic shortcomings of most of the students in our
charge. Society has assigned us our tasks and expects our

services in return. These services we do fairly well in providing—being perhaps less guilty of waste, blunders, corruption, and messiness than some other huge bureaucracies.

Our colleges and universities are in sober fact training scientists and expert specialists—these to find, we expect, their places in our gigantic and ever-more-technological establishments. We are doing research in the natural and social sciences and producing graduates in both. It is not unreasonable to hope that such graduates will contribute to our security in the fight against cancer and in the winning of the arms race; will become research-and-development staff members in industrial corporations; will render counseling and therapy to the newly divorced. Countless other goods may be readily listed. For parents who can afford it, we supply a place and a four-year program during the time their children leave secondary school and enter the work force. Though a generation ago it was hardly requisite, we are distributing degrees to millions who need them as tickets to even an unpretentious niche in the job market. Also, even as we confess our inequities, we have moved a respectable distance in our admission policies and practices toward widening opportunities for the disadvantaged, the minorities, the oppressed, the handicapped. Although militant feminists are restive about our pace and their pay, we are almost as rapidly as possible recruiting women to our faculties and administrative posts. We are doing our bit for women students in fostering self-assertion and aggressiveness, handy traits in the competitiveness of career building. (One may doubt that Harvard is as much the leader as of yore, yet Radcliffe College now has a rugby team worthy of respect.)[9]

If by the multiplying of the student population we have had to adjust our standards downward, possibly this is no disaster: Maybe if youth gets only fragments of liberal education, these are better than none at all. (This of course can be debatable; in Queen Anne's day, one poet thought "a little learning is a

9 See featured article with color photographs: G. M. Denison, "Scrum's the Word," *Harvard Magazine,* 87 (November–December 1984), pp. 53–57.

dangerous thing.") Some can point out, too, that since culturally
ours is the era of postmodernism, the disposal of the past and
decline in humanities studies are not lamentable. Perhaps a new
culture is emerging that needs no grounding in the traditional?
After all, the Middle Ages got by for several centuries when
Europe's links with the ancient civilizations of the Mediterra-
nean were nearly all but lost. Whatever one's view here, it is a
positive fact that in certain arts—I think now of performing arts
like music and the theatre as most familiar to myself—some of
our universities provide superb preparation. Even those dis-
heartened about the study of *litterae humaniores* might have to
grant some chance of gain through our having on numerous
campuses poets and fiction writers in residence. And on another
level: to the multibillion-dollar professional sports industry our
universities are indispensable training grounds for football and
basketball stars. Almost everything for almost everybody? Well,
not quite.

What we cannot hope to educate now in academe—rare
accidents excepted—is the person of "wisdom and character."
I mean those with historic perspective and a broad and deep
sense of human experience, disciplined in the best that has been
thought and said, those faithful to the perdurable virtues and
values of civilization, those who cherish and protect the higher
culture,—in Babbitt's Emersonian phrase, those who can never
forget "the law for man." In sum: not "think tanks" (committees, commissions, or private commercial firms made up of
experts to bring us reports aimed at problem solving); rather,
the sorts of persons equipped with the potential for leadership
in ideas, for a voice of some authority in our world. We used to
hear of a saving remnant, those who might leaven the masses
instead of leveling down to them. From time beyond measure,
though, such creatures have been scarcely a handful.

So, we meet head on the conception of the elite, an unspeak-
able and damned word with everyone who follows the ethos of
contemporary democracy. Is Babbitt, then, to be discarded as a
snob? He actually wrote about the elite as "that aristocracy of
character and intelligence that is needed in a community like

ours to take the place of an aristocracy of birth, and to counter-act the tendency toward an aristocracy of money."

One of the ironies of our problem is that Babbitt's elite designates the same thing Thomas Jefferson intended by his "natural aristocracy." This egalitarian, influenced by Rousseau, is in crucial respects an arch foe of Babbitt's, yet he affords still another irony. That is, anyone who glances at those few pages in his *Notes on Virginia* where he sets forth his plan for public education in his native state will discover that the curriculum he outlines, the subjects he stresses (including Latin, Greek, history), the high standards he exacts for promotion through the schooling system, all these in their rigor surpass anything like what Babbitt expected of those for whom he wrote. Jefferson's proposal was so strenuous because he never doubted that liberal education is an indispensable safeguard of democracy. He and Babbitt are at one in the conviction that America needs leaders with vision. But cannot we somehow manage without?

It is interesting that another critic of American culture and an exact contemporary of Babbitt, John Jay Chapman, saw that our institutions of higher learning were virtually in competition to render social service to the public. At almost the same year *Literature and the American College* appeared, Chapman defined the mission of our universities to be a "guide to the people in true scholarship, to be a light and not a false beacon to the half-educated."[10] The American public and its educators, unwittingly or not, have decided for the second alternative. Evidently we in academe must abide by it. But a doubt keeps nagging, nagging. Some of us remember a prophet of old: "Where there is no vision, the people perish."

10 Chapman's article in *Science* (October 1, 1909).

Irving Babbitt:
A Chronology of His Life and
Major Works, 1865–1933

1865   Irving Babbitt is born in Dayton, Ohio, on August 2, the third son and fourth child of the five children of Edwin Dwight and Augusta (Darling) Babbitt.

He comes of a family founded in America by Edward Bobet, or Bobbett (later spelled Babbitt), an Englishman, who settled at Plymouth, Massachusetts, in 1643.

At the time of Irving's birth, Dr. Babbitt, a physician, is a partner, with Abram Wilt, in a business/commercial school founded in Dayton.

Irving later takes a certain pride in his midwestern origins, feeling there might be a "more robust though unfortunately less combative humanism in the Middle West than on the Atlantic seaboard."

The family moves frequently during his childhood, going as far east as New York City and East Orange, New Jersey, where Irving attends public schools.

He sells newspapers on the New York City streets where he plays with and frequently gives black eyes and bloody noses to street urchins.

1876?   Irving's mother dies when he is about eleven years old. His mother's parents take Irving, his older brother, Tom, and his younger sister, Katharine, to live with them on the Darling farm in Madisonville, Ohio, on the outskirts of Cincinnati.

In Madisonville Irving attends a small district school. He often helps tenant farmers pick fruit and vegetables in the nearby fields and woods.

1881   By this time Dr. Edwin Babbitt has remarried and is living in Cincinnati. Irving and his sister Katharine live at their father's home and attend Woodward High School.

Irving impresses his high school classmates with his knowledge and reading. He graduates second in a class of approximately fifty without seeming to work for grades or to care about them.

At the age of sixteen he receives a high pass in an examination that qualifies him to teach in a district school.

Irving's brother Tom is now a foreman on his uncle Albert Babbitt's Bar-Circle Ranch in Cheyenne, Wyoming. When Irving spends a summer there, sometimes riding horseback for fourteen hours a day, he develops a strenuous robustness and an almost Homeric love of nature. These traits are to surface throughout his later intellectual life.

1882   Not able to go to college because of a lack of funds, Irving returns to high school to study chemistry and civil engineering.

His chief family tie, at this time, seems to be his sister Katharine. Throughout his life he remains deeply attached to her.

1885   With financial help from his uncles—Thomas Babbitt of

Dayton and Albert Babbitt of Cheyenne—Irving goes east to attend Harvard University.

As an undergraduate he studies languages, including French, German, Italian, Spanish, Greek, and Latin.

1887   In the summer Irving and a classmate, A. P. Butterworth, sail to Europe. They stay five days in Paris, then walk to Madrid, Italy, Switzerland, and down the Rhine to Holland. They travel from Havre to Gibraltar, from Naples to the North Sea. They often live like tramps, with knapsacks on their backs, sleeping in fields, or in small inns, shunning the beaten paths.

In 1898, Babbitt's *Atlantic Monthly* essay on "Lights and Shades of Spanish Character" is graced by charming, even lyrical memories of this "European jaunt."

1889   Irving graduates with high honors from the Department of Classics at Harvard.

In September Irving takes the first job offered to him by a teachers' agency. He leaves for Montana, to teach Greek and Latin at the College of Montana, in Deer Lodge.

The two years he spends at this small Presbyterian school are to be the last time he teaches classical languages.

1891   Irving goes to Paris to study Sanskrit and Pāli, along with Indian philosophy, under the direction of Sylvain Lévi, a Hindu scholar, only two years older than Babbitt, at the École des Hautes Études.

1892   Irving returns to Harvard University to study for the M.A. He meets Paul Elmer More. He and Irving are the only two students in Professor Charles Rockwell Lanman's advanced class in Oriental studies.

"I can well remember our first meeting," More reminisced, "in Lanman's marvellously equipped library. Babbitt was rather above the average height, powerfully built, with the complexion of radiant health. . . . But it was his eyes that caught and held one's attention. They were of a dark, not pure blue, and even then, though of a luster that dimmed somewhat in later years, had in repose the withdrawn look of one much given to meditation."

1893   Babbitt is awarded an M.A. by Harvard Graduate School.

In the autumn he is appointed for a one-year instructorship in Romance languages at Williams College. He teaches French, Spanish, and Italian, as well as a course on Dante for juniors and seniors.

Later, reflecting on his year at the college, Babbitt says approvingly, "They do things in style at Williams."

1894   He returns to Harvard to join the Department of Classics, from which he had graduated with honors. But since 1883, when President Charles W. Eliot dropped the classical language requirements from the curriculum, Harvard's Department of Classics has been dwindling. So Babbitt teaches Romance languages, as an instructor of French, from 1894–1902.

1895   He delivers, at the University of Wisconsin, a lecture on "The Rational Study of the Classics."

The lecture's subsequent publication in March 1897, in *The Atlantic Monthly,* marks Babbitt's first appearance in print.

He spends the summer with Frank Jewett Mather, Jr., in Florence.

1896   Probably through the intervention of President Eliot, Babbitt is relieved of teaching elementary French in the first semester of 1896–97.

He teaches advanced "half-courses" for upperclassmen and graduate students.

He begins teaching additional courses at Radcliffe College.

He visits France in the summer and purchases about 300 books in further preparation for teaching more advanced French courses.

1897   The French neoclassical and conservative literary critic Vincent de Paul Marie Ferdinand Brunetière (1849–1906) visits Harvard. Babbitt is one of his hosts.

Babbitt subsequently translates Brunetière's "The French Mastery of Style" and publishes the translation in *The Atlantic Monthly* in October.

1898   He edits, with an essay on Hippolyte Adolphe Taine (1828–93), *Taine's Introduction à l'Histoire de la Littérature Anglaise.*

1900   He marries, in London, his former Radcliffe student, Dora May Drew. Born and brought up in China, Mrs. Babbitt is the twenty-three-year-old daughter of Edward B. Drew, a Protestant missionary to China whose home is in Cambridge, Massachusetts.

The Babbitts rent a three-story house at 6 Kirkland Road, in Cambridge, on the third floor of which Irving has a private study. Among their neighbors are Josiah Royce, William James, and Charles Rockwell Lanman.

Babbitt does most of his writing in subsequent summers at the couple's summer home in New Hampshire.

Katharine Babbitt is a frequent guest at their home.

1901   The Babbitts' daughter, Esther, is born on October 2.

1902   Babbitt is promoted to assistant professor.

He edits, with an Introduction and notes, *Renan's Souvenirs d'Enfance et de Jeunesse.*

1903   The Babbitts' son, Edward Sturges, is born on June 12.

1905   Babbitt edits, with an Introduction, notes, and vocabulary, *Voltaire's Zadig and Other Stories.*

1907   He is awarded a sabbatical leave to finish his first book.

He spends part of his sabbatical in Paris and part visiting England, where he walks in the Lake Country.

1908   Babbitt's first book, *Literature and the American College,* is published.

Abbott Lawrence Lowell becomes president of Harvard.

1909   Student interest in Babbitt's classes swells. T. S. Eliot enrolls in his course on "Literary Criticism in France with Special Reference to the Nineteenth Century."

1910   Babbitt's second book, *The New Laokoon: An Essay on the Confusion of the Arts,* is published.

He edits, with an Introduction and notes, *Racine's Phèdre.*

He teaches larger advanced courses and complains to Paul Elmer More about Harvard's failure to recognize him. He becomes increasingly disenchanted with President Lowell and begins to look elsewhere for a teaching position.

1912   Only after he has been offered a professorship at the University of Illinois is Babbitt promoted to professor of French literature.

His teaching continues to be mainly in the area of comparative literature, however.

His third book, *The Masters of Modern French Criticism,* is published.

1915   He spends part of a "semi-sabbatical" in Dublin, New Hampshire, working on *Rousseau and Romanticism.*

In October, he proofreads the ninth series of Paul Elmer More's *Shelburne Essays.* He and More continue to exchange manuscripts for criticism and proofreading.

1919   His fourth book, *Rousseau and Romanticism,* is published.

In the summer he begins work on a book he intends to call *Democracy and Imperialism,* published in 1924 as *Democracy and Leadership.*

1920   He is Larwill lecturer at Kenyon College in January.

His lecture on "The Discipline of Ideas in Literature" is published in the *English Journal* in February as "English and the Discipline of Ideas."

1921   He is Harvard lecturer at Yale from October 1921 to February 1922.

1922   He is West lecturer at Stanford University in April.

1923   From March to May, Babbitt is James Hazen Hyde Lecturer and exchange professor at the Sorbonne.

He gives two courses—one in French on Rousseau and one in English on the English Romantic poets.

Irving, his wife, and his sister Katharine spend several months at the Hotel des Saints-Pères in Paris.

His reputation in France exceeds even his reputation in America; the lectures are a triumphant success.

Babbitt is often surrounded by Oriental students, not only Chinese, but also Japanese, Korean, and Hindu.

1924   His fifth book, *Democracy and Leadership,* is published.

1925   In November Katharine Babbitt is killed in an auto-
        mobile accident.

        "I was well enough acquainted with her," Paul Elmer
        More writes in a letter to Babbitt, "to know how loyal
        and helpful a sister she had been, and how utterly
        unselfish she was. To me she can be a beautiful memory,
        but I understand what her loss is to you."

1926   Paul Elmer More substitutes at Harvard for Professor
        Charles Burton Gulick in the Department of Classics dur-
        ing the second term of the academic year of 1925–26.

        Babbitt meets with More two or three times a week.

        Babbitt gives an address in October on "Humanist and
        Specialist" at the dedication of the Marston Hall of
        Languages at Brown University in Providence, Rhode
        Island.

        He becomes a corresponding member of the French
        Institute (Académie des Sciences Morales et Politiques).

1927   Babbitt's lifelong interest in Oriental philosophy and
        religion and the relations between East and West is
        crystallized in "Buddha and the Occident," which he
        now begins writing.

        "Buddha and the Occident" later serves as the introduc-
        tion to his translation of the ancient Pāli classic of
        Buddhist wisdom, *The Dhammapada* (published post-
        humously in 1936).

        Selections from this essay subsequently appear as
        "Romanticism and the Orient" (in the *Bookman* in 1931)
        and in *On Being Creative and Other Essays* (1932).

1928   Babbitt publishes in *The Forum* in February one of his
        most comprehensive essays, "The Critic and American

Life," in which he attacks H. L. Mencken and anti-traditionalism.

He goes to Italy, Greece, France, and England on a pleasure trip.

He motors with Paul Elmer More and his daughter Alice in Huntingdonshire, near Little Gidding, the home of an Anglican religious community founded in England in the seventeenth century by Nicholas Ferrar and which figures in the last of T. S. Eliot's *Four Quartets.*

1930   He is Clyde Fitch lecturer at Amherst College.

He is elected to the American Academy of Arts and Letters.

On May 9, he debates Carl Van Doren and Henry Seidel Canby in Carnegie Hall.

Van Doren and Canby are favored by the audience; the loudspeaker system breaks down. "Though it was a very warm day," Babbitt says upon returning to Cambridge, "the occasion might be described as a frost."

Controversy rages over Babbitt's and More's neohumanism. Babbitt publishes an important chapter, "Humanism: An Essay at Definition," in *Humanism and America,* edited by Norman Foerster.

1931   Babbitt delivers the Alexander lectures in Toronto, his last important lecture series.

1932   His health begins to decline in January.

He delivers the commencement address at Drew Seminary in Madison, New Jersey, in May.

He is awarded an honorary Doctor of Humane Letters degree from Bowdoin College in June.

On November 12, he delivers before the American Academy of Arts and Letters his last public lecture,

"Style in a Democracy," published in *Spanish Character ands Other Essays* (1940) as "The Problem of Style in a Democracy."

He sees T. S. Eliot twice in November.

He publishes his sixth book, *On Being Creative and Other Essays.*

1933   In much pain as his health deteriorates, Babbitt fulfills all his academic responsibilities through the final examinations at Harvard.

"When I saw him for the last time, only a few weeks before his death," Babbitt's friend since their freshman year at Harvard, William F. Giese, reminisced, "we had hardly been together a quarter-hour before he was extolling, with serene detachment from present circumstances, the luminous qualities of an article on Marcel Proust by the most intellectually sympathetic and the nearest to his heart of all his friends and companions in arms. And all around him on his bed lay the scattered blue-books and reports of his graduate students, which he made it a matter of professional honor to read, though he could do so only in broken snatches. To my remonstrances he characteristically replied: 'When a man has been hired to do a job, it's only decent to stick to it to the end.' "

Irving Babbitt dies at his home in Cambridge on July 15.

"On an afternoon of July," the Bowdoin College professor G. R. Elliott wrote, "his body lay silent in the chancel of the new Harvard chapel. That final scene was strange, hard to believe; though all of its externals were congruous enough. The service was austerely plain. Passages of excellent moral scripture, Christian and non-Christian, were recited from the high reading-desk, which closed a vista of white walls made whiter by the light of day. But the casket, beneath the desk, was covered with a crimson pall; and the sentences that were uttered above it had in them frequent words of rich and deep color. There came to me and doubtless to others who were present a mysterious, overmastering sense of a glow of life in white light. . . ."

Prepared by Mary E. Slayton

Notes on Contributors

Joseph Baldacchino is president of The National Humanities Institute in Washington, D.C. He did graduate work in political theory at The Catholic University of America. He is the author of *Economics and the Moral Order*. Among his scholarly essays is "The Value-Centered Historicism of Edmund Burke" in *Modern Age*. Baldacchino is associate editor of *Human Events*.

J. David Hoeveler, Jr., professor of history at the University of Wisconsin in Milwaukee, is the author of *The New Humanism: A Critique of Modern America, 1900–1940* and of *James McCosh and the Scottish Intellectual Tradition*. He is currently writing a book on the contemporary conservative intellectual movement in America.

Richard B. Hovey, who received a Ph.D. from Harvard University in 1950, has been publishing articles on education for four decades in journals like *Saturday Review, College English, Modern Age, Journal of Higher Education, AAUP Bulletin,* and others. The subject of his 1959 biography, *John Jay Chapman: An American Mind,* is, like Babbitt, a critic of culture and a defender of the humanities.

T. John Jamieson, a longtime student of the New Humanism, pursued graduate studies in English literature at Northwestern University. He has published widely in such journals and periodicals as *Modern Age, The American Spectator, The University Bookman, The Anglican Theological Review,* and *The Salisbury Review*. He is continuing research into issues of classicism, monarchism, and Anglo-Catholicism.

Russell Kirk, perhaps the most influential American social thinker and man of letters in the last thirty years, is the author of many books, including the celebrated *The Conservative Mind,* which deals at length with Irving Babbitt; *Eliot and His Age; Enemies of the Permanent Things; The Roots of American Order;* and *Decline and Renewal in the Higher Learning.* Kirk has been professor or visiting distinguished professor at several universities and colleges. The only American to earn a Doctor of Letters degree from St. Andrews University in Scotland, he has also been awarded many honorary degrees. Kirk has been a Guggenheim

Fellow and a Senior Fellow of the American Council of Learned Societies. He is chairman of the Academic Board of The National Humanities Institute and president of two cultural foundations.

Folke Leander (1910–1981), the Swedish philosopher, wrote many books and monographs in Swedish, English, and German dealing with subjects of aesthetics, the theory of language, ethics, and logic. All three of his books in English, especially *Humanism and Naturalism* (1937) and *The Inner Check* (1974) but also *The Philosophy of John Dewey* (1939), reflect his close and life-long study of Irving Babbitt and Paul Elmer More.

George A. Panichas, since 1962 professor of English at the University of Maryland, is the editor of *Modern Age: A Quarterly Review.* His teaching and writing have centered on the period between the two world wars and also on the interdisciplinary relations between literature and other humanistic disciplines. His two major books are *The Reverent Discipline: Essays in Literary Criticism and Culture* and *The Courage of Judgment: Essays in Criticism, Culture, and Society.* He is also the editor of *The Simone Weil Reader* and *Irving Babbitt: Representative Writings.*

Claes G. Ryn is professor and former chairman of the Department of Politics at The Catholic University of America. Among his works are *Will, Imagination and Reason: Irving Babbitt and the Problem of Knowledge, Democracy and the Ethical Life,* and *Nykonservatismen i USA,* a book on modern American intellectual conservatism published in Sweden. Ryn has taught at Uppsala University (Sweden) and The University of Virginia. He is chairman of The National Humanities Institute in Washington, D.C.

Mary E. Slayton has been on the staff of the Library of Congress, Washington, D.C., since 1968, working in the area of English language cataloging. During the last ten years she has been on the editorial staff of *Modern Age: A Quarterly Review.* She writes poetry and has reviewed books on modern literature in a number of journals.

Peter J. Stanlis, Distinguished Professor of Humanities at Rockford College, is a member of the National Council for the Humanities. During the past forty years he has worked in the areas of eighteenth-century English literature and the history of ideas. He is the author of numerous works, including his best known and highly influential book, *Edmund Burke and the Natural Law* (1958). He is also the editor of *Edmund Burke: Selected Writings and Speeches* (1963), recently reissued by Regnery Gateway of Chicago.

Index